STUDIES IN
LATE ANTIQUITY AND EARLY ISLAM

8

ARABS AND OTHERS IN EARLY ISLAM

SLAEI

STUDIES IN
LATE ANTIQUITY AND EARLY ISLAM
8

ARABS AND OTHERS IN EARLY ISLAM

SULIMAN BASHEAR

THE DARWIN PRESS, INC.
PRINCETON, NEW JERSEY
1997

Library of Congress Cataloging-in-Publication Data

Bashīr, Sulaymān.
Arabs and others in early Islam / Suliman Bashear.
p. cm. -- (Studies in late antiquity and early Islam ; 8)
Includes bibliographical references (p. -) and index.
ISBN 0-87850-126-6 (hardcover)
1. Arabs and Islam. 2. Nationalism--Religious aspects--Islam. 3. Islam Empire--History--622-661. 4. Islam Empire--History--661-750. I. Title. II. Series.
BP190.5.A67B39 1997
297′.0953′09021--dc21 97-41871
CIP

The paper in this book is acid-free neutral pH stock and meets the guidelines for permanence and durability of the Committee on Production Guidelines for Book Longevity of the Council on Library Resources.

Printed in the United States of America

Second Printing 2008

CONTENTS

Preface vii
Introduction 1
I. Bedouins and Non-Arabs 7
II. The Impact of the Arab Polity in Retrospect 24
III. The Great Fusion 44
IV. Ambivalent Attitudes 67
V. Apocalyptic Insecurities 94
VI. Summary Discussion and Concluding Notes 112
General Bibliography 127
General Index 143

PREFACE

THE PRESENT WORK is the product of teaching and research efforts over more than a decade. The core of it was sketched out in Chapter VIII, *Al-Islām wa-l-'Arab*, of my last major work, *Muqaddima Fī al-Tārīkh al-Ākhar* (Jerusalem 1984, in Arabic). After the loss of my job in the University of Nablus, West Bank, in the wake of the publication of that book, and some unfortunate personal complications which followed, my research work suffered serious interruptions. However, with the moral support of my colleagues at the Hebrew University, above all that of my teacher, Professor M.J. Kister, and a generous grant from the Truman Institute of the University, I was able to resume my work. For this encouragement I am very grateful. I would also like to thank the administrators of the Fulbright Fund for a two-year fellowship in the United States in 1985–87. My visiting fellowship at Princeton University in 1986–87 was especially fruitfull and enabled me to use the rich and well-organized collections of Firestone Library.

Parts of the thesis in this work were presented at various colloquia and seminars, as well as occasionally discussed with some of my colleagues in private. I have greatly benefited from the reactions and criticism evoked, especially when I presented my concluding notes at the Fifth International Colloquium held by the Institute of Advanced Studies of the Hebrew University of Jerusalem in July 1990. To Professor M.J. Kister, who virtually taught me the art of reading years after my father decided that I should learn it, I owe a special debt of gratitude. I have also benefited from the discussions that I have had with Professors Bernard Lewis and Michael Cook of Princeton University, Joseph Sadan of Tel-Aviv University and Moshe Sharon and Albert Arazi of the Hebrew University of Jerusalem.

But the present work could not have been the same without the endless efforts of Dr. Lawrence Conrad of the Wellcome Institute, London, who read the text and offered important suggestions and corrections that at times resulted in rewriting important sections of it. It was Dr. Conrad who insisted on the importance of early Arabic poetry to my research and provided a number of crucial references that convinced me that this material could not be neglected. Several sections of the book were read and their English corrected by Dr. Alex Borg of Tel-Aviv University, and Ms. Monique Villarin of the editorial staff of *Jerusalem Studies in Arabic and Islam* did the work of typing neatly and patiently.

Though I bear sole responsibility for the shortcomings of this work, whatever merits it has are due to the help of all the persons and institutes mentioned here.

Suliman Bashear

Editors' Note

Dr. Suliman Bashear fell seriously ill in the summer of 1991, recovered sufficiently to return to his research for a time, but died at his home in Jerusalem on 28 October 1991, shortly after sending his final handwritten revisions and additions for this book. Upon settlement of the affairs of his estate, his text has been seen through the press by a colleague. The editors of *Studies in Late Antiquity and Early Islam* are grateful to Brenda Hall, MA, for preparing the index, and to the Uriel Heyd Foundation, Institute of Asian and African Studies of the Hebrew University of Jerusalem, where Dr. Bashear taught from 1987 until 1991 in the Department of Arabic Language and Literature, for financial support.

INTRODUCTION

THE QUESTION of whether Muḥammad was initially perceived as a prophet sent to the Arabs or, alternatively, to mankind in general, does not alter the historical fact that the spread of Islam throughout its first two centuries coincided historically with the rise of the Arab polity. Different key terms and aspects of the relationship between Arabism and Islam, which were crucial for the development of both, have been studied by modern scholars. Among these mention may be made of the terms *umma* and *ummī*;[1] Islam as a genuine "national" Arabian form of monotheism;[2] the process of the "arabization of Islam;"[3] the role of Arabic as the language of the Qur'ān;[4] the process and tribal nature of Arab settlement;[5] the question of whether Islam on the whole can

[1]R. Paret, s.v. "Umma," *EI* [1], 4/1015–16; A.J. Wensinck, s.v. "Community" and "Umma" in H.A.R. Gibb and J.H. Kraemer, eds., *Shorter EI*, Leiden 1974, 324–25, 603–604; *idem*, *The Muslim Creed*, London 1965, 6; H.M.T. Nagel, "The Authority of the Caliphate," in G.H.A. Juynboll, ed., *Studies on the First Century of Islam*, Carbondale 1982, 177–97.

[2]J. Fueck, "The Originality of the Arabian Prophet," trans. M. Swartz in his *Studies on Islam*, Oxford 1981, 87–97.

[3]J. Wellhausen, *The Arab Kingdom and its Fall*, trans. M.G. Weir, Khayyāṭ, Beirut 1963, 18–20, 24; A.A. Duri, *The Historical Formation of the Arab Nation*, trans. L.I. Conrad, London, 1987, 41; G.R. Hawting, *The First Dynasty of Islam*, London and Sydney, 1986, 2–3.

[4]W.M. Watt, *Bell's Introduction to the Qur'an*, Edinburgh 1970, 84; A. Guillaume, *Islam*, Edinburgh 1954, 1–2; B. Lewis, *The Arabs in History*, London 1980, 12–13; J. Wansbrough, *Qur'ānic Studies*, Oxford 1977, 93–94, 103.

[5]J. Wellhausen, 26–27. For further information see also I. Hasson, "The Penetration of Arab Tribes in Palestine During the First Century of the Hijra," *Cathedra*,

considered as a bedouin and desert, rather than a sedentary, religion and culture;[6] the relationship between the Arab "conquistador" and the peoples converted to Islam as *mawālī*, and the position and role played by the latter in the different fields of Muslim life;[7] and finally, the emergence of what Syriac-speaking Christians referred to as an Arab *malkūtā* (kingdom) and a perception of an Arab menace in Syriac and Persian apocalypses, respectively.[8]

A few studies have specifically addressed certain aspects of the issue of the relations between Arabs and non-Arabs within the Muslim empire. Among these mention may be made of the works of Goldziher on the Shu'ūbīya and "Arab and *'Ajam*," as well as Wellhausen's views concerning the national and racial motives behind the 'Abbāsid revolution.[9] But the point of departure of these works, as well as that of the critical follow-ups made by some scholars,[10] has been that such relations developed within the historical framework of an Arab "conquistador" on the one hand and those "converted among the conquered," to

32 (1984) 54–65 (in Hebrew) and the sources cited therein, especially Balādhurī (d. 279/892), *Futūḥ al-Buldān*, ed. Riḍwān Riḍwān, Dār al-Kutub al-'Ilmīya, Beirut 1978, 1/140, 150–52, 155–58, 171–75, 211–14.

[6]H.A.R. Gibb, *Islam*, Oxford 1980, 1, 17; G.E. von Grunebaum, *Medieval Islam*, Chicago 1953, 173–74; *idem*, "The Nature of Arab Unity Before Islam," *Arabica*, 10 (1963), 7, 18–23.

[7]I. Goldziher, *Muslim Studies*, ed. and trans. C.R. Barber and S.M. Stern, London 1966, 1/72, 98–103, 125, 142–43, 244; B. Lewis, *Race and Color in Islam*, London 1971, 6–10, 15–18; von Grunebaum, *Medieval Islam*, 199–201, 209–10; D. Pipes, *Slave Soldiers and Islam*, New Haven and London 1981, 108, 124; G. Rotter, *Die Stellung des Negres*, Bonn 1967, 103, 132, 179–80; R. Levy, *The Social Structure of Islam*, Cambridge 1969, 55–62; P. Crone, *Slaves on Horses*, Cambridge 1980, 38, nn. 274, 277, 288; A.J. Wensinck, s.v. "Mawlā," in *EI* [1], 3/417.

[8]S.P. Brock, "Syriac Views of Emergent Islam," in Juynboll, ed., *Studies*, 14–21 (and compare with Ibn al-'Ibrī, *Tārīkh*, Beirut 1985, 91–93, 95); S.S. Hartman "Secrets for Muslims in Parsi Scriptures," in G.L. Tikku, ed., *Islam and its Cultural Divergence*, Chicago 1971, 71 n. 43.

[9]Goldziher as in n. 7 above; Wellhausen, 380–93.

[10]R. Mottahedeh, "The Shu'ūbīyah and the Social History of Early Islamic Iran," *IJMES* 7 (1976), 161, on Goldziher. For the criticism of the kind of views expressed by Wellhausen and others concerning the 'Abbāsid revolution, see the implicit remarks of Lewis, *The Arabs in History*, 81, and especially M. Sharon's thorough investigation in his *Black Banners from the East*, Jerusalem 1983, 51–52, 65–71, 197–98.

use Lewis' words;[11] hence, such studies have concentrated upon the examination of only the early 'Abbāsid and later phases of these relations. Such an approach implies an *a priori* acceptance of the notion that the rise of the Arab polity and Islam were one and the same thing from the beginning, and no serious attempt has been made to use the relevant traditional material to examine the validity of this notion. True, Gibb expressed the view that the cardinal question in the development of Islam was "the whole cultural orientation of the new Islamic Society—whether it was a re-embodiment of the old Perso-Aramaean culture into which the Arabic and Islamic elements would be absorbed, or a culture in which the Perso-Aramaean contributions would be subordinated to the Arab tradition and Islamic values."[12] But this judgement referred only to the Shu'ūbīya movement and did not address the initial phases in the development of Islam. In a sense, von Grunebaum's note that with the rise of Islam the passage of the Arabs from *Kulturnation* to *Staatnation*, as another simultaneous process,[13] has not been elaborated upon.

Such conceptual fixation has been, in my opinion, one of the sources of various difficulties confronting the historical placement of the different currents envisaged from the relevant material. The validity of this observation is not limited to such pioneering scholars as Goldziher, who pointed to the existence of conflicting traditions without dating them, or Wellhausen, who accepted the authenticity of the material on the fusion between Arabism and Islam in the early days of both. It is also true for subsequent attempts that, failing to produce a comprehensive understanding of the traditional and exegetical discrepancies on different issues related to the matter, have reverted to pinpointing certain separate questions and even to raising objections of a semantic character. The question, for example, of whether the Arabs or any of the other ethnic groups and races that eventually constituted the world of classical Islam, could be referred to as "national" or "racial" entities is, in a sense, not their problem, but one of the modern student.[14]

[11]Lewis, *Race and Color*, 19.

[12]H.A.R. Gibb, *Studies on the Civilisation of Islam*, ed. S.J. Shaw and W.R. Polk, Cambridge Mass. 1962, 66.

[13]Von Grunebaum, "The Nature of Arab Unity," 18.

[14]See Mottahedeh's introductory notes on this issue in his "Shu'ūbīyah," 161.

There is nothing extraordinary in the fact that in an area of the utmost diversity of cultural, linguistic, religious, ethnic and even racial differences, people of varying backgrounds would feel distinct from each other and express their prejudices in a discourse eventually formulated in traditional statements in Arabic, which emerged as the pre-dominant linguistic tool of Islam.

The main task that the present enquiry aims to accomplish is to break down the traditional complex of Arabism and Islam into its basic component elements. Our primary hypothesis is that such a complex was the product of a historical confluence between two initially separate elements: the rise of the Arab polity as the only power that could fill the historical gap created by the crumbling of the old regimes in the Near East throughout the seventh century AD, and the prevalence of a mosaic of Judeo–Christian legacies long entrenched in the area. A quick glance at the relevant traditional material at hand may suffice to exemplify the literary fusion that led to the establishment of a firm conceptual association between the two elements in a way that presents the birth of Islam as an Arab religious and political project at one and the same time and right from the outset.

Students of *ḥadīth*, and lately, those of Qur'ānic studies as well, have time and again shown that in both genres there exists a fair representation of almost all and everything that prevailed in the area immediately before and in the course of the emergence of the new religion and polity. The suggested search for orientations at the earliest phase of this emergence may serve to clarify certain issues that, to all intents, have not yet been satisfactorily resolved. Above all, there is the clear testimony to a prominent role played by non-Arabs in the early stage of Islam, together with the existence of a strong current in both *ḥadīth* and Qur'ānic exegesis that demeans the bedouins (*a'rāb*). On the other hand, there are numerous references to certain ethnic overtones in the reported statements and policies of 'Umar I, Mu'āwiya and 'Abd al-Malik where Arabs are clearly preferred over non-Arabs. By dating the relevant Prophetic traditions and the exegetical material on certain Qur'ānic verses concerning the Arab identity of both the Prophet and the language of revelation, as well as those promoting the leading role played by Arabs in spreading the new faith, we may be able to point to the period in which the great fusion between Arabism and Islam did occur. Finally, the position of the Arabs *vis-à-vis* other peoples and races that either adopted Islam or lived in neighbouring lands, both in daily life and as projected in eschatological speculations, will also be examined.

In doing so, a critical approach to the variant contents, as well as the technique of *isnād* analysis of the traditional material previously noted by scholars, will be adopted, and a fresh one with sufficient *isnād* information will be investigated. This will hopefully help us to provide a historical dating and evaluation of the different currents and tendencies envisaged from the relevant material, as well as the possible historical circumstances in which it was circulated. Though use will be made of the main theoretical conclusions advanced by Joseph Schacht from his study of *fiqh*,[15] this does not imply their automatic acceptance: judgement will in each case be made separately.

Other limitations must also be stated from the outset. The present study does not aim to rewrite the history of early Islam, although it may bear some implications for the study of this history. It is basically an attempt to identify the elements of Arabism and religious universalism from traditional Muslim sources in Arabic, follow the literary process of their interaction, and construe whatever historical processes lie behind that interaction. Foremost, it is an attempt to examine the Arabs' consciousness of themselves and of others and the way they perceived their separate roles and destinies within Islam. It is basically not an enquiry into the actual policies adopted by the Muslim state towards *mawālī*, *dhimmī*s or non-Arabs as such, though references to such issues will be made as the need to do so arises. Moreover, though the issue of the Shuʿūbīya as reflected in *adab* sources (in the sense of *belle lettres*) does have a certain relevance to the topic under discussion, the controversy over it will not be a major concern for us here. By "Arabism" we mean a category of ethnic consciousness; and whenever the terms *ʿarab* (Arabs) and *aʿrāb* (bedouins) are interchangeably used, a note of the process of transformative fusion will be made. On the other hand, we do not intend to investigate the socio-cultural as-

[15] J. Schacht, *The Origins of Muhammedan Jurisprudence*, Oxford 1979, 156 (on the tendency of *isnād*s to grow backwards), 165 (on the most perfect and complete *isnād*s being the latest ones).

pects of the interaction between sedentary and bedouin lives in *adab* literature.[16]

We shall also not consider the religious polemics against Jews, Christians, Magians, etc. The issue of whether Muḥammad was perceived as a prophet sent to the Arabs (*ummī*, *'arabī*, *ilā al-'arab*) or to mankind in general (*ilā l-kāffa*) will be addressed only if the statements in question have clear ethnic or racial overtones. The same applies to the term *umma*, which will be considered only when denoting an ethnic rather than religious category. The national overtones of Arab attitudes towards the Byzantines in early Muslim sources have been examined by me on two previous occasions[17] and will not be considered here. Finally, traditions that mention the Persians and Byzantines only with religious connotations will also be disregarded.

[16]For an important contribution in this field see J. Sadan, "An Admirable and Ridiculous Hero," *Poetics Today*, 10 (1989), 471–92, and the references cited therein.

[17]"The Mission of Diḥya al-Kalbī and the Situation in Syria," *JSAI* 14 (1991), 84–114; "Apocalyptic and Other Materials on Early Muslim–Byzantine Wars: a Review of Arabic Sources," *JRAS*, Third Series, 1 (1991), 173–207.

CHAPTER I

BEDOUINS AND NON-ARABS

A CLEARLY PREDOMINANT CURRENT in both Qur'ānic discourse and *ḥadīth* literature is one that demeans bedouins, who are referred to as *a'rāb*. Concerning other people and races, Lewis has already noted that while the Qur'ān reveals a clear "consciousness of difference," on the other hand it actually "expresses no racial or colour prejudice."[1] This supports the earlier view of Goldziher that Sūrat Āl 'Imrān (3), v. 110,[2] "refers to the religious community, not the Arab nation."[3] Together with this, Goldziher and a few later scholars have noted the existence of another current in Qur'ānic exegesis that presents the terms *shu'ūb* (peoples) and *qabā'il* (tribes) in Sūrat al-Ḥujurāt (49), v. 13, as referring to non-Arabs (*mawālī*, *'ajam*) and Arabs, respectively, with the overall meaning of the verse taken as a basis for the promotion of universal equality among all Muslims.[4] The material on these points, as well as other related ones, is important and merits further examination.

---

[1]Lewis, *Race and Color* 6–7, referring to Sūrat al-Rūm (30), v. 22: "Among God's Signs are... the diversity of your languages and of your colours...."

[2]Lit. "You are the best nation (*umma*) ever brought forth to men." For this translation see A.J. Arberry, *The Koran Interpreted*, London 1955, 1/87.

[3]Goldziher, *Muslim Studies* 1/199 n. 1.

[4]Lit. "O mankind, we have created you male and female and appointed you races and tribes that you may know one another. Surely, the noblest among you in the sight of God is the most godfearing of you." See Goldziher, *Muslim Studies* 1/72 n. 4; Lewis, *Race and Color* 6 n. 6; von Grunebaum, *Classical Islam* 204; Levy 55 n. 1; Mottahedeh 168 n. 1.

Several Qur'ānic verses mention the *a'rāb* in contexts of blasphemy, hypocrisy, unbelief, unwillingness to fight for the cause of Islam, and the tendency to convert or submit to that religion only under duress rather than out of true devotion to it.[5] In fact, only one verse, Sūrat al-Tawba (9), v. 99, goes so far as to concede the possibility that a nomad can be a sincere believer: "And some of the bedouins believe in God and the Last Day."[6]

However, there is a clear early tendency in Qur'ānic exegesis to interpret the relevant verses as slandering or praising particular tribes and individuals: i.e. the view is adopted that the verses do not apply to bedouins as a whole, though at the same time, the names of the intended tribes and / or individuals are by no means agreed upon.[7] From 'Abd al-Razzāq (d. 211/826) we learn of an isolated attempt, in the form of a tradition by Qatāda (d. 117–18/735–36), to assert ex-

[5]See especially the comments along these lines in Sūrat al-Tawba (9), vv. 90, 97–98, 101, 120; Sūrat Saba' (34), v. 20; Sūrat al-Fatḥ (48), vv. 11, 16; Sūrat al-Ḥujurāt (49), v. 14.

[6]As translated in Arberry 1/219.

[7]The relevant materials on this are quite extensive. See Muqātil (d. 150/767), *Tafsīr*, Ms. Istanbul, III Ahmet 74/1, fol. 159r; 74/2, fols. 89v, 160v–161r; Mujāhid (d. 102–103/720–21), *Tafsīr*, ed. 'Abd al-Raḥmān al-Sawartī, al-Manshūrāt al-'Ilmīya, Beirut n.d., 2/601, 608; Ibn Qutayba (d. 276/889), *Tafsīr Gharīb al-Qur'ān*, ed. Aḥmad Ṣaqr, Dār al-Kutub al-'Ilmīya, Beirut 1978, 191, 416; Abū 'Ubayda (d. 210/825), *Majāz al-Qur'ān*, ed. F. Sezgin, Maktabat al-Khānjī, Cairo 1954, 1/267; Fīrūzābādī (d. 817/1414), *Tanwīr al-Miqbās Tafsīr Ibn 'Abbās*, Dār al-Jīl, Beirut n.d., 126–27; Ṭabarī (d. 310/922), *Tafsīr*, ed. Maḥmūd and Aḥmad Shākir, Dār al-Ma'ārif, Cairo 1954, 14/418–19, 429, 431, 433; Wāḥidī (d. 468/1075), *Asbāb al-Nuzūl*, 'Ālam al-Kutub, Beirut 1316 AH, 124, 265–66, 296–97; Zajjāj (d. 311/923), *Ma'ānī l-Qur'ān*, ed. 'Abd al-Jalīl Shalabī, 'Ālam al-Kutub, Beirut 1988, 2/464–65, 4/221; Sufyān al-Thawrī (d. 161/774), *Tafsīr*, Dār al-Kutub al-'Ilmīya, Beirut 1983, 276; al-Akhfash (d. 207/822), *Ma'ānī l-Qur'ān*, ed. 'Abd al-Amīr al-Ward, 'Ālam al-Kutub, Beirut 1406/1985, 2/558; al-Farrā' (d. 207/822), *Ma'ānī l-Qur'ān*, ed. Aḥmad Najātī and Muḥammad al-Najjār, al-Hay'a al-Miṣrīya al-'Āmma li-l-Kitāb, Cairo 1980, 1/447–49, 3/65, 79. See also Ibn Sa'd (d. 230/844), *Ṭabaqāt*, Dār Ṣādir and Dār Beirut, Beirut 1957, 1/39; Ibn Sayyid al-Nās, *'Uyūn al-Athar*, Dār al-Jīl, Beirut 1356 AH, 2/250–51; Ibn Ḥabīb (d. 245/859), *al-Muḥabbar*, ed. Ilse Lichtenstädter, Dār al-Āfāq al-Jadīda, Beirut n.d., 86–88; *idem*, *al-Munammaq*, Hyderabad 1964, 286–88; Ibn 'Abd al-Barr (d. 463/1070), *al-Tamhīd*, ed. Muṣṭafā al-'Alawī and Muḥammad al-Bakrī, al-Markaz al-Islāmī li-l-Ṭibā'a, Rabat 1981, 9/248, 12/226.

plicitly that Sūrat al-Ḥujurāt (49), v. 14, did not refer to all *a'rāb*, but only to certain groups (*ṭawā'if*) of them.[8] And both Ṭabarī (d. 310/922) and Ṭabarsī (d. 548/1153) take the trouble to explain the differences between *'arabī* (as a sedentary Arab) and *a'rābī* (as a bedouin) in the context of their commentaries on Sūrat al-Tawba (9), vv. 97–99.[9]

Equally noteworthy is the absence in the Qur'ān of any attempt to identify the early Muslim community along national Arab lines. Goldziher's above-mentioned view that *umma* in Sūrat Āl 'Imrān (3), v. 110, refers to a religious rather than national community is basically correct. Exegetical traditions bearing the names of Ibn 'Abbās, Sa'īd ibn Jubayr (a Kūfan *mawlā*, d. 95/713), 'Ikrima (a Medinese of Berber origin, d. 100–10/718–28) and Muqātil (d. 150/767) either say that those meant were the Companions who made their *hijra* (emigration) with the Prophet or specify a few of them by name. Zajjāj (d. 311/923) says that though individual Companions were meant by this verse, it applies to the Prophet's *umma* as a whole. Ṭabarī and Ibn Abī Ḥātim (d. 237/938) cite traditions asserting that no other *umma* has responded to Islam more (*aktharu istijābatan*) than this *umma*. No authority, however, presents the verse as specifically referring to the Arabs.[10]

---

[8]'Abd al-Razzāq, *Tafsīr*, Ms. Dār al-Kutub, Cairo, *Tafsīr*/242, fol. 138v. See also Muḥammad ibn Naṣr al-Marwazī (d. 394/1003), *Ta'ẓīm Qadr al-Ṣalāt*, ed. 'Abd al-Raḥmān al-Faryawā'ī, Maktabat al-Dār, Medina 1406 AH, 2/566.

[9]Ṭabarī, *Tafsīr* 21/142; Ṭabarsī (d. 548/1153), *Majma' al-Bayān*, Dār al-Fikr and Dār al-Kitāb al-Lubnānī, Beirut 1956, 10/123.

[10]See Zajjāj 1/456; Ṭabarī, *Tafsīr* 4/44; Ibn Abī Ḥātim (d. 327/938), *Tafsīr*, ed. Aḥmad al-Zahrānī, Dār Ṭayba, Riyadh 1408 AH, 2/474; Suyūṭī (d. 911/1505), *al-Durr al-Manthūr*, al-Maṭba'a al-Maymanīya, Cairo 1314 AH, 2/64; *idem*, *al-Khaṣā'iṣ al-Kubrā*, Hyderabad 1320 AH, 2/209; Nasā'ī (d/ 303/915), *Tafsīr*, ed. Sayyid al-Jalīmī and Ṣabrī al-Shāfi'ī, Maktabat al-Sunna, Cairo 1990, 1/319; Wāḥidī 87; Ibn Abī 'Āṣim (d. 287/900), *al-Sunna*, ed. Nāṣir al-Dīn al-Albānī, al-Maktab al-Islāmī, Beirut 1985, 2/615–16, 629–30; al-Ḥākim (d. 405/1014), *al-Mustadrak*, Dār al-Ma'rifa, Beirut 1986, 2/294–95, 4/76; Ibn Jumay' (d. 402/1011), *Mu'jam al-Shuyūkh*, ed. 'Umar al-Tadmurī, Mu'assasat al-Risāla, Beirut 1987, 132; Ibn Abī Shayba (d. 235/849), *al-Muṣannaf*, ed. Mukhtār Nadawī, al-Dār al-Salafīya, Bombay 1982, 12/155; Ibn Ḥajar (d. 852/1448), *al-Maṭālib al-'Āliya*, ed. Ḥabīb al-Raḥmān al-A'ẓamī, Dār al-Ma'rifa, Beirut 1392 AH, 3/315; Ibn Ḥanbal (d. 241/855), *Musnad*, Būlāq, Cairo 1313 AH, 1/273, 319, 324; al-Haythamī (d. 807/1404), *Ma-*

In complete harmony with the Qur'ān, there exists in *ḥadīth* literature a strong current that also demeans and slanders bedouins and bedouin life (*a'rābīya*). In a few traditions *a'rābīya* is contrasted to *hijra*. One says that whoever apostatizes to *a'rābīya* after making *hijra* commits a great sin (*min al-kabā'ir*): he will be cursed by God and the Prophet and will never enter Paradise.[11] The Prophet was quoted as once blaming his Companion al-Zubayr ibn al-'Awwām for not abandoning his *a'rābīya*.[12] In another tradition he is said to have forbidden an *a'rābī* from leading a *muhājir* in prayer (*wa-lā ya'ummanna a'rābīyun muhājiran*),[13] though later Sālim ibn 'Abd Allāh (d. 105–107/723–25) retreats from this prohibition on condition that such an *a'rābī* be a righteous man (*ṣāliḥan*).[14] According to a *mursal* tradition[15] by Ḍamra ibn Ḥabīb (Ḥimṣī, d. 130/747), the Prophet forbade *a'rābīs* from marrying *muhājirāt* women for fear that the latter might revert with their husbands to bedouin life.[16] The same posi-

---

jma' al-Zawā'id, Dār al-Rayyān li-l-Turāth, Cairo, and Dār al-Kitāb al-'Arabī, Beirut, 1987, 6/327.

[11]Ṭayālisī (d. 204/819), *Musnad*, Dār al-Ma'rifa, Beirut 1986, 243; Bukhārī, *al-Adab al-Mufrad*, Cairo 1979, 169–70; al-Khaṭīb al-Baghdādī (d. 463/1070), *Tārīkh Baghdād*, Maktabat al-Khānjī, Cairo, and al-Maktaba al-'Arabīya, Baghdad, 1931, 12/293; Suyūṭī, *al-Jāmi' al-Kabīr*, facs. ed., al-Hay'a al-Miṣrīya al-'Āmma li-l-Kitāb, Cairo 1978, 1/543; *idem*, *Iḥyā' al-Mayt*, ed. Muṣṭafā al-Āghā, Dār al-Jīl, Beirut 1987, 57.

[12]Ibn Qutayba, *'Uyūn al-Akhbār*, al-Hay'a al-Miṣrīya al-'Āmma li-l-Kitāb, Cairo 1973, 1/44; Bayhaqī (d. 458/1065), *Shu'ab al-Īmān*, ed. Muḥammad Basyūnī Zaghlūl, Dār al-Kutub al-'Ilmīya, Beirut 1990, 6/480; al-Muttaqī al-Hindī (d. 975/1567), *Kanz al-'Ummāl*, ed. Bakrī Ḥayyānī and Ṣafwat al-Saqqā', Mu'assasat al-Risāla, Beirut 1979, 3/888 no. 9042. Note that the last two sources cite this tradition as a *mursal* one by al-Ḥasan al-Baṣrī (d. 110/728). On *mursal* traditions see n. 15 below.

[13]Ibn Mukram al-Qāḍī, *Fawā'id*, Ms. Ẓāhirīya, *Majmū'* no. 63, 26–27.

[14]Abū Nu'aym (d. 430/1038), *Ḥilyat al-Awliyā'*, Maktabat al-Khānjī and Maṭba'at al-Sa'āda, Cairo 1938, 9/22.

[15]A *mursal* tradition is one in whose *isnād* there is at least one missing link between its earliest transmitter and the Prophet. Schacht (*Origins*, 39, 165) expressed the view that *mursal* traditions are older, while the ones with full and perfect *isnāds* are the latest. For more information see G.H.A. Juynboll, *Muslim Tradition*, Cambridge University Press, Cambridge 1985, 16 *passim*.

[16]Sa'īd ibn Manṣūr (d. 227/841), *Sunan*, ed. Ḥabīb al-Raḥmān al-A'ẓamī, Dār al-Kutub al-'Ilmīya, Beirut 1985, 1/142.

tion was attributed to 'Umar I, Sha'bī (Kūfan, d. 103–10/721–28) and Ḥasan al-Baṣrī (d. 110/728).[17] Finally, there is a Prophetic tradition that differentiates between the *hijra* of a bedouin (*al-bādī*) and that of a sedentary (*al-ḥāḍir*) and expresses a strong preference for the latter (*ashadduhumā balīyatan wa-a'ẓamuhumā ajran*, "a trial more difficult, but the one with the greater reward").[18]

This contrast is clear in a report on the struggle between Mu'āwiya and 'Alī in which the latter asserts his own pre-eminence based, among other things, on the claim that he is a *muhājir* while Mu'āwiya is an *a'rābī*.[19] But before that, we hear of 'Alī blaming Ṭalḥa and Zubayr for instigating the *a'rāb* to fight against him in the Battle of the Camel.[20] We also notice that Ḥajjāj, in his famous speech upon assuming the governorship of Iraq in 75/694, boasted that he was *muhājirun laysa bi-a'rābī*, "a *muhājir*, not a bedouin."[21] From the story of the Companion Salama ibn al-Akwa', reported in the context of a dialogue between him and Ḥajjāj, we learn that the concession to revert to bedouin life (*ta'arrub*) after one had made *hijra* was granted and even recommended by the Prophet during a civil war (*fī l-fitna*).[22] Another Prophetic statement says that *ta'arrub* after the *hijra* would be the only thing

---

[17]Ibn Abī Shayba 4/346; Ibn Ḥazm (d. 457/1064), *Marātib al-Ijmā'*, Beirut 1978, 73.

[18]Abū 'Alī al-'Abdī, *Ḥadīth*, Ms. Ẓāhirīya, *Majmū'* no. 22, 107; al-Dhakwānī, *Amālī*, Ms. Ẓāhirīya, *Majmū'* no. 63, 18.

[19]Ibn 'Abd Rabbihi (d. 328/939), *al-'Iqd al-Farīd*, ed. Aḥmad Amīn, Aḥmad al-Zayn and Ibrāhīm al-Abyārī, Maṭba'at Lajnat al-Ta'līf wa-l-Tarjama wa-l-Nashr, Cairo 1940–53, 4/304.

[20]*Kitāb Sulaym ibn Qays*, Najaf n.d., 170.

[21]*Anonyme Arabische Chronik* (possibly vol. 11 of Balādhurī's *Ansāb*), ed. W. Ahlwardt, Greifswald 1883, 286; al-Washshā' (d. 340/951), *Kitāb al-Fāḍil*, Ms. British Museum, Or. 6499, fol. 98v (I am indebted to Dr. Lawrence Conrad for drawing this important source to my attention); Ibn Manẓūr, *Lisān al-'Arab*, Būlāq, Cairo 1308 AH, 8/173; Zabīdī, *Tāj al-'Arūs*, Būlāq, Cairo 1307 AH, 4/299. Note also that the contrasts *a'rābī–muhājir* and *a'rābi–ḥāḍir* occur in two poetic verses by Iyās ibn Mālik al-Ṭā'ī and Jarīr, respectively. See for them Abū Tammām (d. 236/850), *Kitāb Ash'ār al-Ḥamāsa*, ed. G. Freytag, Bonn 1828–47, 294 and *Dīwān Jarīr*, Cairo 1353 AH, 56.

[22]Bukhārī, *Ṣaḥīḥ*, Dār al-Fikr, Beirut 1981, 8/24; Muslim, *Ṣaḥīḥ*, Dār al-Fikr, Beirut n.d., 6/27; Ibn 'Asākir (d. 571/1175), *Tārīkh*, facs. ed., Dār al-Bashīr, Amman 1988, 7/501.

that could save people (*yunjī*) towards the end of time.[23] By a third tradition we are told that the best of people in the future *fitan* will be the desert-dwelling Muslims (*muslimū ahl al-bawādī*).[24]

This current of prejudice and discrimination against *a'rāb* is further attested by a group of other traditions attributed to both the Prophet and 'Alī. One mentions bedouins among those who are not allowed to lead in prayer or even to be in the first row during prayer (*lā yataqaddamu al-ṣaffa al-awwala a'rābīyun wa-lā a'jamīyun wa-lā ghulāmun lam yaḥtalim*).[25] Another rejects the testimony of a bedouin (*badawī*) against a sedentary (*ṣāḥib qarya*).[26] A third forbids a *muhājir* from acting as a broker (*simsār*) for the merchandise of a bedouin.[27] The Prophet is said to have forbidden giving bedouin Muslims a share in the booty unless they took part in the fighting, and even then he is said to have given them only half the regular share.[28] There is also a warning against the tendency of *a'rāb* to delay the evening prayer (*al-'ishā'*) until milking the camels after darkness, and hence, altering its name to *al-'atama* (meaning "darkness").[29]

---

[23]Hannād ibn al-Sarī (d. 243/857), *Kitāb al-Zuhd*, Dār al-Khulafā', Kuwait 1985, 2/586.

[24]Ibn 'Asākir 5/391. Further observations on the position of the Arabs during the *fitan* preceding the end of times will be made below in Chapter V.

[25]Dāraquṭnī (d. 385/995), *Sunan*, ed. 'Abd Allāh Hāshim Yamānī al-Madīnī, Medina 1966, 1/281; Daylamī (d. 509/1115), *al-Firdaws*, ed. Sa'īd Zaghlūl, Dār al-Kutub al-'Ilmīya, Beirut 1986, 5/118; Ibn 'Asākir 14/638.

[26]Ḥākim 4/99; Bayhaqī, *Sunan*, Dār al-Ma'rifa, Beirut 1987, 10/250.

[27]Ibn Abī Ḥātim (d. 327/938), *'Ilal al-Ḥadīth*, Dār al-Ma'rifa, Beirut 1985, 1/376; Ṭabarānī (d. 360/970), *al-Mu'jam al-Awsaṭ*, ed. Maḥmūd al-Ṭaḥḥān, Maktabat al-Ma'ārif, Riyadh 1985, 1/160; Haythamī, *Majma'* 3/82; Muttaqī 4/56 no. 9482; Muḥyī l-Dīn al-Ba'albakī, *Mashyakha*, Ms. Ẓāhirīya, *Majmū'* no. 25, 51; Sufyān ibn 'Uyayna, *Ḥadīth*, Ms. Ẓāhirīya, *Majmū'* no. 22, 82; Yūnus ibn 'Ubayd, *Ḥadīth*, Ms. Ẓāhirīya, *Majmū'* no. 103, 140; Ibn al-Ṣawwāf, *Ḥadīth*, Ms. Ẓāhirīya, *Majmū'* no. 105, 163, 166.

[28]Bayhaqī, *Sunan* 6/348; Ibn 'Asākir 2/247.

[29]Ḥumaydī (d. 219/834), *Musnad*, ed. Ḥabīb al-Raḥmān al-A'ẓamī, 'Ālam al-Kutub, Beirut 1383 AH, 2/285; Bazzār (d. 292/904), *Musnad*, ed. Maḥfūẓ Zayn Allāh, Maktabat al-'Ulūm wa-l-Ḥikam, Medina, and Mu'assasat 'Ulūm al-Qur'ān, Beirut, 1988, 3/264; Abū Ya'lā (d. 307/919), *Musnad*, ed. Ḥusayn Asad, Dār al-Ma'mūn li-l-Turāth, Damascus 1984, 2/173; al-Shāshī (d. 335/946), *Musnad*, ed. Maḥfūẓ Zayn Allāh, Maktabat al-'Ulūm wa-l-Ḥikam, Medina 1410 AH, 1/293; Ibn Ḥibbān (d. 354/965), *Ṣaḥīḥ*, ed. Kamāl al-Ḥūt, Dār al-Kutub al-'Ilmīya, Beirut 1987,

Living in the desert is said by one tradition to be the cause of uncouth character (*man sakana l-bādiyata jafā*).[30] Certain Arab habits, like mourning the dead (*niyāḥa*), attacking another's claims to noble descent (*al-ṭa'n fī l-nasab*), prayer for rain (*al-istisqā' bi-l-anwā'*), and so forth, are branded as elements of unbelief (*kufr*) from which, we are told, the Arabs will never free themselves.[31] Their hypocrisy (*riyā'*) and covert sensuality (*al-shahwa al-khafīya*) are causes for concern in another Prophetic tradition.[32] In one apocalyptic vision, the Prophet warns that the bedouins will one day ambush travellers in the passes leading to Mecca, and hence hinder the fulfillment of pilgrimage to the city.[33] 'Abd Allāh ibn 'Amr warns that one day people will follow the *sunna* of *a'rāb* and have hearts like those of *a'ājim* (non-Arabs).[34] A tradition transmitted by Anas ibn Mālik says that nine tenths of all jealousy in the world rests with the Arabs, and the remaining one tenth belongs to the other peoples (*fī l-nās*).[35] Through Abū Hurayra we hear of another tradition in which the Prophet even says that he trusts the *mawālī* (non-Arab clients) more than the Arabs, or at least more than some of them. This was transmitted by the Medinese *mawlā* Ṣāliḥ ibn Abī Ṣāliḥ (d. 125/742).[36] Two *mursal* traditions by 'Aṭā' (possibly al-Khurāsānī, d. 135/752) say that the *abdāl* (mysterious saintly figures)

3/41; Abū Nu'aym 8/385; Bayhaqī, *Sunan* 1/372, quoting Bukhārī and Muslim; Suyūṭī, *Durr* 5/57, quoting Ibn Abī Shayba and Ibn Mardawayh (d. 410/1019); Muttaqī 7/nos. 19468–69, 19504, 19507.

[30]Bayhaqī, *Sunan* 10/101; Ibn 'Abd al-Barr 18/144; Muttaqī 15/no. 41588. Compare also with Abū Nu'aym 3/282, where the same was cited as Mujāhid's statement.

[31]Ibn 'Asākir 6/443.

[32]Ibn al-Mubārak (d. 181/797), *Kitab al-Zuhd*, ed. Ḥabīb al-Raḥmān al-A'ẓamī, Dār al-Kutub al-'Ilmīya, Beirut 1386 AH, 393; Ibn Abī Ḥātim, *'Ilal* 2/124; Abū Nu'aym 7/122; Ibn 'Asākir 8/5; Muttaqī 3/nos. 7538, 8840.

[33]Bayhaqī, *Sunan* 4/341; Muttaqī 5/no. 11820.

[34]Cf. however, Ṭabarī, *Tahdhīb al-Āthār*, ed. Maḥmūd Shākir, Maṭba'at al-Madanī, Cairo 1981, 1/122, and Ibn Ḥanbal, *Musnad* 5/340, where a Prophetic tradition warns against *alsina* ("tongues") instead of *al-sunna* of the Arabs.

[35]Daylamī 2/160; al-Kinānī (d. 963/1555), *Tanzīh a-Sharī'a*, ed. 'Abd al-Wahhāb 'Abd al-Laṭīf and 'Abd Allāh al-Ṣiddīq, Dār al-Kutub al-'Ilmīya, Beirut 1979, 1/177. As this tradition mentions the characteristics of other peoples, a further reference to it will be made below.

[36]Ṭayālisī 326; Tirmidhī (d. 279/892), *Ṣaḥīḥ*, ed. Aḥmad Shākir, Cairo 1937, 5/725; al-Jawraqānī (d. 543/1148), *al-Abāṭīl wa-l-Manākīr*, Varanasi 1983, 2/266.

will be *mawālī* and that an Arab's hatred of a *mawlā* is hypocrisy (*nifāq*, i.e. in the sense of religious dissimulation).[37] Finally, one report has it that the Companion Salmān al-Fārisī used to pray for God's protection (*yata'awwadhu bi-l-lāhi*) from a non-Arab who behaves like an Arab (*al-musta'rib*).[38]

The strongest current in interpreting the term *umma* in Sūrat Āl 'Imrān (3), v. 110, is one that asserts that it refers to the Prophet's Companions (*aṣḥāb al-rasūl*), especially those who made *hijra* with him. This is clearly reflected in the traditions of Sa'īd ibn Jubayr and 'Ikrima from Ibn 'Abbās, as well as those of al-Ḍaḥḥāk ibn Muzāḥim (d. 105–106/723–24) and Suddī (d. 127/744).[39] Other traditions, especially the one reported from 'Ikrima by Ibn Jurayj (d. 150/767), give the names of individual Companions who were referred to by this verse.[40] However, as reported by Yazīd al-Naḥawī (ibn Abī Sa'īd, d. 131/748), 'Ikrima interpreted it as referring to "the people who best treat other people" (*khayru al-nāsi li-l-nās*), explaining that they gave security "to the red and black" (*li-l-aḥmar wa-l-aswad*), meaning "to all mankind."[41] Actually, the statement *khayru al-nāsi li-l-nās* occurs also in traditions bearing the names of Ibn 'Abbās, Mujāhid, al-Rabī' ibn Anas (d. 139–40/756–57), 'Aṭā' al-Khurāsānī and 'Aṭīya al-'Awfī (d. 111–27/729–44).[42] This last one in particular explains that this *umma* was considered the best because it had recognized the prophets who had previously been rejected by their own peoples. And a tradition transmitted from Abū Hurayra by Abū Ḥāzim (Salmān al-Ashja'ī al-Kūfī, d. *ca.* 100/718), justifies the preference over other communities (*umam*) by the notion that this one will bring the others to Islam "in chains" (*bi-l-salāsil*).[43]

---

[37]Abū Bakr ibn al-Khallāl (d. 311/923), *al-Sunna*, ed. 'Aṭīya al-Zahrānī, Dār al-Rāya, Riyadh 1989, 290; Muttaqī 12/no. 34598; al-Ghumārī, *al-Mughīr*, Cairo n.d., 32; the last two sources quoting *al-Kunā* by al-Ḥākim.

[38]Ibn Qutayba, *'Uyūn* 1/269.

[39]Ṭabarī, *Tafsīr* 7/101–102; Ibn Abī Ḥātim, *Tafsīr* 2/470.

[40]Ṭabarī, *Tafsīr* 7/101–102, and compare with Muqātil, 74/1, 59v.

[41]Ibn Abī Ḥātim, *Tafsīr* 2/472. On the use of colours to identify peoples in Muslim literature, see Goldziher, *Muslim Studies* 1/243–44; Lewis 8–9 and the sources cited therein.

[42]Ibn Abī Ḥātim, *Tafsīr* 2/472; Ṭabarī, *Tafsīr* 7/103; Mujāhid 1/133.

[43]Ibn Abī Ḥātim, *Tafsīr* 2/472; Ṭabarī, *Tafsīr* 7/103.

One Shīʿī tradition with the *isnād* Jābir (al-Juʿfī, d. 127–34/744–51) ← Abū Jaʿfar (al-Bāqir, d. 114–19/732–36), says that this verse meant "the best people of the house of the Prophet."[44] And the philological commentary of Abū ʿUbayda interprets *umma* as "a group" (*jamāʿa*). To all intents, the closest attempt to present this verse along ethnic lines is recorded in a tradition of al-Rabīʿ ibn Anas that only says, however, that "no *umma* displayed a greater acceptance (lit. "response," *istijābatan*) of Islam than this one." Note also that in one source, Ibn Abī Ḥātim's *Tafsīr*, the *isnād* has been extended back from al-Rabīʿ to Abū l-ʿĀliya (Rufayʿ ibn Mihrān, d. 93–111/711–29) ← a Companion of the Prophet, Ubayy ibn Kaʿb.[45]

The notion of a messenger who has been sent to people (*li-l-nās*) in general (*jamīʿan*, *kāffatan*), and not to any particular ethnic group, is explicitly advanced in Sūrat al-Nisā' (4), v. 79, Sūrat al-Aʿrāf (7), v. 158 and Sūrat Saba' (34), v. 28. In the ps.-Ibn ʿAbbās *Tafsīr* it is even said that such message was directed to both "spirit beings and humans" (*li-l-jinni wa-l-ins*).[46] Actually, this may not be very far from Ṭabarī's view that Sūrat al-Nisā' (4), v. 79, meant that Muḥammad was God's messenger to all "creatures" (*al-khalq*), assuming that by this word Ṭabarī had in mind something broader than "mankind" in particular.[47] Commenting on the term *jamīʿan* of Sūrat al-Aʿrāf (7), v. 158, Ṭabarī also draws the line between Muḥammad and the prophets preceding him, who, he says, were sent only to some people (*ilā baʿḍ al-nās*).[48] In a few other sources the terms *jamīʿan*, *kāffatan* and *ʿāmman* are applied as synonyms to explain one another.[49]

Commenting on Sūrat Saba' (34), v. 28, the early ʿAbd al-Razzāq cites a tradition that Mujāhid attributes to the Prophet in a *mursal* form. According to this tradition, he mentions being sent to all mankind (lit. "to every red and black") as one of five other things that

---

[44]Ibn Abī Ḥātim, *Tafsīr* 2/473.

[45]*Ibid.*, and compare with Ṭabarī, *Tafsīr* 7/103.

[46]Fīrūzābādī 61, 27. See also Zabīdī, *Itḥāf al-Sāda*, Cairo n.d., 2/35, where a similar view was attributed to both Ibn ʿAbbās and Mujāhid, with Bayhaqī being quoted for it.

[47]Ṭabarī, *Tafsīr* 8/562.

[48]*Ibid.*, 13/170.

[49]Abū ʿUbayda 2/149; Ibn Qutayba, *Tafsīr* 357; Fīrūzābādī 109.

no other prophet before him was granted.[50] We notice, however, that *ḥadīth* and other sources cite variants of this tradition but attribute them to the Prophet through the Companions Abū Dharr, Ibn ʿAbbās, Abū Umāma al-Bāhilī, Jābir ibn ʿAbd Allāh, ʿAwf ibn Mālik, ʿAlī and Abū Hurayra. Still, we believe that the original core of the tradition was circulated around the turn of the first/seventh century and constitutes an early representation of such a current. For in addition to ʿAbd al-Razzāq, an even earlier source, the *Kitāb al-Zuhd* of Ibn al-Mubārak, cites both the *mursal* form of Mujāhid and two other transmissions by him from Abū Dharr and Abū Hurayra.[51] We also notice that the tradition of ʿAlī was transmitted by his grandson, ʿAlī Zayn al-ʿĀbidīn (d. 92–100/710–18), in a family line.[52] Also suggestive is the *mursal* tradition of Khālid ibn Maʿdān (d. 103–108/721–26), which probably represents a cross-section of two conflicting currents. According to it, the Prophet said: "I have been sent to all mankind (*ilā l-kāffa*), but if they fail to respond (*fa-in lam yastajībū*), then to the Arabs... to Quraysh... to Banū Hāshim...," etc.[53]

The notion that the Prophet was sent to all mankind finds important support in the Prophetic statement: "I am the master of the children of Adam / all peoples" (*anā sayyidu wuldi ādam / al-nās*). It occurs in different contexts and was widely circulated through chains of transmitters leading back to ʿĀ'isha, Ḥudhayfa ibn al-Yamān, Abū Saʿīd al-Khudrī, Anas ibn Mālik, Abū Hurayra, Jābir ibn ʿAbd Allah

[50] ʿAbd al-Razzāq, *Tafsīr*, 112v.

[51] For these, as well as the variants transmitted by the other Companions, cf. Ibn al-Mubārak 377, 563; Abū Bakr al-ʿAllāf, *Amālī*, Ms. Ẓāhirīya, *Majmūʿ* no. 67, 120; Ibn Ḥumayd (d. 249/861), *al-Muntakhab Min al-Musnad*, ed. Ṣubḥī al-Sāmarrā'ī and Maḥmūd al-Ṣaʿīdī, Maktabat al-Sunna, Cairo 1988, 215–16; Jāḥiẓ (d. 255/868), *al-Bayān wa-l-Tabyīn*, Dār al-Fikr li-l-Jamīʿ, Beirut 1968, 4/7; *idem*, *Fakhr al-Sūdān*, ed. G. van Vloten, Leiden 1903, 75–76; Ibn Ḥibbān, *Ṣaḥīḥ*, 8/104–105, 127; al-Khaṭīb al-Baghdādī 12/378; Bayhaqī, *Shuʿab* 2/177; Ibn ʿAbd al-Barr 5/221–22; Zabīdī, *Itḥāf* 2/35; Samarqandī (d. 373/983), *Tanbīh al-Ghāfilīn*, Dār al-Fikr, Beirut n.d., 191; Suyūṭī, *Durr* 2/83, 5/237, 240; Muttaqī 11/439–40 nos. 32060–65.

[52] Ibn ʿAsākir 5/112. Compare also with the variant transmitted by Zayn al-ʿĀbidīn's son, al-Bāqir, in a *mursal* form cited by Ibn Saʿd, cf. Muttaqī 11/445 no. 32094.

[53] Suyūṭī, *Khaṣā'is* 2/188; Muttaqī 11/427 no. 32004, quoting Ibn Saʿd.

and Ibn 'Abbās. The wording of 'Ā'isha's tradition is polemical and betrays the existence of an opposite current identifying the Prophet as "master of the Arabs" (*sayyid al-'arab*). For in an answer to 'Ā'isha concerning this latter title, the Prophet says that it refers to 'Alī / var. Abū Bakr (or, in a harmonizing version, 'Alī as "the master of Arab young men," the *shabāb*, and Abū Bakr as the master of the *kuhūl*, the "middle aged," among them), while the Prophet himself retains the title "master of all humanity." There is also one variant, sustained by a clear 'Abbāsid *isnād*, which mentions both 'Alī and al-'Abbās as "the two masters of the Arabs" (*sayyidā l-'arab*).[54]

Another attempt to identify the Prophet along ethnic lines comes in the form of an isolated variant of the widely circulated tradition on the "forerunners" (*al-subbāq*): Muḥammad, Salmān, Ṣuhayb and Bilāl, each mentioned as a representative *sābiq* of his people. It bears the name of 'Alī and attributes to the Prophet the saying, among other things, that Ādam is the master of mankind, while Muḥammad and the three Companions mentioned above are masters of the Arabs, Persians, Byzantines and Abyssinians respectively. The tradition continues to name the masters of trees, mountains, months, days, words, etc.[55]

But all other variants, attributed to the Prophet through Anas, Abū Umāma al-Bāhilī and Umm Hāni', use *sābiq* instead of *sayyid* and limit themselves to specifying the Prophet and his three Companions, each

---

[54]See Ibn Sa'd 1/20; Ibn Ḥanbal, *Faḍā'il al-Saḥāba*, ed. Waṣī Allāh 'Abbās, Mu'assasat al-Risāla, Beirut 1983, 1/394; Bukhārī, *al-Tārīkh al-Kabīr*, Hyderabad 1380 AH, 7/400; Abū l-Ḥasan al-Bazzār, *Faḍā'il Banī Hāshim*, Ms. Ẓāhirīya, *Majmū'* no. 103, 167; Abū Bakr ibn al-Muqri', *Fawā'id*, Ms. Ẓāhirīya, *Majmū'* no. 105, 183; Ṭabarānī, *al-Mu'jam al-Kabīr*, ed. Ḥamdī al-Salafī, Baghdad 1983, 3/88; *idem*, *al-Mu'jam al-Awsaṭ*, 2/36, 279; Ibn Ḥibbān, *Ṣaḥīḥ* 8/129–30, 137; Ḥākim 3/124; Abū Nu'aym 1/63; Nasā'ī, *Tafsīr* 1/648, in connection with Sūrat al-Isrā' (17), v. 3; Muḥibb al-Dīn al-Ṭabarī (d. 694/1294), *Dhakhā'ir al-'Uqbā* 37; *idem*, *al-Riyāḍ al-Naḍira fī Manāqib al-'Ashara*, ed. Muḥammad Abū l-'Ulā, Maktabat al-Najda, Cairo 1970, 1/163–64; al-Khaṭīb al-Baghdādī 11/89–90; Daylamī 1/43; Ibn 'Asākir 3/384, 8/929, 9/621, 12/274–75; Dhahabī (d. 748/1347), *Tārīkh al-Islām*, ed. 'Umar Tadmurī, Dār al-Kitāb al-'Arabī, Beirut 1987–proceeding, 635; Haythamī, *Majma'* 9/131; Ibn Ḥajar, *Lisān al-Mīzān*, Hyderabad 1330 AH, 4/289–90; Sakhāwi (d. 902/1496), *al-Maqāsid al-Hasana*, Cairo 1956, 245–46; Munāwī, *Kunūz al-Haqā'iq*, in the margin of Suyūṭī, *al-Jāmi' al-Ṣaghīr*, Dār al-Kutub al-'Ilmīya, Beirut n.d., 1/148; Muttaqī 11/nos. 33003, 33006, 13/no. 36456; Zabīdī, *Itḥāf* 2/35–36.

[55]Daylamī 2/324.

as the forerunner of his nation. However, one variant of Anas' tradition, transmitted from him by a certain Muḥammad ibn Ḥijāra, refers to the Prophet as "master of the children of Adam." We also notice that Abū Umāma's tradition specifies Paradise as the aim of such precedence (*sābiq... ilā l-janna*). But possibly more substantial is the fact that in our early sources, this tradition was heavily reported not as one of any of the above-mentioned Companions, but in a *mursal* form from the early second/eighth-century Ḥasan al-Baṣrī.[56]

The impact of the rise of the Arab polity on the current to identify the Prophet along Arab ethnic lines is a problem to which we shall turn in the next chapter. Suffice to note at this stage two early Islamic poetic verses, by A'shā Banī Māzin and al-Muṭarraf respectively, in which the Prophet is addressed as "king / master of all peoples and judge of the Arabs" (*yā malika / sayyida l-nāsi wa-dayyāna l-'arab*).[57] As against this, the instances in which other early Muslim figures are referred to by this title are rare indeed.[58] The titles commonly used in both the Umayyad and early 'Abbāsid periods are overwhelmingly related to the Arabs. The clan of Banū 'Abd Shams, for example, was addressed by Arwā bint al-Ḥārith ibn 'Abd al-Muṭṭalib as "masters of the Arabs" (*sādat al-'arab*).[59] In a unique report, 'Umar I is quoted as calling Mu'āwiya "Chosroes of the Arabs."[60] Mu'āwiya's wife, Maysūn bint

[56]For all these variants, see Ibn Sa'd 1/21, 2/232, 4/82; Ibn Ḥanbal, *Faḍā'il* 2/209; Balādhurī (d. 279/892), *Ansāb al-Ashrāf* 1, ed. Muḥammad Ḥamīd Allāh, Dār al-Ma'ārif, Cairo 1959, 181; Ibn Abī Ḥātim, *'Ilal* 2/353; al-Ḥalīmī (d. 402/1011), *al-Minhāj Fī Shu'ab al-Īmān*, Dar al-Fikr, Beirut 1979, 2/178; Samarqandī 129; Ḥākim 2/284–85, 402; Abū Nu'aym 1/149, 185; Daylamī 1/45; Ibn 'Asākir 3/455–56, 7/391, 407, 8/377–78; Ibn Badrān (d. 1346/1927), *Tahdhīb Tārīkh Ibn 'Asākir*, Maṭba'at Rawḍat al-Shām, Damascus 1331 AH, 3/306; Dhahabī, *Tārīkh* 203, 514, 598; al-'Irāqī, *al-Qurab Fī Maḥabbat al-'Arab*, Bombay 1303 AH, 4; Haythamī, *Majma'* 9/305; Suyūṭī, *al-Jāmi' al-Ṣaghīr* 1/107; Munāwī 1/80, 144; Haytamī (d. 973/1565), *Fakhr al-'Arab*, ed. Majdī al-Sayyid Ibrāhīm, Maktabat al-Qur'ān, Cairo 1987, 20; Muttaqī 11/nos. 32082, 33133, 33676.

[57]Ibn Sa'd 7/36–37; Ibn Manẓūr, *Lisān al-'Arab* 17/24; Zabīdī, *Tāj* 9/208.

[58]E.g. where the poet A'shā Banī Rabī'a addressed Bishr ibn Marwān, 'Abd al-Malik's brother and his governor over Iraq, with the verse: *yā sayyida l-nāsi min 'ujmin wa-min 'arabi*, "O master of [all] people from among [both] non-Arabs and Arabs." See Balādhurī, *Ansāb al-Ashrāf* 5, ed. S.D. Goitein, Jerusalem 1936, 171.

[59]Balādhurī, *Ansāb al-Ashrāf* 4B, ed. M. Schloessinger, Jerusalem 1938, 127.

[60]Ibn 'Asākir 16/701.

Baḥdal from the tribe of Kalb, praised her son Yazīd by calling him "the best among Arab young men" (*khayru shabābi l-'arab*).[61] The third Marwānid caliph, al-Walīd I, was addressed by a similar title, namely "master (*sayyid*) of Arab young men."[62] In an attempt to gain al-Manṣūr's pardon for taking part in the uprising of Ibrāhīm ibn al-Ḥasan in 145 AH, the poet Sudayf addressed him by the title "the best among the Arabs" (*khayru l-'arab*).[63] Another poet, 'Abd al-Raḥīm al-Raqqāṣ, called 'Alī, son of the caliph al-Mahdī, "youth (*fatā*) of the Arabs."[64] And a third one, Muṭī' ibn Iyās, praised another early 'Abbāsid dignitary, Ma'n ibn Zā'ida al-Shaybānī, as "master (*sayyid*) of the Arabs."[65]

Sūrat al-Jumu'a (62), v. 3, speaks about certain "others" from among those to whom a messenger was sent, but who have not yet followed them (*wa-ākharīna minhum lammā yalḥaqū bihim*). This verse was sometimes referred to as a basis for the current emphasizing the universal character of Muḥammad's message, namely that he was sent also to the *mawālī*, to the *'ajam* and, more specifically, to the Persians as well.[66]

To support this view, a tradition bearing the name of Abū Hurayra is often cited. It asserts that when this verse was revealed a man enquired about those meant by it; the Prophet put his hand on Salmān al-Fārisī and said: "Had belief / religion / knowledge been suspended from the Pleiades, some of the people of this [man] would seize it."[67] In some *ḥadīth* compilations, variants of this tradition were also attributed to the Prophet through the Companions Qays ibn Sa'd and Ibn Mas'ūd. We notice, however, that the tradition of Abū Hurayra

---

[61]Ibn Ḥabīb, *Munammaq* 434.

[62]Ibn 'Asākir 17/840–41.

[63]Ibn Qutayba, *al-Shi'r wa-l-Shu'arā'*, ed. M.J. de Goeje, Leiden 1902, 480.

[64]Al-Mubarrad, *al-Kāmil*, ed. W. Wright, Leipzig 1864, 1/389.

[65]Abū l-Faraj al-Iṣbahānī (d. 356/966), *Kitāb al-Aghānī*, Dār al-Kutub al-Misrīya, 1950, 13/324.

[66]See Fīrūzābādī 354; Zajjāj 5/169–70; Mujāhid 2/673; Farrā' 3/155.

[67]Bukhārī, *Ṣaḥīḥ* 6/63; Muslim 7/191–92; Nasā'ī, *Tafsīr* 2/428; *idem*, *Faḍā'il al-Ṣaḥāba*, ed. Farūq Ḥamāda, Dār al-Thaqāfa, al-Dār al-Bayḍā' 1984, 157–58; Tirmidhī 5/725–26; Ṭabarī, *Tafsīr* 28/95–96; Bayhaqī, *Dalā'il al-Nubuwwa*, ed. 'Abd al-Mu'ṭī Qal'ajī, Dār al-Kutub al-'Ilmīya, Beirut 1985, 6/333; Jawraqānī 2/262–63; Ibn Ḥibbān, *Ṣaḥīḥ* 9/207; Muttaqī 12/303 no. 35125.

connects this statement with the revelation of Sūrat al-Jumu'a (62), v. 3, and that only when transmitted by the early second/eighth-century Medinese *mawlā* Sālim, nicknamed Abū al-Ghayth.[68] We also notice that when reported through the chain al-'Alā' ibn 'Abd al-Raḥmān (d. 132–39/749–56) ← his father, the tradition of Abū Hurayra is overwhelmingly connected rather with Sūrat Muḥammad (47), v. 38: "And if you turn away, He will replace you with another people."[69]

Sūrat al-An'ām (6), v. 52, warns the Prophet not to expel those who raise supplications to their God on mornings and evenings. Commenting on this, a few early as well as late sources give the names of some Companions, usually of non-Arab origin like Salmān, Ṣuhayb and Bilāl, who are sometimes presented as slaves (*a'bud*) or *mawālī*, rejected by certain Arab or Qurashī aristocratic leaders. Though only individual names are given, the overall values stressed by these commentaries are those of ethnic, racial and social equality, as the Companions concerned are often also described as those weak, poor and common among the Muslims (*ḍu'afā' al-muslimīn*).[70]

As noted by some scholars, Sūrat al-Ḥujurāt (49), v. 13, was often referred to in the heat of Arab / non-Arab controversy.[71] The key term in this verse, *shu'ūb*, is presented by a few sources as denoting the *mawālī* or *'ajam*, while others hold that it referred to great Arab

---

[68]See the sources cited in the previous note and cf. 'Abd al-Razzāq, *Muṣannaf*, ed. Ḥabīb al-Raḥmān al-A'ẓamī, al-Maktab al-Islāmī, Beirut 1983, 11/66; Ibn Abī Shayba 12/207; also Haythamī, *Kashf al-Astār*, Mu'assasat al-Risāla, Beirut 1983, 3/316; *idem*, *Majma'* 10/64–65; Abū Ya'lā 3/23; Ḥalīmī 2/177; Ibn 'Asākir 8/137, 14/686; Ibn Ḥajar, *Maṭālib* 4/158; Suyūṭī, *Khaṣā'is* 2/153; Muttaqī 12/no. 34129, quoting Ṭabarānī.

[69]Ṭabarī, *Tafsīr* 26/66–67; Ibn Ḥibbān, *Ṣaḥīḥ* 9/127; Zajjāj 5/17; Ṭabarsī 26/48; Suyūṭī, *Durr* 6/67; Ḥākim 2/458; Bayhaqī, *Dalā'il* 6/334; Ibn 'Asākir 7/413–14; but compare with Mujāhid 2/600.

[70]Muqātil 74/1, 116v–117r (where they are curiously referred to as *a'rāb*); Fīrūzābādī 87; Thawri 107; Mujāhid 1/215; 'Abd al-Razzāq, *Tafsīr* 35r; Ibn Abī Shayba 12/207–208; Farrā' 1/336; Nasā'ī, *Faḍā'il* 149–50; Ṭabarī, *Tafsīr* 7/201–202, 11/374, 381—cf. also 15/234–36, commenting on Sūrat al-Kahf (18), v. 28, which he notes as a parallel; Zajjāj 2/251; Wāḥidī 162–63; Bayhaqī, *Shu'ab* 7/334; Ibn al-Jawzī (d. 597/1200), *al-Tabṣira*, Dar al-Kutub al-'Ilmīya, Beirut 1986, 1/486; Ibn 'Asākir 3/445, 8/380; Suyūṭī, *Durr* 3/13.

[71]Goldziher, *Muslim Studies* 1/72 n. 4; von Grunebaum, *Medieval Islam* 204; Mottahedeh 168 n. 21; Levy 55 n. 1.

tribal confederations like Muḍar. From the available *isnād* information we learn that the first opinion was advanced by Ja'far al-Ṣādiq (d. 148/765) and 'Aṭā' (al-Khurāsānī, d. 135/752), the latter attributing it to Ibn 'Abbās. But other transmitters from Ibn 'Abbās (such as Sa'īd ibn Jubayr and 'Aṭīya al-'Awfī), as well as the traditions of other early second-century figures (such as Mujāhid, Qatāda and al-Kalbī, d. 146/763), upheld the second opinion.[72] As for "the occasion of revelation" (*sabab al-nuzūl*) of this verse, we also notice that it was revealed in order to rebuke the Companion Thābit ibn Qays, who mentioned somebody's mother in a slanderous way.[73] The narrative reported from Ibn Abī Mulayka ('Abd Allāh ibn 'Ubayd Allāh, d. 117–18/735–36) and Muqātil says that it was revealed when people from Quraysh protested against Bilāl's call to prayer (*adhān*) from the roof of the Ka'ba upon the occupation of Mecca, because of his black colour.[74]

Goldziher also noted that this verse was reportedly recited by the Prophet during his Farewell (*al-wadā'*) Pilgrimage to Mecca, though in some later sources there was added to the address he delivered on that occasion the statement: "The Arab has no advantage over a non-Arab except through mindfulness of God" (*lā faḍla li-'arabīyin 'alā a'jamīyin illā bi-l-taqwā*).[75] Now Goldziher's observation is basically correct, as a cross-examination with major *sīra*, *maghāzī*, *ḥadīth* and historiographical sources reveals that such an addition is indeed absent from them. However, this does not alter the fact that Sūrat al-Ḥujurāt

---

[72]Cf. Fīrūzābādī 325; Mujāhid 2/608; 'Abd al-Razzāq, *Tafsīr* 138r–v; Farrā' 3/72; Ibn al-Yazīdī (d. 237/851), *Gharīb al-Qur'ān wa-Tafsīruh*, ed. 'Abd al-Razzāq Ḥusayn, Mu'assasat al-Risāla, Beirut 1987, 165; Ibn Qutayba, *Tafsīr* 416; Zajjāj 5/37–38; Ibn 'Abd Rabbihi 3/284, 354; Ṭabarī, *Tafsīr* 26/139–40; Ḥalīmī 2/152; Abū Ḥayyān al-Tawḥīdī (d. 444/1052), *al-Baṣā'ir wa-l-Dhakhā'ir*, ed. Wadād al-Qāḍī, Beirut 1988, 1/147; Baghawī (d. 510/1116), *Ma'ālim al-Tanzīl*, Bombay 1273 AH, 4/88; Ṭabarsī 26/96–97; and see the lexicographic work of the early third/ninth-century Abū l-'Umaythil al-A'rābī, *Mā Ittafaqa Lafẓuhu wa-Ikhtalafa Ma'nāhu*, Ms. Ẓāhirīya, *Majmū'* no. 104, 115.

[73]Fīrūzābādī 325; Wāḥidī 295.

[74]Wāḥidī 295; Ibn 'Asākir 3/465; and compare with Fīrūzābādī 325, where the same was reported under the anonymous form *wa-yuqālu*, "and it has been said."

[75]Goldziher, *Muslim Studies* 1/72 n. 3; cf. also Levy 60. The later sources referred to are Ya'qūbī (d. 282/895), *Tārīkh*, ed. M.T. Houtsma, Leiden 1969, 2/123; Jāḥiẓ, *al-Bayān* 2/33; Ibn 'Abd Rabbihi 2/85.

(49), v. 13, which conveys a clear sense of equality, was reportedly recited by the Prophet on that occasion, a fact that renders the above-mentioned addition a mere elaboration on it. In an attempt to establish the date of this additional elaboration, and possible figures responsible for it, we have conducted further investigations into the available *isnād* information and have arrived at the following conclusions:

1. In none of Ibn Isḥāq's traditions (from Yaḥyā ibn ʻAbbād, Layth ibn Sulaym, Ibn Abī Najīh), or those of his mid-second/eighth century contemporaries (like ʻAmr ibn Abī ʻAmr ← ʻIkrima, Saʻīd ibn Abī ʻArūba ← Qatāda, Hishām ibn al-Ghāz ← Nāfiʻ, Qurra ibn Khālid ← Ibn Sīrīn; Jaʻfar al-Ṣādiq ← Muḥammad al-Bāqir, etc.), is there any mention of this additional statement in the Farewell Pilgrimage.[76]

2. The link al-Ṣādiq ← al-Bāqir, which transmits the tradition of Jābir ibn ʻAbd Allāh, is worth noting because of the existence of two similar traditions by Jābir himself and Abū Saʻīd al-Khudrī, both transmitted by Abū Naḍra (al-Mundhir ibn Mālik, d. 108–109/726–27). We notice that the tradition Abū Naḍra ← Jābir includes the additional statement within the context of the Farewell Address only when reported by a certain Shayba al-ʻAbsī, nicknamed Abū Qulāba. On the other hand, when the Abū Naḍra ← al-Khudrī tradition is reported by Saʻīd ibn Iyās al-Jarīrī (d. 144/761), the same statement is given, but without mentioning the context of the Farewell Pilgrimage.[77]

[76] Ibn Hishām, *al-Sīra al-Nabawīya*, ed. ʻAbd al-Raʼūf Saʻd, Dār al-Jil, Beirut 1975, 4/185–87; Wāqidī, *Maghāzī*, ed. M. Jones, ʻĀlam al-Kutub, Beirut 1984, 3/1110–13; Ibn Saʻd 2/183–86; Ṭabarī, *Tarikh al-Umam wa-l-Mulūk*, ed. Muḥammad Abū l-Faḍl Ibrāhīm, Dār Suwaydān, Beirut 1967, 3/150–52. See also Ibn Sayyid al-Nās 2/272–80; Abū Yaʻlā, *al-Mafārīd*, ed. ʻAbd Allāh al-Judayʻ, Maktabat Dār al-Aqṣā, Medina 1985, 100–101; Ibn Ḥibbān, *al-Sīra al-Nabawīya wa-Tārīkh al-Khulafā'*, ed. al-Sayyid ʻAzīz Bek, Dār al-Fikr, Beirut 1987, 395–96; Ibn ʻAbd al-Barr, *al-Durar*, Dār al-Kutub al-ʻIlmīya, Beirut 1984, 201; Bayhaqī, *Shuʻab* 4/386–87; Ibn ʻAsākir 7/441, 19/155; Nasāʼī, *Tafsīr* 1/533–34, who rather cites this speech in connection with the revelation of Sūrat al-Tawba (9), v. 3.

[77] Cf. Ibn Ḥanbal, *Musnad* 5/411; Abū l-Shaykh (d. 369/979), *al-Tawbīkh wa-l-Tanbīh*, ed. Ḥasan Ibn al-Mandūḥ, Maktabat al-Tawʻiya al-Islāmīya, Cairo 1408 AH, 259; Abū Nuʻaym 3/100; Daylamī 4/371; Suyūṭī, *Durr* 6/98–99.

3. A variant similar to the one by al-Jarīrī was transmitted from Jābir by the chain 'Abd Allāh ibn Salama ← Zuhrī ← Abd al-Raḥmān ibn Ka'b, but again, outside the context of the Pilgrimage speech.[78]

4. One tradition by Abū Umāma refers to this verse as a basis for establishing religious piety as the only criterion for preference. This is done in the context of a slanderous statement (*ta'yīr*) by Abū Dharr concerning Bilāl's mother, but again without mentioning the Farewell Address.[79]

5. From a report cited by Balādhurī we learn that during Ziyād's governorship of Iraq under Mu'āwiya the Shī'a there invoked Sūrat al-Mā'ida (5), v. 45 (*al-nafsu bi-l-nafs*), when demanding equal treatment for Arabs and non-Arabs. We also learn that on that occasion they used a statement similar to the above-mentioned Prophetic one, namely: "There is no preference for an Arab over somebody else" (*lā faḍla li-'arabīyin 'alā ghayrih*).[80]

To conclude this discussion, mention may be made of another tradition, noted by Goldziher, which describes the massive conversion of Arabs and non-Arabs in the form of a reported dream of the Prophet. According to this, Muḥammad saw that he was driving black sheep that soon became mixed with and outnumbered by sandy / white ones (*'ufr / bīḍ*)—representing Arabs and non-Arabs, respectively. However, we notice again that this tradition does not date before the turn of the first/seventh century, as it was overwhelmingly attributed to the Prophet in *mursal* forms by Qatāda and Ḥasan al-Baṣrī.[81]

---

[78]Ibn Abī Ḥātim, *'Ilal* 2/161.

[79]Ibn 'Asākir 3/464; Suyūṭī, *Durr* 6/99.

[80]Balādhurī, *Ansāb al-Ashrāf* 4A, ed. M. Schloessinger and M.J. Kister, Jerusalem 1971, 220. This, we are told, they did when Ziyād refused to execute an Arab from Banū Asad for killing a Muslim from non-Arab origin.

[81]Goldziher, *Muslim Studies* 1/112; for the *isnād* information see 'Abd al-Razzāq, *Muṣannaf* 11/66; Ibn Ḥanbal, *Faḍa'il* 1/163; Daraquṭnı, *al-'Ilal al-Warida Fı l-Aḥādīth al-Nabawīya*, ed. Maḥfūẓ al-Salafī, Dār Ṭayba, Riyadh 1985, 1/289; Ḥākim 4/395; Bayhaqī, *Dalā'il* 6/336–37; Muttaqī 11/569 no. 32692, 12/92 no. 34134.

CHAPTER II

THE IMPACT OF THE ARAB POLITY IN RETROSPECT

THE HAZARDOUS TASK of reconstructing the history of the Arab polity during the first Islamic century has long occupied modern scholarship. Admittedly, the cardinal difficulty lies in the fact that almost everything that has reached us concerning this period comes from traditional Muslim compilations, the main aim of which was to establish a paradigm of sacred history for it.[1] In an attempt to contribute to the study of this paradigm, but without going beyond the scope of the present enquiry, we shall proceed to re-examine some of the material on issues of direct relevance to our topic.

As noted by von Grunebaum, the importance of the Arab–Persian battle of Dhū Qār (in *ca.* AD 610) for the future relations between these two peoples cannot be denied.[2] We may concede the truth of the view that without the Arab victory in that battle the future of the region, and with it, that of Islam as well, would have been different. The problem, however, lies in the fact that the only sources on Dhū Qār are traditional Muslim ones that not only present it within the framework of the crucial stage in the birth of Islam, but also advance

[1]See J. Wansbrough, *The Sectarian Milieu*, London 1978; also M. Sharon, "The Military Reform of Abū Muslim," in M. Sharon, ed., *Studies in Islamic History and Civilisation*, Jerusalem 1986, 109 n. 15.

[2]Von Grunebaum, "The Nature of Arab Unity," 18, and compare with an earlier note by Goldziher, *Muslim Studies* 1/100.

the notion that the Prophet himself expressed satisfaction with the Arab victory. A close examination of the relevant traditions, however, reveals that they were basically the product of two mid-second/eighth century figures: Ibrāhīm al-Taymī (his exact death date is unknown) and Muḥammad ibn Sawā' (d. 187/802). A third figure from approximately the same period, Khālid ibn Sā'id al-Umawī, circulated a similar variant of the Prophet's reaction through a family *isnād*. The main elements reiterated by these traditions are 1) the Prophet's statement that the Arabs / var. Banū Bakr gained justice (*intaṣafū*) from the Persians (*'ajam*), 2) the information that the Arabs used Muḥammad's name as their battle slogan (*shi'ār*), and hence, 3) the Prophet's statement: "They were victorious through me" (*bī nuṣirū*), upon hearing the outcome of the battle.[3]

Now, for one who finds history in these traditions there is a good case in all this for a national Arabian position adopted by the Prophet of Islam against the Persians. However, as it stands, and in the absence of any other sources, the only conclusion that can safely be drawn from this material is that this was how the issue was perceived from the point of view of a certain current in Muslim society in the mid-second/eighth century, and no more. As such, it can at most reflect an anti-Persian sentiment during that period, a view supported by a few *rajaz* verses composed by Abū l-Najm al-'Ijlī during the reign of the 'Abbāsid caliph Manṣūr.[4]

Another set of traditions specify the Prophet's assessment of the future of his religious movement *vis-à-vis* Arabs and *'ajam*. This comes in the form of a reported conversation between him and his uncle Abū Ṭālib. This exchange has it that Muḥammad promised that if his people would follow him, the Arabs in general would do likewise and the *'ajam* would pay poll tax (*jizya*) to them. The authorities responsible for

---

[3]Ibn Ḥanbal, *Faḍā'il* 2/829; *idem*, *Kitāb al-'Ilal wa-Ma'rifat al-Rijāl*, ed. Waṣī Allāh 'Abbās, al-Maktab al-Islāmī, Beirut, and Dār al-Khānī, Riyadh, 1988, 1/129; Akram Ḍiyā' al-'Umarī, *Musnad Khalīfa ibn Khayyāṭ* (d. 240/854), Medina 1985, 24; al-'Askarī, *al-Awā'il*, Dār al-Kutub al-'Ilmīya, Beirut 1987, 18; Daylamī 5/548; Abū l-Baqā', *al-Manāqib al-Mazyadīya*, ed. Ṣāliḥ Darādka and Muḥammad Khraysāt, Maktabat al-Risāla al-Ḥadītha, Amman 1984, 422; Haythamī, *Majma'* 6/211; Albānī 2/47–48. Cf. also Ṭabarī, *Tārīkh* 2/193, 207.

[4]Ibn al-Shajarī, *Ḥamāsa*, Cairo 1345 AH, 38.

circulating this tradition are two mid-second/eighth century figures: Sulaymān ibn Mihrān al-A'mash (d. 145–48/762–65) and Ibn Isḥāq, the latter reporting it in an 'Abbāsid family line through al-'Abbās ibn 'Abd Allāh ibn Mi'bad.[5]

The same observation applies to the numerous traditions that attribute to the Prophet statements instigating Arab tribes to fight the Persians and promising his Companions the fall of "Chosroes" (*Kisrā*) and "Caesar" (*Qayṣar*) and the seizure of their treasures.[6] There are also some exegetical traditions on Sūrat al-Fatḥ (48), vv. 116–21, which specify the Persians and Byzantines as the future enemies who will be defeated.[7] Under the same category comes the statement of the local Persian leader, Hurmuzān, that he reportedly made to 'Umar I after falling captive and confessing Islam. "As long as God was neutral in the struggle between the Arab forces (lit. "companies," *ma'āshir*) and the Persians," he said, "the latter were victorious; then He took the side of the Arabs and brought about their victory."[8]

This is not meant as an implicit rejection of the role played by the Arabs in the collapse of Persian and Byzantine rule over the area, nor as a tacit denial of the emergence, on the ruins of this rule, of a local polity in which the Arab element soon became predominant. Indeed, in some

---

[5]Ibn Hishām 2/46; Ibn Isḥāq, *Kitāb al-Siyar wa-l-Maghāzī*, ed. Suhayl Zakkār, Dār al-Fikr, Beirut 1978, 236; Ibn Ḥibbān, *Ṣaḥīḥ* 8/242; Abū Ya'lā 4/455–56; Ibn Ḥanbal, *Musnad* 1/227, 2/362; Ḥākim 2/432; Nasā'ī, *Tafsīr* 2/216–17; Wāḥidī 275; Ṭabarī, *Tafsīr* 23/125; Bayhaqī, *Sunan* 9/188; Suyūṭī, *Durr* 5/295. The *tafsīr* sources cited here quote this tradition in the context of explaining the occasion for the revelation of Sūrat Ṣād (38), vv. 1–5.

[6]For some of these, see Ibn Ḥanbal, *Faḍā'il* 2/865–66; al-Basawī (d. 277/890), *al-Ma'rifa wa-l-Tārīkh*, ed. Akram Ḍiyā' al-'Umarī, Beirut 1981, 1/266–67, 352, 2/514–15; Ibn Abī 'Āṣim (d. 287/900), *al-Awā'il*, ed. Muḥammad Sa'īd Zaglūl, Dār al-Kutub al-'Ilmīya, Beirut 1987, 56; Ibn Abī Ḥatim, *'Ilal* 2/397; Ibn Ḥibbān, *Ṣaḥīḥ* 8/237, 243–44; Ṭabarānī, *al-Mu'jam al-Awsaṭ* 2/492–93; al-Sam'ānī, *Kitāb al-Ansāb*, facs. ed. by D.S. Margoliouth, London 1912, 8r; Ḥākim 4/515, 519; al-Khaṭīb al-Baghdādī 1/186, 190, 5/36, 10/38; Bayhaqī, *Dalā'il* 4/393, 6/322–30; *idem*, *Sunan* 5/225–26, 9/177; Ibn 'Asākir 1/140–41, 9/12; Muttaqī 11/no. 31773, 12/no. 34139, 13/no. 37617.

[7]Mujāhid 2/602–603; Muqātil 74/2, 161v; Yaḥyā ibn Ādam, *Kitāb al-Kharāj*, ed. T.W. Juynboll, Leiden 1895, 22; Fīrūzābādī 320; Farrā' 3/67; Ibn Qutayba, *Tafsīr* 413; Ṭabarī, *Tafsīr* 26/21–22.

[8]Sa'īd ibn Manṣūr 2/252.

reports on the early wars against the Persians we encounter statements describing Hurmuz as a king "most hostile to the Arabs,"[9] while the "Muslim" armies are merely referred to as "the forces (*ma'āshir*) of the Arabs."[10] The point to be stressed here is that such references to the Arabs should be identified and separated from the religious elements that were gradually attached to them in the Muslim material on the conquests (*futūḥ*), a process that, we believe, was the product of the great literary fusion between Arabism and Islam in the second/eighth century. To provide a full examination of this *futūḥ* material would carry us beyound the scope of the present study. We can only call for more attention to the sporadic references to the *'arab* as an element separate from *muhājirūn*, *mawālī*, *anbāṭ*, *'abīd* and even Jews in the reports on the anti-Byzantine wars in Syria.[11]

A group of traditions and reports mention several instances and fields of discrimination in favour of the Arabs within the new Arab polity. The first notion that calls for attention is one stating that no Arab may be enslaved. Noting this, von Grunebaum expressed the view that only under Islam could the application of this principle be rendered effective.[12] However, from the information cited by Bayhaqī on the treatment of the matter by Shāfi'ī (d. 204/819) we learn that such a position was held by Muslim scholars around the turn of the first/seventh century. We are specifically told that Sa'īd ibn al-Musayyib, Sha'bī and Zuhrī held that no Arab could be enslaved and

[9]Ḥākim 3/299; Bayhaqī, *Sunan* 6/311.

[10]Ṭabarī, *Tārīkh* 4/140; Ibn Abī Shayba 12/194; Ḥākim 3/451–52.

[11]For coverage of this subject, see F.M. Donner, *The Early Muslim Conquests*, Princeton 1983, 91 *passim*; Sharon, "Military Reforms," 106–12. This issue was raised by me on a previous occasion; see S. Bashear "Apocalyptic and Other Materials on Early Muslim–Byzantine Wars," 199. More of these separate references may be found in ps.-Wāqidī, *Futūḥ al-Shām*, al-Maktaba al-Sha'bīya, Beirut n.d., 1/12–14, 18, 27, 76–78, 96, 98–99, 101–103, 105; Abū Ḥafṣ Ibn Shāhīn, *Ḥadīth*, Ms. Ẓāhirīya, *Majmū'* no. 83, 102; Ibn Duqmāq, *al-Intiṣār*, ed. K. Vollers, Cairo 1893, 4/5; al-Azdī, *Futūḥ al-Shām*, ed. W.N. Lees, Calcutta 1854, 75. For a modern evaluation of the originality of this last source, see L.I. Conrad, "Al-Azdī's History of the Arab Conquests in Bilād al-Shām: Some Historiographical Observations," in *The Fourth International Conference on the History of Bilād al-Shām*, ed. Muḥammad 'Adnān Bakhīt, Amman 1987, 28–62.

[12]Von Grunebaum, "The Nature of Arab Unity," 19.

reported traditions to that effect from the Prophet, 'Umar I and 'Umar II. On the other hand, certain scholars, whom Bayhaqī does not name, held that Arabs should be treated the same as *'ajam* and that Shāfi'ī, who shared this position, doubted the authenticity of Prophetic traditions that favoured the Arabs.[13]

The only feasible explanation for such discrepancies among the various traditional reports is the recasting of materials reflecting what were initially two separate currents: the Arab policies on the one hand, and the religious position of Islam on the other. The same observation can be made concerning the material exempting the Arabs from payment of tithes (*'ushūr*). One may notice that in the traditions attributed to the Prophet and 'Umar I on this issue, the terms "Arabs" and "Muslims" are used interchangeably.[14] And related to this also are the controversial reports on the positions and fiscal policies attributed to the Prophet, 'Umar I and 'Alī concerning the Arab tribes, especially Banū Taghlib, which refused to convert to Islam and threatened to join the Byzantines. The relevant material on this last issue and other related ones seems to contain two distinct elements that stood at the heart of scholarly controversies: on the one hand, the notion that conversion was obligatory for the Arabs and, on the other, the argument that Christian Arab tribes were not to be treated like non-Arabs.[15] One may also

---

[13]Bayhaqī, *Sunan* 9/73–74. See also Ibn 'Abd al-Barr, *Tamhīd* 3/133–34, 5/195; Ḥalīmī 2/151; Ṭabarānī, *al-Mu'jam al-Kabīr* 20/168; Haythamī, *Majma'* 5/332; and compare between the Prophetic tradition cited by Ibn Abī Ḥātim, *'Ilal* 1/442, which gives priority to freeing someone from among the children of Ismā'īl, and the information, cited by Ibn Abī Shayba 12/192, that the ransom of an Arab during the Battle of Badr was double that of a *mawlā*.

[14]Bishr ibn Maṭar al-Wāsiṭī, *Ḥadīth*, Ms. Ẓāhirīya, *Majmū'* no. 94, 93; al-Qaṭṭān, *Ḥadīth*, Ms. Ẓāhirīya, *Majmū'* no. 31, 178; Ibn Ḥanbal, *Musnad* 1/190, 3/474, 4/322, 5/410; Basawī 1/292; al-Ḥarbī (d. 285/898), *Gharīb al-Ḥadīth*, ed. Sulaymān al-'Āyid, Kullīyat al-Sharī'a, Mecca 1985, 1/153; Abū Ya'lā 2/256; Bayhaqī, *Sunan* 9/199, 211; Baghawī, *Mukhtaṣar al-Mu'jam*, Ms. Ẓāhirīya, *Majmū'* no. 94, 132; Daylamī 5/287; Mughulṭay, *al-Zahr al-Bāsim*, Ms. Leiden, Or. 370, 120v; Haythamī, *Majma'* 3/87; Muttaqī 12/no. 33937.

[15]For such questions as whether one should consider non-Muslim Arabs as *dhimmīs* or *ahl al-kitāb*, whether one may eat meat slaughtered by them and oblige them to pay poll tax, and the taxes that should be levied on their lands, cattle and merchandise, see Yaḥyā ibn Ādam, 10–12; Abū Yūsuf, *Kitāb al-Kharāj*, al-Maṭba'a al-Salafīya, Cairo 1352 AH, 58–59, 66–67, 120; Ibn al-Ja'd (d. 230/844), *Musnad*,

notice that these issues were matters of intense controversy throughout the second/eighth century, with traditions adduced in the names of the Prophet, 'Umar I and 'Alī to support either view. The legal ruling to exempt Banū Taghlib from payment of *jizya* and to collect, instead, a doubled *zakāt* (alms tax) from them, was adopted by Thawrī, Abū Ḥanīfa (d. 150/767), Shāfi'ī and Ibn Ḥanbal—all relying on a Kūfan tradition asserting that such was the policy of 'Umar I. We also learn that no explicit ruling on the matter was reported from Mālik ibn Anas (d. 179/795), although scholars of the Mālikī rite are said not to have treated Banū Taghlib differently from the rest of those from whom *jizya* was levied. Mālik seems to have stood alone also when he ruled that *'ajam* and non-Muslim Arabs should be subject to payment of *jizya* on an equal footing. As for Shāfi'ī and Abū 'Ubayd (al-Qāsim ibn Sallām, d. 224/838), they reportedly adopted a middle path in ruling that *jizya* is to be accepted from Arabs only if they are *ahl al-kitāb* (lit. "people of the book," i.e. Jews and Christians).[16]

One tradition gives a military justification to 'Umar I's pro-Arabian policy. This is a family tradition circulated by Sa'īd ibn 'Amr ibn Sa'īd ibn al-'Āṣ (d. 110/728). According to this tradition, 'Umar I refrained from killing non-Muslim Arabs only because he heard the Prophet saying that God would defend "this religion" (*hādhā l-dīn*) with Christians from the Rabī'a tribal confederation (to whom Banū Taghlib belonged) on the banks of the Euphrates.[17]

The notion that only Islam could be accepted from the Arabs was understood by Wellhausen as part of the policy to rid Arabia of any other religion,[18] and could apparently be taken as a "proof" that Is-

---

ed. 'Abd al-Mahdī ibn 'Abd al-Hādī, Maktabat al-Falāḥ, Kuwait 1985, 1/322; Ibn Ḥanbal, *'Ilal* 3/386; Abū 'Ubayd (d. 224/838), *Kitāb al-Amwāl*, Cairo 1353 AH, 41; Ṭabarī, *Tahdhīb al-Āthār (Musnad 'Alī)*, ed. Maḥmūd Shākir, Maṭba'at al-Madanī, Cairo 1982, 223–24; Abū Ya'lā 1/204; al-Mas'ūdī (d. 345/956), *al-Tanbīh wa-l-Ishrāf*, Maktabat Khayyāṭ, Beirut 1985, 167–68, 206; Ibn al-Mundhir (d. 318/930), *al-Ijtimā'*, ed. 'Abd Allāh al-Bārūdī, Dār al-Jinān, Beirut 1986, 56–59; Māwardī (d. 450/1058), *al-Aḥkām al-Sulṭānīya*, Dār al-Kutub al-'Ilmīya, Beirut 1978, 109; Ibn Ḥazm, *Marātib al-Ijmā'* 44–45; Bayhaqī, *Sunan* 7/173, 9/187, 216–18, 284.

[16]Ibn 'Abd al-Barr, *Tamhīd* 2/117–18, 131–32.

[17]Bazzār, *Musnad* 1/443; cf. also Haythamī, *Kashf* 2/287; *idem*, *Majma'* 5/302; Abū Ya'lā 1/204; Bayhaqī, *Sunan* 9/187; Ibn 'Asākir 7/254, 330.

[18]Wellhausen 24.

lam and Arabism were considered one and the same right from the beginning. This notion was also associated with the name of 'Umar I, especially in the case of the Jews of Khaybar and the Christians of Najrān; but traditions in this spirit were attributed to the Prophet via other Companions, as well as 'Ā'isha.[19] From a note by Ibn Ḥanbal ← Aṣma'ī (d. 217/832), we also learn that what was meant was the territory not previously controlled by the Byzantines or Persians.[20] Even more interesting is the *isnād* information on some of these traditions, which points clearly to the early second/eighth century as the date for the current that equated Arabism with Islam in this respect. We notice, for example, that Zuhrī and Ḥasan al-Baṣrī, who figure as important links in the *isnād*s of some of these traditions, transmit the same in *mursal* forms. From a few sources we also learn that 'Umar II too attributed the same position to the Prophet without specifying his sources, and only by using the phrase "it has reached me that...." (*balaghanī annahu....*).[21]

The name of 'Umar I is prominently associated with the policy of favouring the Arabs and segregating them from *'ajam*, *dhimmī*s and even *mawālī*. Such was the bottom line in his well-known policy of establishing the separate Arab settlements known as *amṣār*. Against this background, the information that in his stipend policy (*'aṭā'*) he treated equally Arabs and *mawālī* who participated in the Battle of Badr[22] seems clearly to be tendentious. One may also note that such a notion contradicts the information that until the Arabization of registers (*dawāwīn*) during the reign of 'Abd al-Malik (d. 86/705) or even that of Hishām (d. 125/742), Arabs and *'ajam* were registered separately.[23]

[19]Ibn al-Jārūd (d. 307/919), *al-Muntaqā Min al-Sunan*, Dār al-Qalam, Beirut 1987, 407; Ibn Ḥibbān, *Ṣaḥīḥ* 6/26; Ṭabarānī, *al-Mu'jam al-Awsaṭ* 2/42; Abū Nu'aym 8/385; Bayhaqī, *Sunan* 6/115; Ibn 'Asākir 8/733, 9/690; Abū Bakr al-Shīrāzī, *Amālī*, Ms. Ẓāhirīya, *Majmū'* no. 63, 5; Ibn 'Abd al-Barr, *Tamhīd* 6/463, 12/13–15; Muttaqī 12/nos. 35147–48, 14/nos. 38160, 38252–54.

[20]'Abd Allāh ibn Aḥmad ibn Ḥanbal, *Masā'il al-Imām Aḥmad*, ed. Zuhayr al-Shāwīsh, al-Maktab al-Islāmī, Beirut 1988, 444.

[21]Ibn al-Ja'd 2/1126–27; Bayhaqī, *Sunan* 9/207–208.

[22]Ibn Abī Shayba 12/207; Bayhaqī, *Sunan* 6/349; Ṭabarī, *Tārīkh* 4/211.

[23]Ibn 'Asākir 7/114. More information on 'Abd al-Malik's or Hishām's Arabization of the registers may be consulted in Balādhurī, *Futūḥ* 1/230, 2/368–69; *The Fihrist of al-Nadīm*, trans. B. Dodge, London and New York 1970, 2/581, 583, 586.

There is also sporadic information that, as in a few *futūḥ* reports, makes a separate identification of *mawālī* and Arab regiments (*bu'ūth*) during Hishām's reign, as well as in a certain summer campaign (*ṣā'ifa*) against the Byzantines under the Umayyad commander Maslama ibn 'Abd al-Malik.[24]

A family tradition that Mālik ibn Anas reports from al-'Alā' ibn 'Abd al-Raḥmān ibn Ya'qūb attributes to 'Umar I a decision forbidding any *a'jamī* to trade in an Arab market (*lā yabī'anna fī sūqinā a'jamīyun*). We also learn from it that al-'Alā' 's grandfather, who was himself a cloth trader (*tājiru bazzin*) of non-Arab origin, personally testified to this order.[25] Another strong expression of 'Umar I's policy comes in a series of widely circulated reports that attribute to him statements forbidding Arabs to learn non-Arab languages (*raṭānat al-a'ājim*), wear their style of clothing (*ziyy*) or adopt their habits (*'ādāt*), and ordering them to adhere, instead, to the rough way of life of their ancestor Ma'add. Goldziher, who noted this tradition, briefly observed that a basic core of it also occurs in a poem of Ḥassān ibn Thābit. However, he did not seem to have felt that it merited further examination and assigned it to the category of later forms of traditional prohibitions on foreign customs.[26] As for 'Umar I's order, it appears within different contexts and was cited by a wide variety of sources. Especially worth noting is the reported attempt to attribute one variant of it to the Prophet in a *mursal* form on the authority of 'Abd Allāh ibn Sa'īd al-Maqburī, who circulated it after the mid-second/eighth century.[27] One also notices that the order attributed to 'Umar I widely varies in content following the different early second-century figures who reported it from its main transmitter, Abū 'Uthmān al-Nahdī ('Abd al-Raḥmān ibn Mall, d. 95–100/713–

---

[24]For some of these, see Ibn 'Asākir, 16/160, 445.

[25]Mālik ibn Anas, *Muwaṭṭa'*, in the recension of Shaybānī (d. 189/804), ed. 'Abd al-Wahhāb 'Abd al-Laṭīf, Dār al-Qalam, Beirut n.d., 283.

[26]Goldziher, *Muslim Studies* 1/143. Ḥassān's verse in question, *wa-lā talbasū ziyyan ka-ziyyi l-a'ājimi*, "and do not wear clothing styled after that of the *a'ājim*," was cited also by Ibn Hishām 4/157

[27]Ṭabarānī, *al-Mu'jam al-Kabīr* 19/40; Ibn 'Asākir 9/102; al-Rāmhurmuzī, *Amthāl al-Ḥadīth*, ed. Aḥmad 'Abd al-Fattāḥ Tamām, Mu'assasat al-Kutub al-Thaqāfīya, Beirut 1988, 161–62; Sakhāwī 163–64; Fattanī 113.

18). And while the context given for the main version is a letter sent by ʿUmar I to Adharbayjān, he is said to have made similar statements when he visited Jābiya in Syria. We also notice that to ʿAbd Allāh ibn al-Zubayr (d. 72/691) too was attributed a prohibition on the wearing of silk that figures centrally in the variants attributed to both ʿUmar and the Prophet. Finally, in two *ḥadīth* sources the term *aʿājim* is replaced by the phrase "the people of polytheism" (*ahl al-shirk*).[28]

The notion that Arabs should not completely dissociate themselves from desert life is also linked with the name of ʿUmar I. One report says that he urged his district governors to order "people" (*al-nās*) to spend some time in the desert during the spring.[29] In another, ʿUmar I is even quoted as specifying knowledge in dealing with Jāhilī matters (*man lam yuʿālij amr al-jāhilīya....*) as one of two things without which the Arabs would perish, the other being companionship with the Prophet.[30] Finally, the reported testament of ʿUmar to his successor does not fail to mention the *aʿrāb* as one of the groups he recommended for good treatment (*wa-ūṣīhi bi-l-aʿrābi khayran*), because they were "the origins of the Arabs and a reinforcement for Islam" (*li-annahum aṣlu l-ʿarabi wa-māddatu l-islām*).[31]

---

[28]Compare al-Muʿāfā ibn ʿImrān (d. 185/801), *Kitāb al-Zuhd*, Ms. Ẓāhirīya, *Ḥadīth* no. 359, 260; Abū l-ʿUmaythil 121; Abū ʿUbayd al-Qāsim ibn Sallām (d. 224/838), *Gharīb al-Ḥadīth*, ed. Muḥammad ʿAbd al-Muʿīd Khān, Hyderabad 1966, 3/326–28; al-Ḥirafī 5; Ibn al-Jaʿd 1/517; Ibn Zanjawayh (d. 251/865), *Kitāb al-Amwāl*, Riyadh 1986, 1/271; Muslim 6/140–41; Ibn Qutayba, *ʿUyūn* 1/132; al-Ḥarbī 2/544–46; Ibn Ḥibbān, *Ṣaḥīḥ* 7/401; Abū Nuʿaym 3/122; Bayhaqī, *Shuʿab* 5/137, 159, 7/43–44; *idem*, *Sunan* 2/18, 423, 3/269–70, 9/234, 10/14; Ibn ʿAsākir 8/125; Ibn al-Jawzī, *Gharīb al-Ḥadīth*, ed. ʿAbd al-Muʿṭi Qalʿajī, Dār al-Kutub al-ʿIlmīya, Beirut 1985, 2/364; Ibn ʿAbd al-Barr, *Tamhīd* 14/252; Zaylaʿī (d. 762/1360), *Naṣb al-Rāya*, Dār al-Ḥadīth, Cairo 1938, 4/226–27; Sakhāwī 165; Fattanī 113; Suyūṭī, *al-Aḥādīth al-Ḥisān*, ed. A. Arāzī, Jerusalem 1983, 48–49; Muttaqī 3/nos. 5732, 6315, 8486, 9034.

[29]Al-Dhakwānī, *Amālī*, Ms. Ẓāhirīya, *Majmūʿ* no. 63, 5.

[30]Ibn al-Jaʿd 2/876; Ibn Abī Shayba 12/193; Ibn Saʿd 6/88; Abū Nuʿaym 7/243; Ḥākim 4/428; Bayhaqī, *Shuʿab* 6/70.

[31]Abū Yūsuf 13–14; Ibn al-Sammāk, *Ḥadīth*, Ms. Ẓāhirīya, *Majmūʿ* no. 103, 25; Ibn al-Jaʿd 1/587; Abū l-ʿArab (d. 333/944), *Kitāb al-Miḥan*, ed. Yaḥyā al-Jabbūrī, Dār al-Gharb al-Islāmī, Qatar 1983, 51; Bayhaqī, *Sunan* 9/206; Ibn ʿAsākir 3/168; ʿIrāqī 5; Haytamī 23. Cf. also Nasāʾī, *Tafsīr* 2/406, where a variant of this tradition

Elaborations on the core of the pro-Arab policy associated with the name of ʿUmar I were made in the course of time and acquired the form of statements also attributed to the Prophet. But before we move on to examine this kind of material, note must be made of the fact that to the Prophet were also attributed several traditions that warn against harming even the non-Muslim *dhimmī* and *muʿāhid* and urge just treatment for them.[32] Our concern, however, is not the official or internal policies towards non-Muslim subjects under Muslim rule,[33] but the cultural and behavioural expressions of the positions towards non-Arabs and non-Arab habits and ways in daily life that were often attributed to the Prophet in traditional forms.

To begin with, the Prophetic tradition circulated in order to abrogate a former prohibition of intercourse with a suckling woman (*al-ghiyāl*) makes a point of basing the new permission on the fact that such a practice was followed by both Persians and Byzantines and did not cause any harm to them.[34] Another testimony, cited in the name of the Companion al-Barrāʾ ibn ʿĀzib, states that the Prophet recommended for Muslims the shaking / clapping of hands (*muṣāfaḥa*) in spite of the objection expressed by al-Barrāʾ that such was the manner of *aʿājim*.[35] But such cases of invoking and consciously conceding the imitation of non-Arab practices are indeed rare ones in our sources, and must be weighed against the numerous traditions rejecting non-Arab habits.

One of these traditions was attributed to the Prophet through Abū Hurayra on the authority of ʿAbd al-Raḥmān ibn Ziyād ibn Anʿam (d. 161/777). This report has it that while in the market, the Prophet was approached by someone who tried to kiss his hand. The Prophet

is cited in connection with Sūrat al-Ḥashr (59), v. 9, but without mentioning the element of *aʿrāb*.

[32]Al-Khaṭīb al-Baghdādī 8/370; Ibn al-Jawzī, *al-Mawḍūʿāt*, Medina 1966, 2/236; Sakhāwī 392–93; Samhūdī (d. 911/1505), *al-Ghummāz ʿAlā l-Lummāz*, ed. Muḥammad ʿAṭā, Dār al-Kutub al-ʿIlmīya 1986, 20.

[33]For coverage of this subject, see A.S. Tritton, *The Caliphs and Their Non-Muslim Subjects*, London 1939.

[34]This tradition was noted by Goldziher, *Muslim Studies* 1/143–44, who quoted for it both Malik's *Muwaṭṭaʾ* and Muslim's *Ṣaḥīḥ*. See also Ibn Ḥanbal, *Musnad* 5/203; Ḥākim 4/69; Ibn ʿAbd al-Barr, *Tamhīd* 13/90.

[35]Ibn ʿAsākir 2/61.

refused to allow him to do so, saying that this was what *a'ājim* did to their kings.[36] One may note, however, that this Prophetic statement is only one element in a longer tradition on markets and trading, and as such, does not occur in all variants. In any case, it is not known to Ibn 'Abd Rabbihi (d. 328/939), who in fact cites a tradition of Ibn Abī Laylā ← Ibn 'Umar according to which the latter testifies that people used to kiss the Prophet's hand.

Another report, with the *isnād* Wakī' (d. 197/812) ← Sufyān, says that Abū 'Ubayda ibn al-Jarrāḥ kissed the hand of 'Umar I when they met in Syria. Other cases of kissing the hands of the caliph 'Abd al-Malik and 'Alī Zayn al-'Ābidīn ibn al-Ḥusayn (d. 92–100/710–18) are also cited by Ibn 'Abd Rabbihi. Actually, this source has it that the only caliphs who refused to allow people to kiss their hands were the late Umayyad Hishām ibn 'Abd al-Malik and the early 'Abbāsids Mahdī (d. 169/789) and Ma'mūn (d. 218/833).[37] The reason Hishām gave for his refusal, we are told, was that "the Arabs do not kiss the hands except out of fear, and the *'ajam* do not do it except in order to make a sign of submission" (*inna l-'araba mā qabbalat al-aydī illā hulu'an, wa-lā fa'alathu l-'ajamu illā khudū'an*). Ma'mūn, in turn, was quoted as saying to a man who wanted to kiss his hand: "A kiss of the hand by a Muslim is an act of humiliation (*dhulla*), and by the *dhimmī* it is an act of treachery (*khadī'a*)."

Another tradition of this sort was attributed to the Prophet through the Companion Abū Umāma al-Bāhilī on the authority of Mis'ar ibn Kaddām (d. 155/771). According to it the Prophet prohibited standing for him like the *a'ājim* do for exalting one another (*lā taqūmū kamā taqūmu l-a'ājimu yu'aẓẓimu ba'ḍuhum ba'ḍan*).[38] From Abū l-Zubayr al-Makkī (Muḥammad ibn Muslim, d. 126/743) we hear of a tradition of the Companion Jābir ibn 'Abd Allāh that tells how once the Prophet,

---

[36]Bayhaqī, *Shu'ab* 5/172; Haythamī, *Majma'* 5/121–22, quoting Abū Ya'lā and Ṭabarānī's *al-Mu'jam al-Awsaṭ*; Suyūṭī, *al-La'ālī l-Maṣnū'a*, Dār al-Ma'rifa, Beirut 1975, 2/263; Albānī 1/126, 2/44.

[37]Ibn 'Abd Rabbihi 2/6–7. He mentions this in a chapter entitled "Kings who Disliked that Their Hands be Kissed" and quotes al-'Utbī for it.

[38]Ibn Ḥanbal, *Musnad* 5/253, 256; Ibn 'Asākir 8/297; Mundhirī (d. 656/1258), *al-Targhīb wa-l-Tarhīb*, Dār al-Hadīth, Cairo n.d., 3/269–70; Albānī 1/351–52. Compare also with Ḥalīmī 3/332.

because he was ill, led his Companions in prayer while he was sitting. When he glimpsed them standing he rebuked them for acting like the Persians and Byzantines, who stand while their kings sit.[39]

More information is available about the controversy over whether a Muslim, when writing a letter, should begin it by mentioning his name or that of the man to whom it is addressed, like the *'ajam* do when writing to a senior person (*al-'ajam yabda'ūna bi-kibārihim*). A prohibition in this spirit is attributed to the Prophet in a tradition that Sa'īd al-Maqburī (d. 117–26/735–42) transmitted from his father.[40] However, reviewing the material that Shaybānī (d. 189/804) cites in the *Muwaṭṭa'* in the name of Mālik ibn Anas, one notices that he either ignores Maqburī's tradition or else is not aware of it. Moreover, he adduces two traditions—one with the *isnād* of Mālik ← 'Abd Allāh ibn Dīnār (d. 127/744), and the other from 'Abd al-Raḥmān ibn Abī l-Zinād (d. 174/790) ← his father (d. 131–32/748–49) ← Khārija ibn Zayd (d. 99–100/717–18)—testifying that both Companions Ibn 'Umar and Zayd ibn Thābit began the letters they wrote to 'Abd al-Malik and Mu'āwiya, respectively, by addressing them. On this basis Shaybānī concluded that there was "no harm" in such a practice.[41]

Another relevant controversy is one concerning the games of dice (*nard*) and chess (*shaṭranj*), which were considered *a'jamī* games of luck (*maysir*). We may note especially the conflicting reports about whether early second/eighth-century figures like Bahz ibn Ḥakīm, Ibrāhīm al-Hajarī, Ḥasan al-Baṣrī, 'Āmir al-Sha'bī, Muḥammad ibn Sīrīn and Hishām ibn 'Urwa did or did not play chess. The position reported from another such figure, Mujāhid, is that Sūrat al-Mā'ida (5), vv. 90–91, which prohibits *maysir*, applies in this case. The same opinion is attributed to both Ḥusayn ibn 'Alī (often through a family line of *isnād*) and the Prophet (by Qatāda in a *mursal* form).[42]

Bedouins are clearly the ones meant by a Prophetic tradition that differentiates between Arabs and non-Arabs in terms of occupation. According to this report, selling camels, cattle and butter are occupations

[39] Ibn Ḥibbān, *Ṣaḥīḥ* 3/282; Bayhaqī, *Sunan* 3/79.
[40] Daylamī 3/89.
[41] Mālik ibn Anas 320.
[42] Bayhaqī, *Sunan* 10/212–13; *idem*, *Shu'ab* 5/240–41.

suitable for Arabs, while non-Arabs sell cloths and wheat and run shops in general.[43] From another report we learn that professional and trade segregation was also the predominant situation during Ziyād's governorship over Iraq.[44] An anonymous poet, cited by Jāḥiẓ, notes that *mawālī* run shops in all the markets of Iraq.[45] Of some relevance are also two traditions of Ibn 'Abbās commanding merchants to be honest with their scales and measures: a Prophetic one transmitted by 'Ikrima and a *mawqūf* one (whose *isnād* ends with the name of a Companion, in this case Ibn 'Abbas, and is not attributed to the Prophet) circulated by Kurayb (ibn Abī Muslim, *mawlā* of Ibn 'Abbās, d. 98/716). One should notice that in this second variant, the word "merchants" (*tujjār*) is replaced with "non-Arabs" (*a'ājim*).[46]

Another occupation that was strongly disapproved for Arabs was agriculture. For both 'Alī and 'Abd Allāh ibn 'Amr, planting (*zar'*) was tantamount to apostasy (*ridda*).[47] Abū l-Ghayth (Sālim, an early second/eighth-century *mawlā* of Ibn Muṭī') warns that if the Arabs "follow the tails of cows" (i.e. plough the land) God will humiliate them and make the Persians their masters.[48]

Also of some relevance is a unique report concerning the circumstances in which Ḥajjāj had to dismiss the dark-skinned *mawlā* Sa'īd ibn Jubayr from the position of judge (*qāḍī*) of Kūfa. From it we learn that the Kūfans protested against his appointment to this post, saying that it did not suit a *mawlā* and that only an Arab was fit for the position.[49] Later, we are told, Sa'īd joined the rebels under Ibn al-Ash'ath and when caught by Ḥajjāj was put to death.

But the most important field in which one detects a clear current of discrimination between Arabs and non-Arabs, and one that seems to

---

[43]Abū l-'Abbās al-Aṣamm, *Ḥadīth*, Ms. Ẓāhirīya, *Majmū'* no. 31, 142; Ibn Abī Ḥatim, *'Ilal* 1/383.

[44]Ibn 'Asākir 8/430–41.

[45]"I looked at the markets of Iraq and // found only *mawālī* running its shops" (*ta'ammaltu aswāqa l-'iraqi fa-lam ajid // dakākīnahā illā 'alayhā l-mawāliya*); see Jāḥiẓ, *Rasā'il*, ed. 'Abd al-Salām Harūn, Maṭba'at al-Khānjī, Cairo 1964–65, 2/251.

[46]Bayhaqī, *Sunan* 6/32. More on *mawqūf* traditions in Juynboll, *Muslim Tradition*, 16–17, *passim*.

[47]Abū Nu'aym 1/292; Suyūṭī, *Durr* 2/83, quoting Ibn Abī Ḥatim.

[48]Suyūṭī, *al-Jāmi' al-Kabīr* 1/207.

[49]Ibn 'Abd al-Barr, *Tamhīd* 2/262.

have raised a sharp controversy, was the issue of worthiness (*kafā'a*) in marriage. Roughly noting the relevant group of traditions, Goldziher expressed his view that they reflect "the prevailing sentiments of the Arab aristocracy in the first two centuries in Islam."[50] One of these traditions attributes to the Prophet, through 'Ā'isha and the Companions Mu'ādh ibn Jabal and Ibn 'Umar, the saying that Arab men and tribes are worthy of each other and *mawālī* are worthy of each other, except for a tailor or a cupper (*illā ḥā'ik aw ḥajjām*). No *isnād* details are given for Mu'ādh's tradition. From one source we learn that 'Ā'isha's version was transmitted through the link Zuhrī ← Sa'īd ibn al-Musayyib. Ibn 'Umar's tradition enjoyed the widest circulation through two early second-century chains: his Medinese *mawlā* Nāfi' (d. 117–20/735–37) and Ibn Abī Mulayka (d. 117–18/735–36), a Meccan who acted as *qāḍī* for Ibn al-Zubayr.[51]

Of direct relevance to this issue are traditions and reports on cases of Arab–*mawālī* mixed marriages. Noteworthy among these are ones that bear the name of Salmān al-Fārisī, whose name is symbolic because of his Persian descent. He is usually quoted as saying that "we" (i.e. non-Arabs or *mawālī*) do not lead "you" (i.e. Arabs) in prayer and do not marry "your women" (*lā na'ummukum wa-lā nankaḥu nisā'akum*). Some variants explain that this preference was granted to the Arabs because the Prophet came from among them (*nufaḍḍilukum bi-faḍli rasūli l-lāhi*). Note also that while most variants give the statement as Salmān's own (*mawqūf*), others attribute this prohibition through him—i.e. in a *marfū'* form—to the Prophet saying: "The Prophet forbade us to marry your women" (*nahānā rasūlu l-lāhi an nankaḥa nisā'akum*).[52]

A special case that calls for attention is the refusal of Banū Layth to give Salmān a wife from among them and their consent to give

[50]Goldziher, *Muslim Studies* 1/125.

[51]Abū l-'Abbās al-Aṣamm, *Ḥadīth* 142; Ibn Abī Ḥātim, *'Ilal* 1/412, 421, 423–24; Ḥalīmī 2/175–76; Bayhaqī, *Sunan* 7/134–35; Daylamī 3/89; Zayla'ī 3/197–98; Haythamī, *Majma'* 4/275; Ghumārī 73.

[52]'Abd al-Razzāq, *Muṣannaf* 5/153; Ibn al-Ja'd 1/375; Ibn Sa'd 4/90; Ibn Abī Shayba 4/418–19; Ibn Abī Ḥātim, *'Ilal* 1/110, 406; Ibn 'Adī (d. 365/975), *al-Kāmil fī Ḍu'āfa' al-Rijāl*, Dār al-Fikr, Beirut 1984, 3/1297; Abū Nu'aym 1/189; Bayhaqī, *Sunan* 7/134; Ibn 'Asākir 7/424–25; Haythamī, *Majma'* 4/275.

her to the Arab Companion Abū l-Dardā'. We also learn that Abū l-Dardā' acted as a marriage broker for Salmān seemingly because, according to an early source, the Prophet had associated the two as brothers (*ākhā baynahumā*). Abū l-Dardā', we are told, apologized to Salmān and took the women for himself.[53] In another case, that of Bilāl and his brother, the provided *isnād* information is more conclusive. From a *maqṭū'* report (i.e. one whose *isnād* is broken up with at least one chain missing) by Qatāda (d. 117–18/735–36) we learn that Bilāl actually married an enslaved Arab woman from the tribe of Zuhra.[54] The traditions of Sha'bī (d. 103–10/721–28), 'Amr ibn Maymūn (d. 74–75/693–94) and al-Ḥuṣayn ibn Numayr (d. 63–64/682–83) say that Bilāl tried to obtain an Arab wife for his brother and possibly for himself too, but some variants do not make it clear whether he succeeded or not.[55]

A clear relevance to the issue of worthiness, and one with an indirect bearing on the case of the black-skinned Bilāl, can be found in a group of traditions attributed to the Prophet through 'Ā'isha, 'Umar and Anas. According to them the Prophet basically said: "Choose for your seed and marry the worthy" (*takhayyarū li-nuṭafikum wa-nkaḥū l-akfā'*). We notice, however, that in the variants of Sufyān ibn 'Uyayna (d. 198/813) ← Ziyād ibn Sa'd ← Zuhrī (d. 124/741) from Anas, and those of a certain Hishām, *mawlā* to the family of 'Uthmān ibn 'Affān, and Suddī (d. 127/744), both transmitting from Hishām ibn 'Urwa (d. 145–47/762–64) ← his father ← 'Ā'isha, an addition is made advising the avoidance of black "because it is a trait of disfigurement" (*wa-'jtanibū hādhā al-sawāda fa-innahu khalqun mushawwah*). There are even two variants, by 'Āmir ibn Ṣāliḥ al-Zubayrī (d. 182/798) and Maslama ibn Muḥammad (death date uncertain), both from Hishām ← 'Urwa ← 'Ā'isha, which limit themselves to citing only the last part of the statement on avoiding blacks.[56]

---

[53]Ibn 'Asākir 7/429; Haythamī, *Majma'* 4/275; Ibn Sa'd 4/84.

[54]Balādhurī, *Ansāb* 1/189.

[55]Cf. Balādhurī, *Ansāb* 1/189; Ibn Sa'd 3/237–38; Ḥākim 3/283; Bayhaqī, *Sunan* 7/137; Ibn 'Asākir 5/157–58, 421.

[56]Cf. Yaḥyā ibn Ma'īn (d. 233/847), *Tārīkh*, ed. Aḥmad Nūr Sayf, Markaz al-Baḥth al-'Ilmī, Mecca 1979, 1/338; Ibn Māja (d. 275/888), *Sunan*, ed. Muḥammad 'Abd al-Bāqī, Dār al-Ḥadīth, Cairo n.d., 1/633; Ibn Abī Ḥātim, *'Ilal* 1/403–404;

There is a striking complaint, made by Jāḥiẓ in the name of the blacks, that the *kafā'a* principle applied to their disadvantage was a Muslim innovation unknown in the Jāhilīya.[57] The dearth of relevant information, however, renders it impossible to pursue this assertion beyond noting that 'Umar I, 'Umar II, Ḥasan al-Baṣrī, Zuhrī, Thawrī and other prominent figures in early Islam are indeed reported to have stood strongly against mixed marriages and in favour of the strict application of the *kafā'a* principle.[58] Only 'Alī is reported to have not preferred an Arab woman over a *mawlāt* one.[59] Mu'āwiya is said to have sent a letter to Ziyād, his governor over Iraq, instructing him to follow the *sunna* of 'Umar I and, among other things, not to allow a *mawlā* to marry an Arab woman.[60] Ibn Jurayj (d. 150/767) even circulated a Prophetic tradition that branded those who enter mixed marriages as the worst among both Arabs and *mawālī*.[61] Sulaymān al-A'mash circulated another tradition through Ibn Mas'ūd prohibiting the marrying of Khazars in particular.[62] A half-breed son (*hajīn*, i.e. one whose mother was non-Arab) could not easily find a wife of aristocratic Arab descent even though his father was none other than the caliph 'Abd al-Malik.[63] And during the struggle between the late

Ibn Ḥibbān, *Kitāb al-Majrūḥīn*, ed. Maḥmūd Zāyid, Dār al-Wa'y, Aleppo 1402 AH, 2/286; Ibn 'Adī 5/1737; Ḥākim 2/163; Abū Nu'aym 3/377; al-Khaṭīb al-Baghdādī 1/264; Tammām al-Rāzī (d. 414/1023), *Fawā'id*, ed. Jāsim al-Dawsarī, Dār al-Bashā'ir al-Islāmīya, Beirut 1989, 2/373; al-Quḍā'ī (d. 454/1062), *Musnad*, ed. Ḥamdī al-Salafī, Mu'assasat al-Risāla, Beirut 1985, 1/390; Dāraquṭnī, *Sunan* 3/299; Bayhaqī, *Sunan* 7/133; Ibn 'Asākir 5/241; Zayla'ī 3/197; Ibn Ḥajar, *Tahdhīb al-Tahdhīb*, Hyderabad 1325–27 AH, 10/148; Suyūṭī, *La'ālī* 1/445; *idem*, *al-Jāmi' al-Ṣaghīr* 1/130; Samhūdī 78; Kinānī 2/32; al-Qārī (d. 1014/1605), *al-Asrār al-Marfū'a*, ed. Muḥammad Sa'īd Zaghlūl, Dār al-Kutub al-'Ilmīya, Beirut 1985, 332; Shawkānī (d. 1250/1834), *al-Fawā'id al-Majmū'a*, Cairo 1960, 415–16; Albānī 2/159; Muttaqī 16/no. 44558.

[57]Jāḥiẓ, *Fakhr al-Sūdan*, in G. van Vloten, ed., *Tria Opuscula*, Leiden 1903, 68. For an interesting evaluation of the motives behind this work, see Lewis, *Race and Color* 19.

[58]'Abd al-Razzāq, *Muṣannaf* 5/152–54; Ibn Abī Shayba 4/418–19, 12/194–95.

[59]Bayhaqī, *Sunan* 6/349.

[60]*Kitāb Sulaym ibn Qays* (d. 90/708), Najaf n.d., 140–43.

[61]Daylamī 5/288–89, with the full *isnād* for the tradition quoted from *Zahr al-Firdaws* 4/281, in the margin.

[62]Daylamī 5/190, with the full *isnād* quoted from *Zahr* 4/190, in the margin.

[63]Ibn 'Abd Rabbihi 3/366.

Umayyads Yazīd III and Walīd II, the fact that one was a *hajīn* was a reason for the rejection of his claim to the throne.[64]

Of the Umayyad rulers, Mu'āwiya is the one most frequently reported as loving, preferring and recommending the good treatment of Arabs. Moreover, he is said to have expressed his fear that the *ḥamrā'* ("red ones," i.e. non-Arabs) would overpower the Arabs and urged the latter to bring to fruition the mission of the Prophet, least others do it in their stead.[65] The role played by non-Arabs in religious life during 'Abd al-Malik's reign was stressed in the famous conversation between 'Abd al-Malik and Zuhrī. As noted by Goldziher, Zuhrī told 'Abd al-Malik that it was actually people of non-Arab origin who ran the religious and legal affairs in the major provincial centers of his empire.[66] However, the version cited by Goldziher lacks the most important element in this report, a phrase in which 'Abd al-Malik expresses his deep concern over this state of affairs and his relief when told by Zuhrī that in one place, Kūfa, the leading religious authority is Ibrāhīm al-Nakha'ī, an Arab.[67]

'Abd al-Malik's son Sulaymān is reported to have expressed a similar dissatisfaction over the continued dependence upon *'ajam* in running the affairs of the state.[68] About 'Umar II we learn that he advised a governor of his to rely primarily upon Arabs,[69] though this caliph is of course more commonly known for his meaures in favour of the *mawālī*.

---

[64]Note especially the poetical verse attributed to Walīd II when he was deposed (cited in Ibn 'Asākir, 5/241): *atankuthu bay'atī min ajli ummī // wa-qad bāya'tumū qablī hajīnā*?, "Will you break your pledge of allegiance to me because of my mother, // when you have pledged allegiance to a *hajīn* previously?" In another verse of his (cited in Ibn Manẓūr, *Lisān al-'Arab* 4/416 and Zabīdī, *Tāj* 2/504) he says: *'allili l-qawma qalīlan // bi-bni binti l-fārisīya*, "Cherish the hopes of people for a short while // with the son of a Persian daughter."

[65]For such statements of Mu'āwiya, see Ibn Abī 'Āṣim, *Sunna* 35–36; Ṭabarānī, *al-Mu'jam al-Kabīr* 19/307–308; Haythamī, *Majma'* 9/358; Ibn 'Abd Rabbihi 3/364, 370–71.

[66]Goldziher, *Muslim Studies* 2/110, citing Ibn al-Ṣalāḥ (d. 643/1245).

[67]For this version, see Ibn 'Asākir 2/853, 11/643–44, 16/140–41.

[68]Al-Zubayr ibn Bakkār (d. 256/869), *al-Akhbār al-Muwaffaqīyāt*, ed. Samī al-'Ānī, Maṭba'at al-'Ānī, Baghdad 1980, 186.

[69]Ibn al-Jawzī, *Sīrat wa-Manāqib 'Umar ibn 'Abd al-'Azīz*, ed. Na'īm Zarzūr, Dār al-Kutub al-'Ilmīya, Beirut 1984, 241.

On the whole, the basic orientation during the Umayyad period seems clearly to have been an Arab one.[70] There is an isolated tradition that even describes the death of Ḥusayn ibn ʿAlī as the first humiliation (*awwalu dhullin*) that the Arabs suffered,[71] an idea that, if considered outside the context of this general Arab orientation, would seem quite extraordinary, especially against the background of the pro-*mawālī* position of the Shīʿa. The uprising of Ibn al-Ashʿath in Iraq in the year 82/701 was noted for being dominated by a *mawālī* element, probably ex-prisoners of war, and Ḥajjāj's reportedly harsh treatment of them bears a clear ethnic colouring.[72]

We shall see below how the civil wars in the late Umayyad period were feared for threatening the perdition (*halāk*) of the Arabs and, as such, for being an eschatological sign of the end of times. As for the ʿAbbāsids, the views expressed by Wellhausen and other nineteenth-century scholars, that the strong non-Arab element in their movement was a sign that it was a Persian national and an Arian racial revolution against the Arabs, have been heavily criticized by later scholars. These latter have shown that in spite of the massive *mawālī* and specifically Persian elements, the *daʿwa* (religious movement) remained basically Arab in leadership and political aspirations.[73] Non-Arabs, it is true, were reportedly recruited to the ʿAbbāsid army in substantial numbers during Manṣūr's reign (136–58/753–74).[74] It is also true that Abū

[70]On the need of *mawālī* to be affiliated to the Arabs and acquire Arab names, see Wellhausen 24 and Levy 60. Ibn ʿAbbās' reported preference to call his servants by Arab names seems indeed to be the rule. For this see Muḥammad ibn Naṣr al-Marwazī (d. 394/1003), *Taʿẓīm Qadr al-Ṣalāt*, ed. ʿAbd al-Raḥmān al-Faryawāʾī, Maktabat al-Dār, Medina 1406 AH, 1/503.

[71]Ṭabarānī, *al-Muʿjam al-Kabīr* 3/123; Ibn ʿAsākir 4/551; Haythamī, *Majmaʿ* 9/196.

[72]Cf. Balādhurī, *Ansāb* V, 246, 294 and Ibn ʿAbd Rabbihi 3/367, who quotes Jāḥiẓ' *al-Mawālī wa-l-ʿArab*, with the Syriac contemporary source of Bar Penkāyē, cited in P. Crone, *Slaves on Horses*, Cambridge 1980, 156 n. 647; and see Levy 58–59.

[73]Lewis, *The Arabs in History* 81, and especially M.A. Shaban, *The ʿAbbāsid Revolution*, Cambridge 1970, and M. Sharon, *Black Banners From the East*, Jerusalem 1983, 51–52, 65–71, 197–98. For Wellhausen's views see his *Arab Kingdom* 380–93.

[74]Crone, 84, referring to the Syriac source in J.B. Chabot (ed. and trans.), *Chronique de Denys de Tell Maḥre*, Paris 1895. More on Manṣūr's recruitment of Turks will be said below. See also Ibn Khaldūn's note (in his *Tārikh*, Fez 1936,

Muslim al-Khurāsānī, Manṣūr's military right-hand man at one stage, was reportedly no great lover of Arabs.[75] However, Manṣūr himself is said to have ordered different treatments for each of the groups of Qurashīs, Arabs and *mawālī* who took part in the uprising of al-Nafs al-Zakīya against him in the year 145/762.[76]

A report in which the caliph Ma'mūn (d. 218/833) expresses his dissatisfaction and resentment about the political behaviour of the main Arab tribal confederations towards the 'Abbāsid state[77] may reflect the actual state of affaits, or at least the beginning of a certain shift in the political and military situation during his own time. However, the main orientation—with the Arabs standing in the core of the new religion and constituting its predominant element—seems to have taken root by the era of the early 'Abbāsids. This is clear from the fact that in the late second/eighth century, only the Khārijites were reported, and this in order to blame them, as having treated Arabs and non-Arabs equally.[78] Also of some relevance is the fact that of the merits of the famous third/ninth-century *ḥadīth* scholar Aḥmad ibn Ḥanbal, a special note that he did not boast of his Arab descent was made by his contemporary, Yaḥyā ibn Ma'īn.[79]

Such stress on one's descent was even stronger during the second/eighth century, when it was used in the struggle against those legal scholars who favoured the exercise of independent legal reasoning (*al-ra'y*): Abū Ḥanīfa, 'Uthmān al-Battī (ibn Muslim, d. 143/760) and Rabī'a ibn Abī 'Abd al-Raḥmān (nicknamed Rabī'at al-Ra'y, d. 133–42/750–59). In order to undermine their rulings, a Prophetic tradition was circulated in a *mursal* form by Hishām ibn 'Urwa (d. 145–47/762–64) warning against the rise of "the sons of slave girls from among the

3/177) that in the army of Yaḥyā, brother of the caliph Saffāḥ (d. 136/753), there were four thousand blacks (*zanj*).

[75]Ibn 'Asākir 10/190; Ibn Khaldūn 3/103.

[76]Al-Zubayr ibn Bakkār, *al-Akhbār* 186.

[77]Noted by Goldziher, *Muslim Studies* 1/138, who quotes Ṭabarī (*Tārīkh*, ed. M.J. de Goeje *et al.*, Leiden 1897–1901, III/1142). See also Ibn 'Asākir 19/269. Ma'mūn, we are told, expressed such grudges when he visited Syria and was approached by a man from the Quḍā'a tribal confederation who complained to him that "the Arabs are lost in Syria (*al-shām*)."

[78]Abū Yūsuf 59.

[79]Cited in Ibn 'Asākir 2/122–23.

nations" (*abnā' al-sabāyā min al-umam*) to high positions in legal (*fiqh*) matters.[80]

However, taking such advantage does not always seem to have been done. Shurayk (ibn 'Abd Allāh al-Nakh'ī, d. 177/793) is quoted as saying that religious knowledge (*'ilm*) is exclusively the occupation of Arabs and the tribal notables of kings (*mā kāna hādhā l-'ilmu illā fī l-'arabī wa-ashrāfi l-mulūk*).[81] But when the Arab Sufyān al-Thawrī died (in 161/777), 'Abd Allāh ibn al-Mubārak (d. 181/797), who was a *mawlā*, was considered his successor to the title "legal authority of the Arabs" (*faqīhu l-'arab*).[82] Finally, the statement attributed to Ibn al-Muqaffa' (d. *ca.* 145/762) that the Arabs were "the most intelligent of all nations" (*a'qal al-umam*), though most probably not authentic in itself, clearly reflects a pro-Arab current in the struggle against the Shu'ūbīya.[83]

[80]Abū Bakr al-Marwazī, *Akhbār al-Shuyūkh*, Ms. Ẓāhirīya, *Majmū'* no. 120, 42; Ibn Māja 1/21; Basawī 3/20–21; al-Khaṭīb al-Baghdādī 13/394.

[81]Abū Nu'aym 5/48.

[82]*Ibid.* 8/163.

[83]Ibn 'Abd Rabbihi 3/372.

CHAPTER III

THE GREAT FUSION

THE TERMS MOST FREQUENTLY USED in the Qur'ān to identify the Prophet and those to whom he was sent are *ummī* and *ummīyūn*, respectively. In other instances a certain people are directly addressed or indirectly referred to as those from among whom (*min anfusikum / anfusihim*) a messenger was sent, though they are not explicitly said to be the Arabs. In many verses, however, the Qur'ān is described as one revealed in the Arabic tongue so that it would be understood. It will be interesting to examine the literary process through which Muḥammad was identified as an Arab prophet sent to the Arabs, and the effect this had on promoting their role in Islam.

Sūrat al-Baqara (2), vv. 129, 151, Sūrat Āl 'Imrān (3), v. 164, Sūrat al-Tawba (9), v. 128, and Sūrat al-Mu'minūn (23), v. 32, address or mention certain people to whom a messenger was sent. We notice, however, that most early exegetical traditions and commentary views do not explicitly say that those meant are the Arabs. Instead, it is generally stated that the ones referred to are the *umma* of Muḥammad, as represented by the Muslim "who has not been contaminated by a pre-Islamic birth" (*lam yuṣibhu shay'un min wilādat al-jāhilīya*).[1]

This does not mean, of course, that attempts at ethnic identification were not recorded. From Muqātil we learn that those addressed by Sūrat al-Tawba (9), v. 128, were the people of Mecca who knew the

[1]Mujāhid 1/92; Muqātil 74/1 22r, 25r; 74/2, 30r; 'Abd al-Razzāq, *Tafsīr* 54v; Ṭabarī, *Tafsīr* 3/82–86, 209–10, 14/585; Ibn Abī Ḥātim, *Tafsīr* 1/388–89.

Prophet and did not deny him (*ta'rifūnahu wa-lā tunkirūnah*).[2] Concerning the same verse, Farrā' says that *min anfusikum* meant that there was no Arab tribal branch (*baṭn*) that did not have a share in his birth.[3] The ps.-Ibn 'Abbās source presents Sūrat al-Baqara (2), vv. 129 and 151, as meaning the genealogy of the descendants of Ismā'īl.[4] As for Sūrat al-Tawba (9), v. 128, this passage says that the ones being addressed were the people of Mecca, and that *rasūlun min anfusikum* meant that he was "an Arab, Hāshimite like you."[5] And both Zajjāj and Ṭabarī upheld their own understanding that vv. 129 and 151 of Sūrat al-Baqara (2) addressed the Arab polytheists and Arabs in general, respectively.[6]

Sūrat al-Qaṣaṣ (28), v. 59 mentions Umm al-Qurā (lit. "the mother of towns") as a place in which a messenger was sent. This title was often presented as indicating Mecca, though a few commentaries limit themselves to giving its literal meaning as "the greatest among them" (*a'ẓamuhā*), that is, without specifying its ethnic identity or that of the Prophet.[7]

The ones to whom a messenger was sent "from among themselves" are named in Sūrat Āl 'Imrān (3) as *mu'minūn*, "believers." Two traditions, one by Qatāda and the other by Ibn Isḥāq, understand this term as denoting the *umma* or the *ahl al-īmān*, the "people of faith."[8] On the other hand, a unique tradition of Zuhrī (from 'Urwa ← 'Ā'isha) says that the Qur'ānic verse was revealed "especially for the Arabs" (*li-l-'arabi khāṣṣatan*).[9] The ps.-Ibn 'Abbās source in turn interprets the phrase *min anfusihim* in this verse as meaning "a Qurashī, Arab like them."[10]

---

[2]Muqātil 74/1, 162r.

[3]Farrā' 1/456.

[4]Fīrūzābādī 14, 17.

[5]*Ibid.*, 130.

[6]Zajjāj 1/228; Ṭabarī, *Tafsīr* 3/210, 14/584.

[7]See Fīrūzābādī 243; Farrā' 2/309; Abū 'Ubayda 2/108; Ibn al-Yazīdī 139; Ibn Qutayba, *Tafsīr* 334.

[8]Ṭabarī, *Tafsīr* 7/37.

[9]Ibn Abī Ḥātim, *Tafsīr* 2/647–48; Qurṭubī (d. 671/1272), *al-Jāmi' li-Aḥkām al-Qur'ān*, Dār al-Sha'b, Cairo n.d., 4/264; Suyūṭī, *Durr* 2/93, quoting Ibn Abī Ḥātim, Ibn al-Mundhir (d. 318/930) and Bayhaqī.

[10]Fīrūzābādī 48.

The term *ummīyūn* is the one usually used to denote those to whom a messenger was sent from among themselves. Special attention must be given to Sūrat al-Jumu'a (62), v. 2, where such use is made. In Sūrat Āl 'Imran (3), vv. 20, 75, *ummīyūn* are differentiated from "people of the book." A call to believe in the *ummī* prophet is made in Sūrat al-A'rāf (7), vv. 157–58. On the basis of these as well as other occurrences, a strong current equating *ummī* and *ummīyūn* with "an Arab" and "Arabs" emerged in Muslim sources.[11] In what follows, however, we shall re-examine the *tafsīr* material in an attempt to reconstruct this process and possibly detect the existence of other early currents.

To begin with, there exists a strong tendency in early *tafsīr* sources to present *ummīyīn* in Sūrat Āl 'Imrān (3), vv. 20, 75, and Sūrat al-Jumu'a (62), v. 2, as those who either did not have / recite "a book" or ones to whom "books" were not revealed. Views like these were reported from Ibn Isḥāq ← Muḥammad ibn Ja'far (d. 110–20/728–37), Ma'mar (ibn Rāshid, d. 152–54/769–70) ← Qatāda and some of their contemporaries, or else occur as the personal interpretation of some early commentators.[12]

Clearly, what was meant by "a book" in these contexts was a scripture: hence, in some sources, *ummīyūn* were understood as Arab polytheists (*min mushrikī l-'arab*).[13] However, a process of literary abridgment was soon underway, and the Arab polytheists who did not recite a book soon became "the illiterate ones" (*al-ladhīna lā yaktubūn*), a

---

[11]Wensinck, "Community" and "Umma." See also Bayhaqī, *Shu'ab* 2/232; Ḥalīmī 2/47; Ibn Sa'd 1/21; Ibn Ḥibbān, *Ṣaḥīḥ* 2/60, 8/137–38; Ibn Abī Ḥātim, *'Ilal* 2/418; Muttaqī 1/no. 961; Ibn Sayyid al-Nās 2/315; Abū Yūsuf 32–33; Ibn Hishām 2/115; Bāyazid al-Bisṭāmī, *Risāla*, Ms. Ẓāhirīya no. 4690, 90; Ibn 'Asākir 1/539–41, 544; *Nawādir al-Makhṭūṭāt*, ed. 'Abd al-Salām Hārūn, Maṭba'at Lajnat al-Ta'līf wa-l-Tarjama wa-l-Nashr, Cairo 1954, 290, 329. For the interchangeable occurrence of *ummī* and *'arabī* as titles of the Prophet in the context of the reports on Muḥammad's contacts with Heraclius, see Bashear, "Diḥya al-Kalbī and the Situation in Syria," esp. nn. 100–105 and the sources cited therein. However, compare also with Wāḥidī, 258–59 where, in a commentary on Sūrat al-Rūm (30), v. 1, the Persians of pre-Islam are also referred to as *ummīyūn*.

[12]Ṭabarī, *Tafsīr* 2/257–58, 6/282; Ibn Abī Ḥātim, *Tafsīr* 2/158; Abū 'Ubayda 1/90; Ibn al-Yazīdī 40; 'Abd al-Razzāq, *Tafsīr* 151v.

[13]Ṭabarī, *Tafsīr* 6/281, 522; Ibn Abī Ḥātim 2/251. Note that this view was also traditionally reported through the link Ma'mar ← Qatāda.

notion that Ibn Jurayj attributed to Ibn ʻAbbās and that was also reported by some commentators in an anonymous form.[14] The second step was to drop both polytheism and illiteracy and simply to equate *ummīyūn* with Arabs, a notion traditionally connected with the names of Saʻīd ibn Abī ʻArūba (d. 156–57/772–73) ← Qatāda, Asbāṭ ← Suddī and al-Rabīʻ ibn Anas, or cited as the personal interpretation of some early scholars.[15] Concerning the term *ummī*, which occurs as an epithet of the Prophet, curtailing the element of polytheism must have been a convenient outlet, a dynamic that also set forth the notion that he was illiterate.[16]

In conclusion to this section a note must be made of the existence in *ḥadīth* literature of a current parallel to the one just reviewed in Qur'ānic exegesis: namely, that of identifying the Prophet with the Arabs or attributing to him statements promoting their position and merits. We hear, for example, of his wish to dye his beard and his command that others should do so in order to differentiate themselves from *aʻājim*.[17] He also combed his front hair like the Arabs did (*farq al-ʻarab*) after having formerly combed it like the *ahl al-kitāb*,[18] recommended the wearing of turbans in order to establish a point of difference from other preceding communities (*iʻtammū, khalifū l-umama qablakum*), and praised turbans as Arab crowns (*al-ʻamā'imu tījān al-*

[14] Ṭabarī 6/282; Ibn Abī Ḥātim 2/158; Abū ʻUbayda 2/258; Ibn al-Yazīdī 180; Zajjāj 5/169.

[15] Ṭabarī, *Tafsīr* 6/521–22; Ibn Abī Ḥātim, *Tafsīr* 2/250; Fīrūzābādī 36, 41, 354; Ibn Qutayba, *Tafsīr* 106–107. Compare also with Muqātil 74/1, 56v, where the same was given as an interpretation of Sūrat Āl ʻImrān (3), v. 75. As for v. 20 of this last Sūra, it is worth noting that Muqātil drops the word *ummīyūn* from the codex altogether. See for that his *Tafsīr* 74/1, 51r.

[16] See Muqātil 74/1, 137r; Ibn al-Yazīdī 40; Ṭabarī, *Tafsīr* 13/157, 163 (where such a view was reported from the link Saʻīd ibn Abī ʻArūba ← Qatāda); Fīrūzābādī 109, where he avoids interpreting this epithet altogether and only says that "it means (*yaʻnī*) Muḥammad."

[17] Ibn ʻAsākir 9/988. See also the tradition of Ibn ʻAbbās, cited in Suyūṭī's *Durr* 1/115, which attributes to the Prophet the saying: "Do not look like *aʻājim*; change your beards" (*lā tashbbahū bi-l-aʻājim, ghayyirū l-liḥā*). However, as cited by another source, Ibn ʻAbd al-Barr, *Tamhīd* 6/76, the same was reported through Ibn ʻUmar except for substituting "the Jews" (*al-yahūd*) for *al-aʻājim*.

[18] Al-Khaṭīb al-Baghdādī 8/438; Tirmidhī, *Shamā'il*, Ms. Ẓāhirīya, *Majmūʻ* no. 83, 50.

'arab) that add forebearance (*ḥilm*) to their wearers.[19] However, we notice that some of these traditions were also reported as Zuhrī's own statements or else were related in *maqṭū'* form from Khālid ibn Ma'dān (d. 103–108/721–26).[20] In a few traditions, also reported in this form, the Prophet was quoted as praising the Arab bow (*al-qaws al-'arabīya*), as against the Persian one, and also the Arabian horse.[21] Finally, the tradition attributed to both the Prophet and 'Umar forbidding people to inscribe an Arabic inscription on their signet rings (*wa-lā tanqushū fī khawātīmikum 'arabīyan*) was explained by Bukhārī as an order not to imitate the formula "Muḥammad is the messenger of God," a fact that clearly points to the identification of the inscription of the Prophet's name and epithet as an Arabian stamp.[22]

As against the lack in the Qur'ān of any explicit identification of the Prophet and his *umma* along clear ethnic lines, there are numerous verses in which the adjective *'arabī* is used to denote the scripture or its language.[23] And once, in Sūrat al-Ra'd (13), v. 37, the Qur'ān is referred to as "an Arab judgement" (*ḥukman 'arabīyan*). In the eyes of some commentators, the contexts in which this adjective occurs asserted either the idea that the Qur'ān was revealed in Arabic so that it would be understood (*li-yafqahūhu*),[24] or else, as in the case of Sūrat al-Naḥl (16), v. 103, that it involved a rebuttal against an implicit accusation of non-Arab (*a'jamī*) influence.[25]

---

[19]See also the information that Ibn Ḥanbal and other scholars recommended that the turban (*'imāma*) be worn in a way that differentiates one from the *'ajam*; Suyūṭī, *al-Aḥādīth al-Ḥisān*, 27–28.

[20]Ḥākim 4/193; Bayhaqī, *Shu'ab* 5/176; Ibn 'Asākir 5/684; Muttaqī 7/nos. 19460, 19477, 15/nos. 41130, 41136–37.

[21]Ibn Ḥanbal, *'Ilal* 3/404; Nasā'ī, *Sunan*, Dār al-Ḥadīth, Cairo 1987, 6/223; Ḥākim 2/92, 144; Bayhaqī, *Sunan* 10/14.

[22]Bukhārī, *Tārīkh* 1/455. For this tradition, see also Ibn Ḥanbal, *Musnad* 3/99; *Musnad Khalīfa* 21; Nasā'ī, *Sunan* 8/176; Ibn 'Abd al-Barr, *Tamhīd* 17/111; Muttaqī 6/no. 17393; Suyūṭī, *Durr* 2/66, quoting Ibn Ḥumayd, Ṭabarī, Abū Ya'lā, Ibn al-Mundhir, Ibn Abī Ḥātim and Bayhaqī.

[23]E.g. Sūrat Yūsuf (12), v. 2; Sūrat Ṭāhā (20), v. 113; Sūrat al-Shu'arā' (26), v. 195; Sūrat al-Zumar (39), v. 28; Sūrat Fuṣṣilat (41), vv. 3, 44; Sūrat al-Shūrā (42), v. 7; Sūrat al-Zukhruf (43), v. 3; Sūrat al-Aḥqāf (46), v. 12.

[24]See especially Muqātil 74/1, 177r, 207v; 74/2, 7r, 54r, 123v, 136r, 137r, 141r, 152r, 190r–v.

[25]Ṭabarī, *Tafsīr* 14/177; Zajjāj 3/219–20; Fīrūzābādī 174.

Concerning Sūrat Fuṣṣilat (41), v. 44, several commentators set forth the notion that Muḥammad was an Arab prophet,[26] a view also stated in Muqātil's commentary on Sūrat al-Ra'd (13), v. 37, where he adds: "... when he [Muḥammad] made a summons to the religion of his fathers" (*... ḥīna da'ā ilā dīni ābā'ihi*).[27] For Abū 'Ubayda, Ṭabarī and Ṭabarsī, *ḥukm* in this verse meant both legal judgements (*aḥkām*) and religion (*dīn*).[28]

A few other nuances are worth noting. In the ps.-Ibn 'Abbās work the adjective *'arabīyan* in most of the above-noted examples is explained as meaning "as expressed in the language of the Arabs" (*'alā majrā lughat al-'arab*).[29] Zajjāj, in turn, understands the word *qur'ān* as "a collection" (*majmū'*) and interprets Sūrat Fuṣṣilat (41), v. 3, as meaning: "Its verses were made evident when it was collected in Arabic" (*buyyinat āyātuhu fī ḥāli jam'ihi 'arabīyan*).[30] For Ṭabarī, the contexts of Sūrat al-Shūrā (42), v. 7, and Sūrat al-Zukhruf (43), v. 3, imply also that Muḥammad, like other prophets, was sent to his own people—the Arabs,[31] a notion that clearly echos the traditional controversy over whether Muḥammad was sent only to his people or to mankind in general.

Elaborating on the phrase *qur'ānan 'arabīyan* in Sūrat Yūsuf (12), v. 2, a traditional current emerged linking eloquence (*faṣāḥa*) with revelation.[32] This appears in the form of a tradition stating that Muḥammad's ancestor Ishmael / var. Abraham, learned the Arabic lan-

---

[26]Muqātil 74/2, 190r–v; Mujāhid 2/572; Ibn Qutayba, *Tafsīr* 389–90; Abū 'Ubayda 1/368; 'Abd al-Razzāq, *Tafsīr* 127r; Ṭabarī, *Tafsīr* 13/164–65; Ṭabarsī 13/182; Zajjāj 4/389; Fīrūzābādī 298; Farrā' 3/19; al-Akhfash 2/685. See also Abū Ḥayyān, *Ḥadīth*, Ms. Ẓahirīya, *Majmū'* no. 93, 23, 32. Cf. also Thawrī 267, where the *isnād* chains cited for this latter view are Abū Bishr ← Ibn Jubayr ← Ibn 'Abbās and Sa'īd (ibn Abī 'Arūba) ← Mujāhid.

[27]Muqātil 74/2, 136r.

[28]Abū 'Ubayda 1/334; Ṭabarī, *Tafsīr* 13/164–65; Ṭabarsī 13/183.

[29]Fīrūzābādī 146, 159, 174, 198, 233, 287, 295, 300.

[30]Zajjāj 3/87, 4/379. For this unusual interpretation of *qur'ān*, see also 'Abd al-Wahhāb al-Ḥunaṭī, *al-Risāla al-Wāḍiḥa*, Ms. Ẓāhirīya, *Majmū'* no. 18, 61.

[31]Ṭabari, *Tafsīr* 25/8, 47–48. See also 16/219, 23/212–13, 24/91 concerning Sūrat Ṭāhā (20), v. 113, Sūrat al-Zumar (39), v. 28, and Sūrat Fuṣṣilat (41), v. 3, respectively, and compare with Ṭabarsī 25/39 concerning Sūrat al-Shūrā (42), v. 7.

[32]Noted by J. Wansbrough, *Quranic Studies*, Oxford 1977, 93–94, 103.

guage by way of revelation (*ulhima ismā'īlu / ibrāhīmu hādhā l-lisāna l-'arabīya ilhāman*). A close look at the *isnād* of this tradition shows that it originated in the early second/eighth century, as it was attributed to the Prophet in a *mursal* form through the *isnād* Sufyān ← al-Ṣādiq ← al-Bāqir (d. 114–18/732–36), though later forms insert the Companion Jābir ibn 'Abd Allāh between al-Bāqir and the Prophet.[33] Also worth noting are two similar traditions cited by Jāḥiẓ: one by the same al-Bāqir, but "from his fathers" (*'an ābā'ihi*), and the other circulated by Qays ibn al-Rabī' (d. 165–68/781–88), who does not specify his sources (*'an ba'ḍi shuyūkhihi*).[34]

There is also a traditional attempt to connect eloquence with revelation to the Prophet himself. In a unique tradition, 'Umar curiously asks the Prophet about the source of his eloquence, since Muḥammad is "not one of us / not one who came from amongst us" (*arāka afṣaḥanā wa-lasta minnā / wa-lam takhruj min bayni aẓhurinā*). To this the Prophet replies that Arabic had degenerated (*indarasat*) until the angel Gabriel came and taught it to him in revelation.[35] But opposed to this trend are the traditions that attribute the Prophet's eloquence to his having been born in the tribe of Quraysh and brought up by the tribe of Sa'd ibn Bakr. These reports were circulated by two figures who were active in the second quarter of the second/eighth century, Mubashshar ibn 'Ubayd and Yaḥyā ibn Yazīd al-Sa'dī, the latter's transmission being also in a *mursal* form.[36]

Dating these traditions is crucial for the assessment of the process through which Arabic acquired the position of a sacred language of revelation, a process that we believe occurred around the turn of the first/seventh century. This assessment is supported by another unique tradition, one by Wahb ibn Munabbih (d. 110/728) occurring in an early source, the *Kitāb al-Tījān* attributed to him. This says that God

---

[33]See Ḥākim 2/343–44, 439; Bayhaqī, *Shu'ab* 2/233–34 (who comments on the *mursal* form by saying: "... and it is the one [more favourably] remembered" ... *wa-hwa l-maḥfūẓ*); Suyūṭī, *Durr* 4/3; Muttaqī 11/490 no. 32311.

[34]Jāḥiẓ, *al-Bayān*, 4/5–6.

[35]Bayhaqī, *Shu'ab* 2/158; Ibn 'Asākir 15/375; Muttaqī 2/no. 2963, 7/no. 18683, 11/nos. 32309, 32313, 12/no. 35462; Suyūṭī, *al-Jāmi' al-Kabīr* 1/207.

[36]See Daylamī 1/42; Haythamī, *Majma'* 8/218; Suyūṭī, *al-Jāmi' al-Ṣaghīr* 1/107; Muttaqī 11/402, nos. 31873, 31884.

created Paradise and chose Arabic out of all other languages for it, and then chose the Arabs for Arabic.[37]

From another early source we learn of this statement by Wahb's younger contemporary, Zuhrī (d. 124/741): "The tongue /speech of the people of Paradise is Arabic" (*lisānu / kalāmu ahli l-jannati ʿarabī*).[38] However, one generation after Zuhrī, a certain elaboration on this notion acquires the form of a tradition attributed to the Prophet through the chain Zuhrī ← Saʿīd ibn al-Musayyib ← Abū Hurayra. This *ḥadīth* asserts that revelation to all previous prophets was initially made in Arabic, and then each prophet delivered it to his people in his own language. From the debate of scholars over the authenticity of this tradition, one may conclude that such elaboration was made by Sulaymān ibn al-Arqam, the reporter from Zuhrī.[39]

We shall deal later with the favourable position the Arabs acquired through the statements presenting them as the people from whom the Prophet descended and in whose language scripture was revealed. Meanwhile, note must be made of certain late second/eighth, early third/ninth-century controversial elements that were added to the idea that Arabic was the speech of Paradise. In one tradition, the Antichrist (*al-dajjāl*) was described as one who would have the guise of Magians (*hay'at al-majūs*), a Persian bow and Persian speech.[40] Another says that Persian is a language hated most by God, that Khūzistānī is the speech of demons, and that Bukhārī is the language used in Hell. We notice that the person held responsible for circulating this tradition was Ismāʿīl ibn Ziyād (d. 246–48/860–62), who attributed it to the Prophet in a chain leading back through Abū Hurayra.[41]

---

[37]Wahb ibn Munabbih, *Kitāb al-Tījān*, ed. F. Krenkow, Hyderabad 1347 AH, 26.

[38]Nuʿaym ibn Ḥammād (d. 227/841), *Ziyādāt al-Zuhd*, in the margin of Ibn al-Mubārak, 71. Compare this also with the version in Ibn Kathīr (d. 774/1372), *al-Nihāya Fī l-Fitan wa-l-Malāḥim*, ed. Aḥmad ʿAbd al-ʿAzīz, al-Maktab al-Thaqāfī, Cairo 1986, 2/412.

[39]Cf. Ibn ʿAdī 3/1101; ʿIrāqī 14; Haythamī, *Majmaʿ* 10/53; Haytamī 76; Abū l-Shaykh (d. 369/979), *Ṣifat Ahl al-Janna*, Dār al-Ma'mūn, Damascus 1987, 117; Fattanī (d. 986/1578), *Maʿrifat Tadhkirat al-Mawḍūʿāt*, Bombay 1342 AH, 113.

[40]Ibn al-Murajjā (d. 492/1098), *Faḍā'il Bayt al-Maqdis*, Ms. Tübingen 27, 79v.

[41]Ibn Ḥibbān, *al-Majrūḥīn* 1/129; Jawraqānī 2/260–61; Ibn al-Jawzī, *al-Mawḍūʿāt*, ed. ʿAbd al-Raḥmān ʿUthmān, al-Maktaba al-Salafīya, Medina 1966, 1/111; Suyūṭī, *La'ālī* 1/11; Kinānī 1/137; Ibn Ḥajar, *Tahdhīb* 1/299; Fattanī 113.

Daylamī attributes the same statement to 'Abd Allāh ibn 'Amr, but without any *isnād* details.[42] From him, as well as from other sources, we also learn of a Prophetic tradition through Ibn 'Umar stating that Arabic is the speech of the people in Paradise, in the Heavens and at the place where people will stand (*mawqif*) before God on the Day of Judgement. Note again that the authority held responsible for circulating it is the late second/eighth-century 'Uthmān ibn Qā'id.[43]

Also noteworthy is another late second/eighth-century current that adds the element of forbidding people from speaking Persian to the original core of urging them to learn Arabic. 'Umar ibn Hārūn (d. 194/809) is usually held responsible for circulating a tradition stating says that whoever could speak Arabic well should not speak Persian because it encourages hypocrisy (*tūrithu al-nifāq*).[44] Also around the late second/eighth century, Ṭalḥa ibn Zayd al-Raqqī circulated another Prophetic tradition that asserts that speaking Persian increases one's deviousness / meanness / insanity / wickedness and decreases his manliness (*muruwwa*).[45]

Other traditions whose authorities are not specified say that "Persian / non-Arabic is the speech of the people of Hell" (*kalāmu l-a'jamīyati kalāmu ahl al-nār*),[46] that "the speech most hated by God is Persian" (*abghaḍu l-kalāmi ilā l-lāhi l-fārisīyatu*),[47] etc. On the other hand, a few traditions tried to save some place for Persian by saying that it is the language of the carriers of God's seat (*kalāmu ḥamalati l-'arshi*),

---

[42]Daylamī 1/368.

[43]Ibn Ḥibbān, *al-Majrūḥīn* 2/101; Daylamī 3/85; Ibn 'Asākir 2/229; Dhahabī, *Mīzān* 3/51. Compare also with Fattanī 112 and Ibn al-Qaysarānī (d. 507/1113), *Ma'rifat al-Tadhkira*, ed. 'Imād al-Dīn Ḥaydar, Mu'assasat al-Kutub al-Thaqāfīya, Beirut 1985, 181.

[44]Abū Sa'īd al-Naqqāsh, *Amālī*, Ms. Ẓāhirīya, *Majmū'* no. 20, 41; Ḥākim 4/88; 'Irāqī 15; Ibn al-Ṣiddīq al-Ghumārī, *al-Mughīr 'Ala Ḍa'īf al-Jāmi' al-Ṣaghīr*, Cairo n.d., 93–94; Haytamī 76; Albānī 2/12. Compare also with Daylamī 3/516, where the same tradition was attributed to the Prophet not through Ibn 'Umar, but through 'Umar. For more traditions that urge the learning of Arabic, see below, 50–52.

[45]For the different vocalisations (*khabbihi*, *khissihi*, *jinnihi*, *khubthihi*) see Ibn 'Adī 4/1428; 'Irāqī 15; Fattanī 113; Haytamī 76.

[46]Daylamī 3/300; Ḥalīmī 2/169.

[47]Al-Shawkānī (d. 1250/1834), *al-Fawā'id al-Majmū'a*, ed. 'Abd al-Raḥmān al-Mu'allimī al-Yamānī, Maṭba'at al-Sunna al-Muḥammadīya, Cairo 1960, 414.

or that God uses it when he wants to reveal a matter involving tenderness or contentment (*idhā arāda amran fīhi līnun / riḍan*), while he uses Arabic for something involving harshness or anger (*fīhi shiddatun / ghaḍabun*).[48]

The improvement of the position not only of Arabic, but also of the Arabs, was part of the process of fusion that resulted in the Arabisation of Islam and the Islamisation of the Arab polity. One dimension of this process is clearly reflected in traditions that rehabilitate the previous position of bedouins (*a'rāb*), reconcile them with Islam and result in the emergence of an Arab ethnic entity related to its bedouin roots.

This development is clearly expressed in a tradition according to which the Prophet rebuked 'Ā'isha for refusing to accept a present from a bedouin woman from Banū Sulaym, saying: "O 'Ā'isha, *a'rāb* who have professed Islam (*aslamū*) are no [longer] *a'rāb*, but the people of our desert [periphery] (*ahlu bādiyatinā*), while we are the people of their sedentary center (*ahlu ḥāḍirihim*). If we call them they respond to us, and if they call us we respond to them."[49]

It is worth noting that the *isnād* of this tradition leads through the link Ṣāliḥ ibn Kaysān (d. 130–40/747–57) ← 'Urwa ibn al-Zubayr (d. 94/712). From another report we learn that the contemporary Zuhrī used to take it upon himself to dwell among the *a'rāb* in order to teach them (*kāna yanzilu bi-l-a'rābi yu'allimuhum*).[50] About a third figure from this period, the caliph 'Umar II (d. 101/719), we learn that he recommended to a man who asked him about heretical tendencies (*al-ahwā'*) that he should follow "the religion of the bedouin and that of the child of school age" / var. "in the book" (*'alayka bi-dīni l-a'rābīyi wa-l-ghulāmi l-ladhī fī l-kuttābi / l-kitābi*).[51] On the other hand, there is a unique tradition that attributes to the Prophet the saying: "I belong to the Arabs, but the bedouins do not belong to me" (*anā min*

---

[48]Ḥalīmī 2/168–69; Daylamī 3/300; Kinānī 1/136; Fattanī 113; al-Qārī, *al-Asrār al-Marfū'a* 182–83.

[49]Bayhaqī, *Shu'ab* 6/480; Ibn al-Jawzī, *Sīra wa-Manāqib 'Umar ibn 'Abd al-'Azīz*, 83.

[50]Abū Nu'aym 3/363.

[51]Bayhaqī, *Shu'ab* 1/95; the latter reading is surely a scribal or editorial error. Compare also with Muttaqī 11/144 no. 30164, quoting Ibn 'Adī for a similar tradition attributed to the Prophet through 'Abd Allāh ibn 'Amr.

l-'arabi wa-laysat al-a'rābu minnī).[52] One may compare this with a poetical verse in which Jarīr says that the right name to be called by is Arabs and not *a'rāb*, which is a pejorative name used by non-Arabs.[53] Finally, there is the statement of Ḥasan al-Baṣrī in which he interprets the Qur'ānic phrase *dhū l-qurbā* as denoting the Prophet's "relatives from among the Arabs."[54]

Nothing is said here to imply that the rehabilitation of the position of *a'rāb*–Arabs was a smooth one. On the contrary, the troubled style and content of some of the above-cited traditions reflect the complexity of a process throughout which different cross-currents were in effect. And the same observation may be made concerning reports describing the policies of certain first/seventh and second/eighth-century figures promoting the learning of Arabic. One of them says that 'Umar I did so because he believed that knowledge of Arabic "increases *muruwwa* and strengthens the intellect" (*tazīdu fī l-muruwwa wa-tuthabbitu l-'aql*). This was circulated by 'Abd al-Wārith ibn Sa'īd (d. 179/795) from a certain Abū Muslim.[55] From a tradition of 'Aṭā' ibn Abī Rabāḥ (d. 114/732) we learn that 'Umar I heard a man speaking Persian and urged him to pursue the study of Arabic (*ittabi' ilā l-'arabīyati sabīlan*).[56] However, one tradition circulated by the mid-second/eighth century Ghālib al-Qaṭṭān says that 'Umar I urged the learning of both genealogy and Arabic, and attributes to him the saying that through knowledge of the latter people would know the scriptures.[57]

It is worth noting that the appearance of this additional element of knowledge of the scripture in the policy attributed to 'Umar I occurs also in a *mursal* tradition by the early second-century Ḥasan al-Baṣrī.[58] We also notice that almost the same was attributed to the Prophet in

---

[52]Ibn Taymīya, *Aḥādīth al-Quṣṣāṣ*, Beirut 1972, 100.

[53]"They call us bedouins, but Arabs is our name // And their names amongst us are the necks of provision bags" (*yusammūnanā l-a'rābu wa-l-'urbu ismunā // wa-asmā'uhum fīnā riqābu l-mazāwidi*); for this, see al-Mubarrad 1/264; *Simṭ al-La'ālī*, Cairo 1354 AH, 1/598.

[54]Al-Barqī, *Kitāb al-Maḥāsin*, Najaf 1964, 109–10.

[55]Abū l-Qāsim al-Ḥirafī, *Fawā'id*, Ms. Ẓāhirīya, *Majmū'* no. 87, 5; Bayhaqī, *Shu'ab* 2/257; Muttaqī 3/no. 9037, 10/no. 29355.

[56]Al-Ḥirafī, *Fawā'id* 5; Bayhaqī, *Shu'ab* 2/257; Muttaqī 3/no. 9038.

[57]Samarqandī, *Ḥadīth*, Ms. Ẓāhirīya, *Majmū'* no. 40, 307.

[58]Bayhaqī, *Shu'ab* 2/257.

another tradition, that of ʿAṭāʾ ibn Abī Rabāḥ from Abū Hurayra, though here a modest knowledge of astronomy is also mentioned.[59]

One report of ʿAbd Allāh ibn Burayda (d. 115/733) says that Muʿāwiya urged his son Yazīd to learn the same three arts—genealogy, astronomy and Arabic—but knowledge of the scriptures is not mentioned here as a motive for learning Arabic.[60] The caliph ʿAbd al-Malik ibn Marwān is also reported to have urged his sons to learn Arabic grammar, saying to his adviser, Rawḥ ibn Zinbāʿ: "No one should rule the Arabs except one who speaks their language" (*lā yanbaghī an yalī amra l-ʿarabi illā man yatakallamu bi-kalāmihā*).[61]

A tradition circulated in Baṣra in the first half of the second century AH by ʿAwf al-Aʿrābī (d. 146–48/763–65) ← Khulayd al-Baṣrī, reflects the great advantage the Arabs acquired by being those whose language was recognized as the sacred tool of revelation. According to this tradition, Salmān al-Fārisī refused to lead in Qurʾānic recitation and explained that since the Qurʾān was Arabic, an Arab should be asked to recite it.[62]

The statement attributed to Salmān does not stand alone, and must be considered together with a whole group of polemical traditions concerning the issue of whether or not slaves and *mawālī* are permitted to lead the believers in prayer. Though some traditions may appear in a form that projects this controversy back to earlier periods, the fact that Ibn Jurayj (d. 150/767) is one of the main figures reporting the pros and cons proves that this was a burning issue in his own lifetime. Also suggestive is the criterion stated for permitting such leadership in prayer, namely that no man may do so unless he knows Arabic and does not have an *aʿjamī* tongue.[63]

Mention has already been made of another set of traditions, associated with the name of Salmān al-Fārisī, in which the reluctance of non-Arabs to lead Arabs in prayer and marry Arab women was con-

---

[59] *Ibid.*, 2/269–70.

[60] Ibn ʿAsākir 2/269–70.

[61] Ibn ʿAsākir 17/840–41; cf. also 2/853.

[62] Ibn Abī Shayba 10/460, 12/192 and the biographical note on Khulayd in Ibn Ḥajar, *Tahdhīb* 3/159. Compare also with a tradition bearing the name of Ibn Masʿūd in Bayhaqī, *Shuʿab* 2/541.

[63] Bayhaqī, *Sunan* 3/88–89. Cf. also Ibn ʿAbd Rabbihi 3/363–64.

strued from the due preference of the Arab Prophet. However, the emergence of Arabic as the sacred language of revelation seems to have become the main focal point for the new religious polity. From a unique tradition of Zuhrī we learn that ʿAbd al-Malik once asked an eloquent man whether he was a *mawlā* or an Arab. The man, we are told, responded by saying: "If Arabic is a father then I do not relate to it, but if it is a tongue then I do" (*in takun al-ʿarabīyatu aban fa-lastu minhā, wa-in takun lisānan fa-innī minhā*). ʿAbd al-Malik, the report says, expressed his agreement with this and referred to the phrase *bi-lisānin ʿarabīyin mubīn*, "in clear Arabic speech," the Qur'ānic locution of Sūrat al-Shuʿarā' (26), v. 195.[64] We may only add here that almost the same notion occurs in a tradition attributed to the Prophet in a *mursal* form by Abū Salama ibn ʿAbd al-Raḥmān (d. 94–104/712–22) and reported by none other than Zuhrī. According to this tradition, the Prophet became angry on hearing that his non-Arab Companions, the ethnic symbolic representatives Salmān, Ṣuhayb and Bilāl, had been reminded of their foreign descent. Muḥammad protested: "O people, [your] God is one, [your] father is one, and Arabic is neither a father nor a mother to any of you; [it is] but a language, so whoever speaks Arabic is an Arab."[65]

Still, the Arabs undoubtedly emerged as the one ethnic group with a position second to none in Islam, a fact expressed by numerous traditions extolling their merits and enjoining love and respect for them since they were both the people of the Prophet and speakers of the language of the Qur'ān. A widely circulated tradition associated with the name of Abū Hurayra attributes to the Prophet the saying: "I am an Arab, the Qur'ān is Arabic and the speech of the people of Paradise is Arabic." Another, bearing the name of Ibn ʿAbbās, attributes to the Prophet a statement identifying these three elements as reasons for loving the Arabs (*aḥibbū l-ʿaraba li-thalāthin....*). A

[64]Abū Ḥayyān al-Tawḥīdī 8/35; Ibn ʿAsākir 19/326.

[65]See Abū al-Ḥasan al-Sukkarī al-Khuttalī, *Ḥadīth*, Ms. Ẓāhirīya, *Majmūʿ* no. 118, 6; Ibn ʿAsākir 3/464, 7/407, 8/378–79; Muttaqī 12/47; al-Albānī, *Silsilat al-Aḥādīth al-Ḍaʿīfa*, al-Maktab al-Islāmī, Beirut 1384 AH, 2/325, quoting Ibn Taymīya's *Iqtiḍā'* too. This tradition is cited by Mottahedeh 179, who notes that al-Qummī quotes it in his *Tafsīr* (Najaf, 1387 AH, 2/322) in a commentary on Sūrat al-Ḥujurāt (49), v. 13.

close examination of the available *isnād* information reveals that the Ibn ʿAbbās tradition was actually circulated by Ibn Jurayj, who took it from ʿAṭāʾ. However, the link of Yaḥyā ibn Yazīd al-Ashʿarī ← al-ʿAlāʾ ibn ʿAmr al-Ḥanafī, which reported it from Ibn Jurayj, was the one blamed for it by *ḥadīth* scholars who questioned its authenticity. Note also that the information concerning the existence of another informant for this tradition from Ibn Jurayj, a certain Muḥammad ibn al-Faḍl al-Khurāsānī, was completely ignored by these scholars.[66] As for the Abū Hurayra tradition, it was also reported around the middle of the second/eighth century by Shibl ibn al-ʿAlāʾ ibn ʿAbd al-Raḥmān in a family line from his father, al-ʿAlāʾ (d. 132/749) ← grandfather ← Abū Hurayra.[67]

In another group of traditions, extolling the merits of Arabs and enjoining love for them was closely connected with the notion of establishing the leadership of Quraysh as *imāms* of the Arabs.[68] One of these traditions, with the *isnād* Thābit al-Bunānī ← Anas, opens with the Prophetic statement: "Loving Quraysh is belief and hating them is infidelity." This is immediately followed by a statement to the effect that "whoever loves the Arabs loves me and whoever hates them hates me" (*man aḥabba l-ʿaraba fa-qad aḥabbanī wa-man abghaḍahum fa-qad*

---

[66]See al-Dhuhalī, *Fawāʾid*, Ms. in private possession, 17v; Ibn Abī Ḥātim, *ʿIlal* 2/375–76; al-ʿUqaylī (d. 322/933), *Kitāb al-Ḍuʿafāʾ al-Kabīr*, ed. ʿAbd al-Muʿṭī Qalʿajī, Dār al-Kutub al-ʿIlmīya, Beirut 1984, 3/348–49; Ṭabarānī, *al-Muʿjam al-Kabīr* 11/185; Ḥākim, *al-Mustadrak* 4/87; *idem*, *Maʿrifat ʿUlūm al-Ḥadīth*, Dār al-Kutub al-ʿIlmīya, Beirut, and al-Maktaba al-ʿIlmīya, Medina, 1977, 161–62; Bayhaqī, *Shuʿab* 2/159, 230; Abū l-Shaykh, *Ṣifat al-Janna* 116; Ibn ʿAsākir 6/458; Dhahabī, *Mīzān al-Iʿtidāl*, Cairo 1963, 3/103; al-ʿIrāqī, *al-Qurab Fī Maḥabbat al-ʿArab*, Bombay 1303 AH, 4, 14; Haythamī, *Majmaʿ* 10/52; Ibn Ḥajar, *Lisān al-Mīzān*, Hyderabad 1330 AH, 2/185; Sakhāwī 22; Suyūṭī, *Laʾālī* 1/442; *idem*, *al-Jāmiʿ al-Kabīr* 1/23; *idem*, *al-Jāmiʿ al-Ṣaghīr* 1/11; al-Qārī (d. 1014/1605), *al-Asrār al-Marfūʿa*, Beirut 1985, 182; al-Kinānī (d. 963/1555), *Tanzīh al-Sharīʿa*, Beirut 1979, 2/30; al-Haytamī (d. 973/1565), *Fakhr al-ʿArab*, Cairo 1987, 20; al-Fattanī (d. 986/1578), *Tadhkirat al-Mawḍūʿāt*, Bombay 1342 AH, 112; Shawkānī 413; al-Ḥūt al-Bayrūtī (d. 1276/1859), *Asnā al-Maṭālib*, Beirut 1319 AH, 20; Albānī 1/189–90.

[67]Sakhāwī 22–23; Suyūṭī, *Laʾālī* 1/442–43; Kinānī 2/30–31; Albānī 1/192–93; and, without sufficient *isnād*, also in Ḥalīmī 2/170; ʿIrāqī 4, 14; Haythamī 10/52–53; Munāwī 1/80; Haytamī 20; Fattanī 112; Shawkānī 413; Muttaqī 12/43 no. 33922, quoting Abū l-Shaykh's *Thawāb*.

[68]Ibn Abī ʿĀṣim, *Sunna* 2/636; Ḥalīmī 2/167; Daylamī 1/121.

abghadanī).[69] In another tradition, by Abū l-Ḥuṣayn ← Abū l-Aḥwaṣ ← Ibn Mas'ūd, Quraysh is described as a bird's breast (*ju'ju'*) without whose wings, the Arabs, it cannot fly.[70]

The traditional correlation between preference for Quraysh and preference for the Arabs is clear in another group of statements describing the choices made by God from the time of Creation until the appearance of the Prophet. One of these, bearing the name of Ibn 'Umar, enjoyed the widest circulation. It was mostly transmitted by 'Amr ibn Dīnār (d. 125–26/742–43), and sometimes by Ibn 'Umar's son, Sālim (d. 105–107/723–25). In reaction to Abū Sufyān's slander of Banū Hāshim, we are told, the Prophet said that God chose human beings (*ikhtāra banī ādam*) out of all his creatures. His second stage was choice of the Arabs out of all human beings, and then, consequently, Muḍar, Quraysh, Banū Hāshim and finally the Prophet himself. We also notice that this tradition ends with what seemingly became a standard literary slogan in the second/eighth century, namely, that whoever loves or hates the Arabs does so because he loves or hates the Prophet.[71]

The existence of other variants similar to this one suggests that it originated during the lifetime of 'Amr ibn Dīnār. For we also find that 'Amr reports it from al-Bāqir, who attributes it to the Prophet in a *mursal* form. The main differences between the two variants are the absence of the introductory element of Abū Sufyān's slander, the final standard statement on love and hatred, and the appearance of Banū Kināna as an additional chain between the Arabs and al-Naḍr ibn Kināna.[72] Exactly the same statement was attributed to the Prophet in another *mursal* tradition, that of 'Abd Allāh ibn 'Ubayd Allāh ibn

---

[69]Bazzār, *Musnad*, cf. Haythamī, *Kashf* 1/51; *idem*, *Majma'* 1/89, 10/7, 32; Haytamī 19–20.

[70]Ibn 'Abd Rabbihi 3/270.

[71]Ṭabarānī, *al-Mu'jam al-Kabīr* 12/455–56; Ibn 'Adī 2/665–66; Ḥalīmī 2/47; Ḥākim 4/73, 86–87; Bayhaqī, *Shu'ab* 2/139–40; *idem*, *Dalā'il* 1/171–72; Dhahabī, *Mīzān* 3/55; Ibn Kathīr, *al-Bidāya wa-l-Nihāya*, Cairo 1932, 2/257; 'Irāqī 3; Haythamī, *Majma'* 8/215; Suyūṭī, *Khaṣā'iṣ* 1/38; *idem*, *Durr* 3/294–95; Haytamī 17; Muttaqī 12/43 no. 33918. Compare also with Bayhaqī, *Shu'ab* 2/229 and Suyūṭī, *Durr* 4/193, where the same tradition was attributed to 'Umar I.

[72]Ibn Sa'd 1/20; cf. also Muttaqī 11/451 no. 32121 (who calls it "problematic" (*mu'ḍil*)); Basawī 1/498; Bayhaqī, *Dalā'il* 1/167; *idem*, *Sunan* 7/134; Suyūṭī, *Khaṣā'iṣ* 1/38; *idem*, *Durr* 3/295.

'Umayr (d. 113/731).[73] When this tradition was reported from al-Bāqir by his son al-Ṣādiq, slight changes occurred, such as the removal of the Banū Kināna element and the addition of a new introductory one, namely that God split the land into two parts, put the Prophet in the better part, etc. (*qasama l-lāhu l-arḍīnā qismayn fa-ja'alanī fī khayrihimā*).[74]

The element of an act of splitting by God at every new stage of choice until the birth of Muḥammad, with the latter's part being always the better, appears also in traditions associated with the name of Abū Hurayra. We notice, however, that in some variants the *'ajam* also appear as a unit of choice besides the Arabs, though God's best was placed, according to them, amongst the latter (*wa-kānat khīratu l-lahi fī l-'arab*).[75] Another tradition that follows the pattern of consecutive splitting was reported from both al-'Abbās and 'Abd al-Muṭṭalib ibn Rabī'a. However, it fails to identify the different units and choices and speaks only in general terms about tribes, houses and souls, stressing the idea that the Prophet came from the best of them.[76] There is also the tradition of Ḥabashī ibn Junāda that speaks about the Arabs being chosen from all peoples (*iṣṭafā l-'araba min jamī' al-nās*), but ends by adding some Shī'ī figures from the Prophet's house to the list of God's chosen ones.[77]

There is an interesting tradition associated with the name of the Companion Wāthila ibn al-Asqa' and transmitted through the Syrian link Awzā'ī (d. 157/773) ← Shaddād Abū 'Ammār. After Awzā'ī it splits into two branches of transmission: one by al-Walīd ibn Muslim (d. 194–95/809–10) continues the Syrian line, and another moves with Muḥammad ibn Muṣ'ab al-Qirqisānī (d. 180/796) to circles of scholarship in Baghdad. The common feature about these two variants is that neither one mentions the Arabs within the series of God's choices. In-

---

[73]Ibn Sa'd 1/21; cf. also Muttaqī 11/450–51 nos. 32119–20 (where it is wrongly assigned to the father, 'Ubayd ibn 'Umayr); Suyūṭī, *Durr* 3/295.

[74]Ibn Sa'd 1/20; Suyūṭī, *Durr* 3/295.

[75]Bībī bint 'Abd al-Ṣamad (d. 477/1084), *Juz'*, ed. 'Abd al-Raḥmān al-Faryawā'ī, Dār al-Khulafā' li-l-Kitāb al-Islāmī, Kuwait 1986, 79; 'Irāqī 3; Haythamī, *Majma'* 8/217; Haytamī 17–18.

[76]Ibn Abī 'Āṣim, *Sunna* 619; Suyūṭī, *Durr* 3/294.

[77]Ibn 'Asākir 5/45; cf. also Muttaqī 11/756 no. 33680.

stead, they speak about the choice of Banū Kināna from among Banū Ismā'īl, of Quraysh from among Banū Kināna, etc. We notice, however, that Walīd's variant ends with an element attributing to the Prophet the saying "and thus I am the master of [all] human beings" (*fa-anā sayyidu wuldī ādam*).[78] Finally, preference for the Arabs over all creatures is expressed by one variant of a tradition of Abū Mūsā al-Ash'arī in the context of a discourse on the Day of Judgement. According to this, the Prophet made an invocation to God on behalf of the Arabs, adding that on the Day of Judgement they would be the closest of all creatures to his banner (*wa-inna aqraba l-khalqi min liwā'ī yawma'idhin al-'arab*).[79]

The Prophet's concern to secure preferential treatment for the Arabs is reflected in a tradition according to which he required 'Alī ibn Abī Ṭālib to ensure their well being (*awṣāhu bi-l-'arabi khayran*),[80] a notion that seems designed to pre-empt any possible anti-Arab sentiment among the Shī'a. As such, this tradition must be considered together with another widely circulated *ḥadīth* specifically aimed at the Persians. This one was circulated in the name of Salmān al-Fārisī, who we are told was warned by the Prophet that hating the Arabs would mean hating him, and hence, departure from religion (*lā tabghaḍnī fa-tufāriq dīnaka... tabghaḍu l-'araba fa-tabghaḍnī*).

Since Goldziher noted this tradition and believed that it originated as part of the Arab defensive reaction against the rise of non-Arab elements to predominance in the third/ninth century,[81] it is important to try to date it. The available information on its *isnād* to Salmān shows that it leads exclusively to the family link Qābūs (Kūfan, d. *ca.* 132/749) ← his father, Abū Ẓibyān (d. 90/708). The only recorded transmitter of this tradition is the Kūfan Abū Badr Shujā' ibn al-Walīd (d. 203–205/818–20), from whom it was cited by several scholars, a

---

[78]Ibn Sa'd 1/20; Ibn Ḥanbal, *Musnad* 4/107; Ibn Ḥibbān, *Ṣaḥīḥ* 8/47, 81–82; Ibn Abī 'Āṣim, *Sunna* 618; Ibn 'Asākir 17/704; Suyūṭī, *Durr* 3/294; Haytamī 18.

[79]Bazzār, *Musnad*, cf. Haythamī, *Kashf* 3/315; *idem*, *Majma'* 10/52; Bayhaqī, *Shu'ab* 2/231–32; Suyūṭī, *Durr* 4/86; Haytamī 25; Muttaqī 12/46 no. 33929; 'Irāqī 6.

[80]Bazzār, *Musnad* 2/318; cf. also Haythamī, *Kashf* 3/315; *idem*, *Majma'* 10/52; Ṭabarānī, *al-Mu'jam al-Kabīr* 4/8; 'Irāqī 5; Hatamī 22–23.

[81]Goldziher, *Muslim Studies* 1/142.

fact suggesting that it originated in the course of the second/eighth century.[82]

Some time earlier, another tradition was circulated in Kūfa, warning that whoever cheated the Arabs would not receive the Prophet's intercession (*shafā'a*) or love (*mawadda*). This was done by al-Ḥuṣayn ibn 'Umar (d. 180–90/796–805) in a line leading back to the Prophet through the caliph 'Uthmān ibn 'Affān.[83] From the link Muṭarraf ibn Ma'qil ← Thābit al-Bunānī (Baṣran, d. 123–27/740–44), we learn of a tradition of 'Umar I that attributes to the Prophet the saying: "Whoever slanders the Arabs is a polytheist" (*man sabba l-'araba fa-ūlā'ika humu l-mushrikūn*).[84] Another tradition, by Jābir ibn 'Abd Allāh, says: "If the Arabs are humiliated, then Islam is humiliated" (*idhā dhalla l-'arabu dhalla l-islām*). This *ḥadīth* was reported through the line Muḥammad ibn al-Khaṭṭāb ← 'Alī ibn Zayd (ibn Jud'ān, Baṣran d. 129–31/747–48).[85] The same Muḥammad ibn al-Khaṭṭāb was also held responsible for circulating from 'Aṭā' ibn Abī Maymūna (Baṣran, d. 131/748) a tradition of Abū Hurayra urging people to love Arabs because "their survival is light in Islam and their perdition is darkness in

---

[82]See Baghawī, *Mukhtaṣar al-Mu'jam*, Ms. Ẓāhirīya, *Majmū'* no. 94, 135; Muḥibb al-Dīn al-Ṭabarī, *Dhakhā'ir al-'Uqbā*, Ms. Ẓāhirīya, General no. 4808, 6; Ibn Ḥanbal, *Musnad* 5/440–41; Tirmidhī 5/723 (where he notes that Abū Ẓibyān did not see Salmān); Ibn Abī Ḥātim, *al-Marāsīl*, ed. Aḥmad 'Iṣām al-Kātib, Dār al-Kutub al-'Ilmīya, Beirut 1983, 47 (noting the same as Tirmidhī); Ḥākim 4/86 (insisting that its *isnād* is *ṣaḥīḥ*); al-Khaṭīb al-Baghdādī 9/248 (and compare 14/366, a different tradition advocating a similar theme); Bayhaqī, *Shu'ab* 2/230; Daylamī 5/388; Muttaqī 12/44 no. 33921; 'Irāqī 4–5; Suyūṭī, *al-Jāmi' al-Kabīr* 1/964; Haytamī 21 (insisting that there are no gaps in its *isnād*: *lā inqiṭā'a fī ṭarīqihi*); Ibn Ḥajar, *Tahdhīb* 4/314.

[83]Ibn Abī Shayba 12/193; Ibn Ḥanbal, *Musnad* 1/72; 'Abd ibn Ḥumayd (d. 249/863), *al-Muntakhab Min al-Musnad*, ed. Subḥī al-Sāmarrā'ī and Maḥmūd al-Ṣa'īdī, Maktabat al-Sunna, Cairo 1988, 48; Tirmidhī 5/724; Bazzār, *Musnad* 2/16; Daylamī 3/533; 'Irāqī 5; Suyūṭī, *al-Jāmi' al-Kabīr* 1/804; *idem*, *al-Jāmi' al-Ṣaghīr* 2/176; Haytamī 23; Munāwī 2/114; Muttāqi 12/44 no. 33920; Albānī 2/24.

[84]This was sometimes reported as Anas' tradition, clearly because in some variants he stands between Thābit al-Bunānī and 'Umar I. See 'Uqaylī 4/217; Ibn 'Adī 6/2376; Ḥalīmī 2/151; al-Khaṭīb al-Baghdādī 10/295; Bayhaqī, *Shu'ab* 2/231; Dhahabī, *Mīzān* 4/126; Muttaqī 12/44.

[85]Abū Ya'lā 3/402, 4/74; Ibn Abī Ḥātim, *'Ilal* 2/376; Dhahabī, *Mīzān* 3/537; 'Irāqī 4; Ibn Ḥajar, *Lisān* 5/155; Haythamī, *Majma'* 10/53; Haytamī 21; Muttaqī 12/44 no. 33923; Albānī 1/194–95.

Islam" (*fa-inna baqā'uhum nūrun fī l-islām wa-fanā'uhum ẓulmatun fī l-islām*). Parallels to this were also transmitted from Anas (by the same 'Aṭā' ibn Abī Maymūna), Nubayṭ ibn Sharīṭ (through a family *isnād*, but with unidentified figures) and possibly Ibn 'Abbās too.[86] Finally, 'Aṭā' ibn Abī Maymūna seems also to be responsible for circulating another tradition of Ibn 'Abbās that attributes to the Prophet the saying: "The numerousness / var. and belief of the Arabs are a delight to my eye" (*kathratu l-'arabi / wa-īmānuhum qurratu 'aynin lī*).[87]

Sporadically, some traditions combined advocation of love for the Arabs with love of the poor, explaining that they are the Prophet's *umma* and that they themselves or some of their customs constitute the pillars of religion (*qiwāmu / 'imādu l-dīn*). Such traditions were attributed to the Prophet through chains leading to Abū Hurayra, Ibn 'Abbās and Ibn 'Umar.[88] Note, however, that one of them occurring in an early source is transmitted through the *isnād* al-Jarrāḥ ibn Malīḥ ← Arṭāṭ ibn al-Mundhir (Ḥimṣī, d. 162–63/778–79) ← "from their authorities, that the Prophet said...." (*'an ashyākhihim anna l-nabīya qāla....*).[89]

More diversified and informative from the point of view of *isnād* investigation is the group of traditions that follow the standard equation of loving the Arabs (together with certain other groups and persons) with belief, and hating them with hypocrisy, infidelity, etc. One attributes to the Prophet through 'Umar a saying that hating the Arabs is a break (*thulma*) in Islam.[90] Another, through Abū Rāfi', reiterates what became a standard statement, namely: "No one except a hypocrite hates the Arabs" (*lā yabghaḍu l-'araba illā munāfiq*). From the son of Abū Rāfi' it was reported by the link Zayd ibn Jubayra ←

---

[86]Daylamī 3/89; 'Irāqī 4, quoting Abū l-Shaykh's *Thawāb*; Sakhāwī 23; Suyūṭī, *al-Jāmi' al-Kabīr* 1/23; Haytamī 20; Munāwī 2/20; Muttaqī 12/43 no. 33922; Albānī 2/46–47.

[87]Ibn Abī Ḥātim, *'Ilal* 2/367; Daylamī 3/301; Albānī 2/163. See also Muttaqī 12/46 no. 33932, where Abū l-Shaykh was quoted for a similar tradition bearing the name of Anas.

[88]Daylamī 2/199; Ibn 'Asākir 1/384; Suyūṭī, *al-Jāmi' al-Kabīr* 1/23; *idem*, *al-Jāmi' al-Ṣaghīr*, 1/11.

[89]Al-Mu'āfā ibn 'Imrān (d. 185/801), *Kitāb al-Zuhd*, Ms. Ẓāhirīya, *Ḥadīth* no. 359, 250.

[90]Daylamī 2/31.

Dāwūd ibn al-Ḥuṣayn (d. 135/752), the former being held responsible for it.[91]

Various elaborations on this standard core were connected with the names of various other Companions. One by Ibn ʻUmar occurs in three variants:

1. "Loving the Arabs is belief, and hating them is hypocrisy" (*ḥubbu l-ʻarabi īmānun wa-bughḍuhum nifāq*), without naming any authority for it.[92]

2. "No believer hates the Arabs, and no believer / no one except a believer / loves Thaqīf" (*lā yabghaḍu l-ʻaraba mu'minun wa-lā yuḥibbu thaqīfan / illā / mu'min*). A certain Sahl ibn ʻĀmir is held responsible for circulating this version.[93]

3. "He who loves the Arabs does so out of love for me, and he who hates the Arabs does so out of hate for me" (*man aḥabba l-ʻaraba fa-bi-ḥubbī aḥabbahum wa-man abghaḍa l-ʻaraba fa-bi-bughḍī abghaḍahum*). This is transmitted by ʻAmr ibn Dīnār as part of a longer tradition of his on God's choices from among His creation, noted above.[94]

As mentioned above, this last variant seems to have become a standard statement one generation after ʻAmr ibn Dīnār. We notice that it occurs *en bloc* in a tradition attributed to Anas through the link Haytham ibn Jummāz ← Thābit al-Bunānī (Baṣran, d. 123–27/740–44), the former being held responsible for it. It is also worth noting that this statement is preceded by one similar to what has otherwise been attributed to Ibn ʻUmar. The only difference between the two is the substitution, in this one, of *kufr* for *nifāq* (*ḥubbu l-ʻarabi īmānun wa-bughḍuhum nifāq*),

[91] Ibn ʻAdī 3/1059. Cf. Muttaqī 12/47 no. 33935, where it was also attributed to ʻAlī.

[92] ʻIrāqī 5; Haytamī 22; Sakhāwī 23, quoting Dāraquṭnī's *Afrād*.

[93] ʻIrāqī 5; Haytamī 22; Haythamī, *Majma'* 10/53; Muttaqī 12/47 no. 33934, quoting Ṭabarānī.

[94] ʻIrāqī 4, quoting Ṭabarānī's *al-Mu'jam al-Kabīr*. Compare also with Muttaqī 12/47 no. 33933, who quotes Abū l-Shaykh for a similar statement bearing the name of Ibn ʻAbbās.

and the additional specification, in one variant, of love and hatred of Quraysh.[95]

In another variant of Anas' tradition, love and hatred of the Anṣār, Muḥammad's followers in Medina, were also specified in the same way, a formulation that raised some scholarly concern as to whether this was not actually a confusion with a similar saying attributed to another Companion, al-Barrā' ibn 'Āzib.[96] This riddle may be solved by the *isnād* information given in Ibn 'Asākir to yet another variant from Anas, namely the one through 'Alī ibn Zayd (Baṣran, d. 129–31/746–48), and not his contemporary Thābit al-Bunānī. Here, love and hatred of the Anṣār, as well as of Abū Bakr and 'Umar I, were specified as *sunna* vs. *kufr*, respectively.[97] But new complications arise from comparing Ibn 'Asākir with his alleged third/ninth-century source, Ismā'īl ibn Muḥammad al-Ṣaffār. Such a comparison strikingly reveals the absence of the Anṣār element from the original version of al-Ṣaffār,[98] a fact that proves that tampering with texts by changing the location of such standard formulae or dropping them altogether was still being done long after the third/ninth century.

To carry our investigation any further would take us beyond the scope of the present enquiry. One may simply note the existence of an isolated variant of Anas' tradition that states that loving Abū Bakr and 'Umar I is belief and hating them is unbelief, without mentioning either the Arabs or the Anṣār. We also notice that this variant was transmitted by the line Abū Isḥāq al-Khamīsī (Khāzim ibn al-Ḥusayn) ← Mālik ibn Dīnār (Baṣran, d. 123–31/740–48) ← Anas.[99]

From Jābir ibn 'Abd Allāh two variant traditions were reported by certain unidentified authorities named al-Ḥusayn and Abū Sufyān. We can only observe that the former applies the formula of faith / unbelief = love / hatred of both Abū Bakr and 'Umar / the Anṣār and Arabs, respectively. The latter, in turn, confines itself to mentioning Abū

---

[95]See 'Uqaylī 4/355; Abū Nu'aym 2/333; 'Irāqī 4–5; Ḥākim 4/87; Munāwī 1/99; Haytamī 22; Haythamī, *Majma'* 10/27, 53, quoting Bazzār and Ṭabarānī's *al-Mu'jam al-Awsaṭ*, respectively; Muttaqī 12/44 no. 33924, quoting Ḥākim.

[96]Compare Bayhaqī, *Shu'ab* 2/230, and Sakhāwī 23, quoting Daylamī.

[97]Ibn 'Asākir 9/601.

[98]Ismā'īl ibn Muḥammad al-Ṣaffār, *Ḥadīth*, Ms. Ẓāhirīya, *Majmū'* no. 31, 222.

[99]Ibn 'Asākir 9/601.

Bakr and 'Umar and substitutes the pair of "believer" vs. "hypocrite" for "faith" vs. "unbelief."[100]

In a tradition attributed to 'Alī, a warning was issued that "no one but a *munāfiq* hates the Arabs."[101] Another tradition argues: "Whoever does not recognize the right of my family (*'itratī*) or that of the Anṣār and the Arabs is one of three things: a *munāfiq*, a son of adultery (*walad zinā*) or one whose mother conceived him without being pure (*li-ghayri ṭuhrin*)."[102] Comparing the *isnāds* of these two traditions, one notices that they share the same links up to Ismā'īl ibn 'Ayyāsh (Ḥimṣī, d. 181–82/797–98). From him, the first variant was circulated by Ismā'īl Abū Ma'mar (ibn Ibrāhīm ibn Ma'mar, who originally came from Harāt and died in Baghdad in 236/850), and the second by Hishām ibn 'Ammār (Damascene, d. 245/859).

As noted above, the occurrence of the element of loving the Arabs and, in this case, recognizing their rights as well (in traditions attributed to 'Alī) must seem as a possible pre-emptive defence against any tendency to the contrary in Shī'ī circles. Needless to add, introducing the element of loving the family (*'itra*) of 'Alī had a special appeal to such circles.

Other elements were sporadically added to the standard formulae reviewed so far in traditions that did not, however, gain much circulation. One by Ibn 'Abbās warns that "hatred of Banū Hāshīm and the Anṣār is unbelief, and hatred of the Arabs is hypocrisy."[103] Another, by Ibn Mas'ūd, praises certain qualities of the Arabs, expresses his confidence in their benevolent willingness to grant requests and ends with the statement: "Whoever hates the Arabs, God hates him."[104] And a third one, by 'Uthmān ibn 'Affān, simply reiterates the other standard Prophetic statement viewing love and hate for the Arabs as springing from love and hate for the Prophet.[105] It will already have been no-

---

[100] *Ibid.*

[101] Ibn Ḥanbal, *Musnad* 1/81; Haythamī 10/53; Haytamī 22.

[102] For minor variations, compare Ibn 'Adī 3/1060; Bayhaqī, *Shu'ab* 2/232; Dhahabī, *Mīzān* 2/99–100.

[103] Haythamī, *Majma'* 10/27; Suyūṭī, *al-Jāmi' al-Ṣaghīr* 1/126, both quoting Ṭabarānī. Compare also with Haytamī, 39.

[104] Ibn 'Abd Rabbihi 3/271.

[105] Ibn 'Adī 2/803.

ticed that the authorities for the last two traditions (Abū l-Ḥuṣayn for Ibn Mas'ūd's and al-Ḥuṣayn ibn 'Umar al-Aḥmasī for 'Uthmān's) are familiar to us from the current of other pro-Arab traditions examined in the course of this study.

CHAPTER IV

AMBIVALENT ATTITUDES

AS QUOTED by Ibn 'Abd Rabbihi, a Shu'ūbī response to an anti-Shu'ūbī treatise by Ibn Qutayba noted that the latter actually advocated equality for all human beings born out of dust and for replacing pride in their genealogies (*ansāb*) by the ideals of mindfulness (*taqwā*) and obedience to God (*ṭā'at al-lāh*).[1] Between these scholastically acculturated ideals and the basic realities of contempt, mistrust and downright enmity in daily life, there existed ambivalence, a complex of acceptance and rejection that comprised the dominant feature of Muslim literature on inter-ethnic and inter-racial relations. As Goldziher rightly noted: "The Muslim teaching of the equality of all men in Islam remained a dead letter for a long time, never realised in the concious-ness of Arabs and roundly denied in their day-to-day behaviour."[2] Ultimately, such ambivalence probably reflects the balance between interdependence and particularism in the Arab attitude towards neighbouring ethnic groups. In what follows some aspects of these ambivalences will be reviewed.

Goldziher's observation on the traditional notion relating the Persians to the Arabs by saying that the former descended from Isaac[3] can also be applied to similar attempts at accommodation with respect to other peoples. Such attempts may be viewed as Islam's traditional way of sketching interdependence between the different ethnicities of

[1] Ibn 'Abd Rabbihi 3/362.
[2] Goldziher, *Muslim Studies* 1/98.
[3] *Ibid.* 1/135.

that faith along the lines of family relations; a clear parallel to this can be traced in the Old Testament concerning the relations between the Israelites and neighbouring peoples.

The idea that the Persians are sons of Isaac was advanced by a variety of traditions attributed to the Prophet. Their main aim was to enhance the role of Persians in the establishment of Islam, and at least some of them bear a clear colouring from the 'Abbāsid period. Thus, while two of them, associated with the names of Ibn 'Umar and Abū Hurayra, simply state this notion, a third one, bearing the name of Ibn 'Abbās, adds that being sons of Isaac and cousins to the sons of Ishmael, "the Persians are a band [related] to us, the people of the house [of the Prophet]" (*fāris 'uṣbatunā ahl al-bayt*).[4] The *isnād* of this last tradition is Sufyān al-Thawrī (d. 161/777) ← Mu'āwiya ibn Qurra (Baṣran, d. 113/731) ← Sa'īd ibn Jubayr ← Ibn 'Abbās ← the Prophet.

However, promoting such ideal harmony and co-operation between relatives was not always the aim of relating the Persians to Isaac, since this relationship sometimes stood at the center of controversies over preference. In the aforementioned family tradition of 'Īsā ibn 'Alī ibn 'Abd Allāh al-Hāshimī (d. 164/780), from his father ← grandfather, Ibn 'Abbās, 'Alī ibn Abī Ṭālib was quoted as saying that for him an Arab woman was not better than a *mawlāt* one because he could not find in the Book of God (i.e. the Qur'ān) any preference for the sons of Ishmael over the sons of Isaac.[5] Ḥalīmī, on the other hand, based his preference for Arabs over *'ajam* on the ground that Ishmael was better than Isaac.[6]

Arab Muslim relations with the Copts of Egypt provide a valuable example of an attempt to assimilate another people that came under Arab rule and, while capable of causing great trouble,[7] was eventually Islamized and even Arabized. Overtures towards the Copts were made along lines similar to those adopted in the case of the Persians. The idea

---

[4]Daylamī 1/410, 418, 3/146; Abū Nu'aym, *Dhikr Akhbār Iṣbahān*, ed. S. Dedering, Leiden 1934, 1/11; Jawraqānī 2/265.

[5]Bayhaqī, *Sunan* 6/349.

[6]Ḥalīmī 2/162–65.

[7]On the continuous uprisings of the Copts during the second/eighth century, see Maqrīzī, *al-Khiṭaṭ*, Cairo 1324/1906, 2/91–100.

that the Copts not only enjoyed *dhimma* (protection by the Muslims), but also had *raḥm* (kinship) relations with the Arabs and hence should be treated well, was conveyed by a group of traditions often attributed to the Prophet. In some of these, Eqypt was described as "a country where the *qīrāṭ* [measure] is used" (*yudhkaru fīhā l-qīrāṭ*) and its people (*ahlu miṣr*) as ones who "have curly [hair on] their heads" (*ju'dun ru'ūsuhum*). They were recommended for good treatment (*istawṣū bihim khayran / aḥsinū ilā ahlihā*) because of their *dhimma* and *raḥm* relations with the Muslims, and because they were expected to become a source of support and reinforcement against the enemy (*fa-innahum quwwatun lakum wa-balāghun ilā 'aduwwikum*).[8]

The *isnād*s through which these traditions were variously attributed to the Prophet, and the comments made on them by a few early scholars, are highly suggestive. Already Yaḥyā ibn Ma'īn (d. 234/848) implies that the variant transmitted by 'Amr ibn Ḥurayth (who in other sources is mentioned in a "group *isnād*" together with Abū 'Abd al-Raḥmān al-Ḥubulī, 'Abd Allāh ibn Yazīd al-Ma'āfirī al-Miṣrī, d. *ca.* 100/718) is a *mursal* one, since 'Amr "did not hear from the Prophet and was only a man from the people of Egypt." The variant attributed to the Prophet through Abū Dharr was also carried by a clear Egyptian line of Ḥarmala ibn 'Imrān al-Tujībī al-Miṣrī (d. 160/776) ← 'Abd al-Raḥmān ibn Shumāsa al-Muhrī (Abū Baṣra, Egyptian, d. *ca.* 100/718). However, Muhrī's transmission from Abū Dharr was as seriously doubted as the transmission of 'Amr ibn Ḥurayth from the Prophet.[9] We also note that the late second-century Egyptian 'Abd Allāh ibn Wahb (d. 197/812), who was the main reporter from Ḥarmala, also reported from Layth ibn Sa'd (d. 175/791) and Mālik ibn Anas a similar tradition that the last two took from Zuhrī in an *isnād* leading back to the Prophet through the Companion Ka'b ibn Mālik.

---

[8]Yaḥyā ibn Ma'īn 1/327; Ibn Ḥanbal, *Musnad* 2/499; Muslim 7/190; Ḥarbī 3/1203; Abū Ya'lā 3/51; Ibn Ḥibbān, *Ṣaḥīḥ* 8/238–39; Ḥalīmī 3/256; Ḥākim 2/553; Bayhaqī, *Sunan* 9/206; *idem*, *Dalā'il* 6/321–22; Abū l-Baqā' 332; Haythamī, *Majma'* 10/63–64; Ibn Ḥajar, *al-Maṭālib* 4/164; Sakhāwī 388; Suyūṭī, *al-Jāmi' al-Kabīr* 1/107; *idem*, *Khaṣā'iṣ* 2/111; 'Ajlūnī (d. 1162/1748), *Kashf al-Khafā' wa-Muzīl al-Ilbas*, ed. Muḥammad al-Qallāsh, Maktabat al-Turāth, Aleppo, and Dār Iḥyā' al-Turāth al-'Arabī, Beirut, n.d., 2/212; Muttaqī 12/65 nos. 34019–20.

[9]For these doubts see Ibn Ḥajar, *Tahdhīb* 6/195, 8/18–19.

Other Prophetic sayings were associated with the names of 'Umar, Umm Salama and Rabāḥ al-Lakhmī, but they do not seem to have enjoyed wide circulation and no *isnād* details are available on them. From one source, al-Zubayr ibn Bakkār (d. 256/869), we also learn of a similar notion attributed to the Prophet by a certain 'Umar, *mawlā* of Ghufra, and circulated by the link Ibn Wahb ← Ibn Lahī'a (Egyptian, d. 174/790).[10]

The tradition enjoying the widest circulation by far was the above-mentioned one bearing the name of Ka'b ibn Mālik; this was transmitted by Zuhrī through Ka'b's son 'Abd al-Raḥmān, who was sometimes wrongly identified as Ubayy. From Zuhrī it was reported by several prominent second/eighth-century scholars like Mālik ibn Anas, Layth ibn Sa'd, Awzā'ī, Ma'mar ibn Rāshid, Isḥāq ibn Asad and 'Abd Allāh ibn Abī Bakr ibn Muḥammad ibn Ḥazm, and was commented upon by Sufyān ibn 'Uyayna (d. 198/813). There are sufficient grounds for concluding that this is actually Zuhrī's tradition, which in the early Ibn Sa'd actually appears in a *mursal* form.[11] From Ḥākim we learn of a supplementary comment by Zuhrī explaining that *raḥm* meant that the mother of Ishmael (i.e. Hagar, wife of Abraham) came from among the Egyptians (*qāla l-zuhrīyu: fa-l-raḥmu anna umma ismā'īl minhum*). Other sources note that Sufyān ibn 'Uyayna, when asked about Zuhrī's tradition, said: "Some people say that Hagar, the mother of Ishmael, was a Copt, while others say that Māriya, the mother of Ibrāhīm (son of the Prophet), was a Copt."[12] Moreover, we hear from Ibn Sa'd, as well as other sources, of *mursal* traditions transmitted by Zuhrī and his two contemporaries, Makḥūl al-Shāmī (d. 118/736) and al-Bāqir, that say: "Had Ibrāhīm (the son of the Prophet) lived, no maternal uncle of his (i.e. from among the Egyptians) would have suffered poverty / slavery" (*mā raqqa lahu khālun*)/var. "all Copts would have been exempted from payment of the *jizya*" (*la-wuḍi'at al-jizyatu 'an kulli qibṭī*).[13]

---

[10]Al-Zubayr ibn Bakkār (d. 256/869), *al-Muntakhab Min Kitāb Azwāj al-Nabī*, ed. Sukayna al-Shihābī, Mu'assasat al-Risāla, Beirut 1983, 60.

[11]Ibn Sa'd 1/144; cf. also Muttaqī 12/66 no. 34021.

[12]Ḥākim 2/553; Bayhaqī, *Dalā'il* 6/321–32; Ibn 'Asākir 19/556; Sakhāwī 388; 'Ajlūnī 2/212.

[13]Ibn Sa'd 1/144; cf. also Muttaqī 11/455, 469–70, nos. 32206–207, 35557, quoting Abū Nu'aym's *Ma'rifa* as well.

Some attempts were made to integrate Turks, Abyssinians, Slavs and other peoples with the Arabs within the above-mentioned tribal genealogical scheme were made, but proved to be more difficult to justify since, unlike the Persians and Egyptians, the former group of peoples either displayed a prolonged enmity before they were Islamized or were never converted at all. Through Abū Hurayra we hear of a tradition stating that Shem was the father of the Arabs, Persians and Byzantines (*al-rūm*), adding "and the good resides amongst them" (*wa-l-khayru fīhim*). We are also told that Japheth was the father of Gog and Magog (Ya'jūj and Ma'jūj), the Turks and Slavs (*ṣaqāliba*) "and no good resides amongst them;" and finally, Ham is specified as the father of the Copts, Berbers and blacks (*al-sūdān*).[14]

Another tradition, associated with the name of Ibn Mas'ūd, confirms the notion that the blacks are the descendants of Noah's son Ham. It states, however, that they acquired their dark colour as a punishment inflicted upon Ham because he saw his father naked. This tradition was circulated by Muḥammad ibn 'Abd al-Raḥmān ibn Abī Labība (d. *ca.* 150/767) through a family line, and was cited in the form of a commentary on Sūrat Nūḥ (71), v. 1.[15]

Concerning the Turks, we shall see below that the prolonged menace they posed during the second/eighth century gave rise to eschatological speculations that identified them with Gog and Magog. However, from the third/ninth-century scholar Jāḥiẓ we learn of another attempt, associated with the name of Haytham ibn 'Adī (d. 207/822), to identify the Turks as relatives of the Arabs, a notion that clearly reflects their increasingly prominent role in the life of the caliphate by Haytham's time. This was effected by saying that they were sons to a third wife of Abraham, Keturah. Hence, even the Wall of Gog and Magog is also called "the wall of the sons of Keturah" (*sudd banī qanṭūrā'*).[16]

---

[14]Ibn 'Adī 7/2725; Daylamī 5/178 (slandering only the Slavs); 'Irāqī 3–4; Suyūṭī, *Durr* 5/278; *idem*, *al-Jāmi' al-Kabīr* 1/871. Compare also with Ibn Ḥanbal, *Musnad* 5/9, 11; Ḥākim 2/546; and Ṭabarānī, *al-Mu'jam al-Kabīr* 7/210, who cite a similar tradition by the Companion Samura ibn Jundab that fails, however, to mention the Persians among the sons of Shem.

[15]Ḥākim 2/546; Fattanī 114; Ibn Kathīr, *Bidaya* 1/116.

[16]Jāḥiẓ, *Risāla Ilā l-Fatḥ ibn Khāqān wa-Manāqib al-Turk*, ed. G. van Vloten in his *Tria Opuscula*, Leiden 1903, 48–51.

The fact that Islam considered itself a universal creed, and adopted past prophets and saints that it recognized as having been sent to other peoples, undoubtedly helped to create this concept of close relations with these peoples. The classic case is of course the connection not only between Judaism and Islam, but between Jews and Arabs as well. And though similar traditional attempts in the case of prophets sent to other peoples enjoyed a more limited circulation, they were certainly not completely absent. An isolated Prophetic tradition transmitted through Abū Hurayra says that Ilyās and al-Khiḍr were two prophets who were also brothers born to a Persian father and a Byzantine mother.[17] Fairly well represented in widely circulated traditions, on the other hand, was recourse to the case of the black saintly figure Luqmān, as well as other pious personalities from early Islam, to ease the acceptance of blacks into the Muslim community. Three of these traditions, transmitted from Ibn Abbās, Anas and Wāthila ibn al-Asqa', variously mention the names of Luqmān, the Negus, Bilāl and Mihjā' (a *mawlā* of either the Prophet or 'Umar I) as "masters of the people of Paradise" (*sādāt ahl al-janna*) and urge people to acquire black servants for this reason. In one variant of Wāthila's tradition, as well as another *mursal* one by 'Abd al-Raḥmān ibn Yazīd ibn Jābir (Syrian, d. 154–56/770–72), these figures are merely given the title "masters of the blacks" (*sādāt al-sūdān*) and the element of urging people to acquire black servants is dropped.

The available *isnād* information points to 'Uthmān al-Ṭarā'ifī as responsible for circulating Ibn 'Abbās' tradition through the line Ubayn ibn Sufyān al-Maqdisī ← Khalīfa ibn Salam ← 'Aṭā' ibn Abī Rabāḥ (d. 114/732). The common link in Wāthila's tradition is Awzā'ī, who at least once transmitted it in a *mursal* form as well. Another *mursal* tradition, this time from 'Abd al-Raḥmān ibn Yazīd ibn Jābir, was also reported from him by Ibn al-Mubārak. Information about the *isnād* of Anas' tradition, however, is insufficient for any conclusion to be drawn.[18]

---

[17]Daylamī 1/427.

[18]For the different variants and *isnāds* of these traditions, see Ibn Ḥibbān, *al-Majrūḥīn* 1/179–80; Ṭabarānī, *al-Mu'jam al-Kabīr* 11/198; Ḥākim 3/284; Daylamī 1/83; Ibn 'Asākir 3/463; Ibn al-Jawzī, *Mawḍū'āt* 2/231–32; Haythamī, *Majma'* 4/235–36; Sakhāwī 207; Qārī 119; Suyūṭī, *La'ālī* 1/448; *idem*, *al-Jāmi' al-Kabīr*

Allying non-Arab Muslims to the Arabs in this way undoubtedly raised their status in Islam, but such status remained, according to a very strong traditional current, secondary to that of the Arabs. One tradition of 'Alī ibn Abī Ṭālib says that Arabs are the best of all peoples (*afḍalu l-nāsi l-'arab*), the best of the *'ajam* are the Persians, the best of the blacks are the Nubians..., etc.[19] The order that a tradition of Ibn 'Umar gives of groups on behalf of which the Prophet would intercede on the Day of Judgement leaves no doubt that Arabs are placed before the *'ajam*.[20] According to a tradition of Mu'ādh ibn Jabal, the peoples previously under Persian and Byzantine rule may enter Paradise simply because while serving the Arabs, these others praise the Arabs by saying "God have mercy on you" or reciting similar blessings.[21] Overdependence on such service, however, was portrayed as a bad omen in a few traditions that strongly warned against the dangerous laxity (*muṭayṭā'*) associated with it.[22]

According to a very strong current, the *'ajam* were seen as a genuine potential danger. One tradition of patently Shī'ī colouring attributes to 'Alī ibn Abī Ṭālib an implicit welcoming of the rise to power of non-Arabs (variously referred to as *ḥamrā'*, *'ajam* and *mawālī*) by saying that eventually they will strike the Arabs for the sake of religion (*la-yaḍribūnakum 'alā l-dīni 'awdan*) as the Arabs had initially done to them (*kamā ḍarabtumūhum 'alayhi bad'an*).[23] But viewing such a contingency in a positive light was the exception rather than the rule.

1/516; *idem*, *al-Jāmi' al-Ṣaghīr* 1/7, 2/8–9; Munāwī 1/126; Kinānī 2/33; Fattanī 113; Ghumārī 9; Muttaqī 9/no. 25001, 11/nos. 33156, 33159; 'Ajlūnī 1/36; Shawkānī 417; Albānī 2/131–32.

[19]Daylamī 2/178; Suyūṭī, *al-Jāmi' al-Kabīr* 1/517; Kinānī 2/36; Fattanī 112–13; Shawkānī 414; Muttaqī 12/87 no. 34109.

[20]Suyūṭī, *al-Jāmi' al-Kabīr* 1/339; *idem*, *al-Jāmi' al-Ṣaghir* 11/112, quoting Ṭabarānī; Ghumārī 31.

[21]Ibn al-Ja'd 2/968; Ḥākim 2/444; Ibn 'Asākir 7/486–87; Suyūṭī, *Durr* 6/8, quoting also Ṭabarī, Ibn al-Mundhir and Ibn Abī Ḥātim.

[22]Nu'aym ibn Ḥammād, *Ziyādāt al-Zuhd* 52; Ṭabarānī, *al-Mu'jam al-Awsaṭ* 1/121; Ibn Ḥibbān, *Ṣaḥīḥ* 8/253; Tirmidhī 3/245; Ibn al-Athīr, *al-Nihāya Fī Gharīb al-Ḥadīth*, al-Maṭba'a al-Khayrīya, Cairo 1322/1904, 4/340; Haythamī, *Majma'* 10/237; Muttaqī 11/123 no. 30819.

[23]Dāraquṭnī, *'Ilal* 4/23; Ibn Ḥajar, *al-Maṭālib* 4/157–58, quoting the *Musnads* of Isḥāq ibn Rāhawayh, al-Ḥārith ibn Abī Usāma, Ibn Abī Shayba and Abū Ya'lā. See also Ḥalīmī's response to this in his *Minhāj* 2/174–75.

Elsewhere, I have drawn attention to a widely circulated Prophetic tradition that warns of the ominous flocking of nations against the Arabs, just as hungry eaters attract one another to a bowl of food (*yūshiku an tadā'ā 'alaykum al-umamu kamā tadā'ā l-akalatu 'alā qaṣ'atihā*).[24]

Another widely circulated tradition warning the Arabs against the danger of being overpowered by the *'ajam* sometime in the future was attributed to the Prophet through the Companions Anas, Ḥudhayfa, Abū Hurayra, Abū Mūsā al-Ash'arī, Ibn 'Amr and Samura ibn Jundab. This *ḥadīth* states: "God, may He be praised and exalted, is about to fill your hands with *'ajam*, but they will not run away; they will kill your fighting men and consume your booty" (*yaqtulūna muqātilatakum wa-ya'kulūna fay'akum*). The most widely circulated variant of this tradition was transmitted from Samura ibn Jundab by Yūnus ibn 'Ubayd (Baṣran, d. 139/756) ← Hasan al-Baṣrī, with the former being its common link.[25] That of Ḥudhayfa was reported in a family *isnād* by Muḥammad ibn Zayd / Yazīd ibn Sinān (al-Jazarī, d. 220/835) ← his father (d. 155/771) who, we are told, was responsible for its circulation through the chain al-A'mash ← Shaqīq (ibn Salama, Abū Wā'il, Kūfan, d. 82–100/701–18).[26] From Anas we hear through al-Barrā' ibn Yazīd al-Ghanawī ← Qatāda, a link whose credibility was seriously doubted by *ḥadīth* scholars.[27] About the traditions of Abū Hurayra and Abū Mūsā al-Ash'arī we know virtually nothing except for the fact that they were cited on the authority of Ṭabarānī by two late sources.[28] Ibn 'Amr

[24]Bashear, "Apocalyptic and Other Materials," 182 and n. 42, with reference to Ṭayālisī 133; Ibn Ḥanbal, *Musnad* 5/278; Abū Dāwūd (d. 275/888), *Sunan*, ed. Muḥammad 'Abd al-Ḥamīd, Dār al-Kutub al-'Ilmīya, Beirut n.d. 4/111; Ṭabarānī, *al-Mu'jam al-Kabīr* 2/102–103; Abū Nu'aym, *Ḥilya* 1/182; Daylamī 5/527; Ibn Ṭāwūs (d. 665/1265), *al-Malāḥim wa-l-Fitan*, Najaf 1963, 129, 166–67; Qurṭubī (d. 671/1272), *al-Tadhkira Fī Aḥwāl al-Mawtā wa-Umūr al-Ākhira*, ed. Ahmad al-Saqqā, Maktabat al-Kullīyāt al-Azharīya, Cairo 1985, 2/315; Haythamī, *Majma'* 7/287; Ibn Ḥajar, *al-Maṭālib* 8/75.

[25]Ibn Ḥanbal, *Musnad* 5/11, 21; Ḥākim 4/512; Abū Nu'aym, *Ḥilya* 3/24–25; Ibn 'Asākir 15/777; Qurṭubī, *Tadhkira* 2/328; 'Uqaylī 2/16; Haythamī, *Majma'* 7/310; Suyūṭī, *al-Jāmi' al-Kabīr* 1/1019; *idem*, *Khaṣā'iṣ* 2/153.

[26]Ḥākim 4/519; Haythamī, *Majma'* 7/311. See also Daylamī 5/526; Suyūṭī, *al-Jāmi' al-Kabīr* 1/1019; *idem*, *Khaṣā'iṣ* 2/153; Muttaqī 11/188 no. 31165.

[27]'Uqaylī 2/116; Haythamī, *Majma'* 7/310; Suyūṭī, *Khaṣā'iṣ* 2/153 (the last two sources quoting Bazzār).

[28]Haythamī, *Majma'* 7/311; Suyūṭī, *Khaṣā'iṣ* 2/153.

was once confused with Ibn 'Umar, a mistake sometimes overlooked by late scholars.[29] One may also note a statement reported in the name of Ibn 'Amr by Abū l-Aswad al-Du'alī (d. 69/688) that, on the other hand, speculates that in the lands of the Arabs there would remain no one from among the *'ajam* except for those who had been killed or taken prisoner.[30]

Needless to say, the late scholars who questioned the credibility of this tradition did so by targeting certain "weak" links in the *isnād* of this or that variant.[31] However, the current considering non-Arabs as a potential enemy to be thoroughly mistrusted is represented by other statements. One, bearing the name of Ḥudhayfa, sometimes also acquires the status of a Prophetic tradition through Abū Hurayra and Jābir ibn 'Abd Allāh. This *ḥadīth* speaks about the *'ajam* (this time in a clear reference to the Persians) and the Byzantines as a future potential threat to Arab rule in Iraq, Syria and Egypt. This is done in an apocalyptic statement warning that the income levied in these lands is about to be stopped by the *'ajam* and Byzantines (*yūshiku ahlu l-'iraqi an lā yujbā ilayhim dirhamun wa-lā qafīzun yamna'u min dhālika l-'ajam*).[32]

The second/eighth-century fusion of Arabism and Islam, however, meant that the faith was eventually engulfed by other peoples and cultures; this new situation lent renewed impetus to the early universalist elements, or at least saved them from total suppression, granted a recognized position to such non-Arab symbolic representatives as Salmān, Ṣuhayb and Bilāl, and hence provided a solid ground for the traditional current that kept alive the recognition of their role in early Islam. An example of this is the tradition of Wakī' ibn al-Jarrāḥ (d. 197/812) with the *isnād* Isrā'īl (ibn Yūnus, d. 160–62/776–78) ← Jābir (ibn Yazīd al-Ju'fī, Kūfan, d. 128–32/745–49) ← Sha'bī (d. 103–10/721–28), which says that six non-Arabs (*a'ājim*) actually took part in the

[29]As in Suyūṭī, *al-Jāmi' al-Kabīr* 1/1019.

[30]Haythamī, *Majma'* 7/312, quoting Abū Ya'lā.

[31]E.g. Haythamī, *Majma'* 5/304, 7/310–11; Suyūṭī, *Khaṣā'iṣ* 2/153 (both quoting Bazzār's *Musnad* and Ṭabarānī's *al-Mu'jam al-Kabīr* and *al-Mu'jam al-Awsaṭ*.

[32]Nu'aym ibn Ḥammād, *Kitāb al-Fitan*, Ms. London, British Museum Or. no. 9449, fol. 192r; Ibn Ḥanbal, *Musnad* 2/262, 3/317; Ḥākim 4/454; Muttaqī 11/no. 31163; Ibn 'Abd al-Barr, *Tamhīd* 6/456, 15/141.

Battle of Badr.[33] In another tradition, this time a highly isolated one, the whole controversy over the Arab–*'ajam* contest for precedence is presented in a new light. An *isnād* reporting through Qatāda (d. 117–18/735–36) ← al-Muṭarraf ibn ['Abd Allāh] ibn al-Shikhkhīr (Baṣran, d. 87–95/705–13) ← 'Iyāḍ ibn Ḥimār, attributes to the Prophet the saying that God looked at the people of the earth and detested them all, Arabs and *'ajam*, except for remnants from among the People of the Book (*naẓara l-lāhu naẓratan ilā ahli l-arḍi fa-maqatahum jamī'an 'arabahum wa-'ajamahum illā baqāyā min ahli l-kitāb*).[34]

However, of all the ethnic groups, the Persians received the lion's share in the current to stress the important, albeit secondary role of non-Arabs, a trend that gained a further impetus with the rise of the 'Abbāsids to power. An expression of this current is a tradition that calls the people of Khurāsān "the army of God" (*jundu l-lāh*) on earth, a title given by some variants also to the angels in heaven.[35] Another urges people to treat Persians well "because our regime depends upon them" (*istawṣū bi-l-fursi khayran fa-inna dawlatanā ma'ahum*).[36] A third one grants a Persian who converts to Islam the position of a Qurashī.[37]

One may note that the position expressed in this last tradition is reminiscent of the well-known Prophetic statement: "Salmān is one of us, the people of the house," whatever the phrase *ahlu l-bayt*, "people of the house," might specifically have meant.[38] Note also that a similar notion was attributed to Sa'īd ibn al-Musayyib (d. 93–100/711–18), who, we are told, placed the people of Persia, particularly those coming from Iṣbahān, second in rank only to Quraysh.[39] From another report we learn that al-Layth ibn Sa'd, who was originally from Iṣbahān, expressed the request that its people should be treated well, using the

---

[33]Ibn Abī Shayba 12/206.

[34]Ibn Ḥanbal, *Musnad* 4/162; al-Khaṭīb al-Baghdādī 8/458; Ibn 'Asākir 15/649–50.

[35]Fattanī 113.

[36]Shawkānī 411, quoting al-Khaṭīb al-Baghdādī.

[37]Ghumārī 94, quoting Ibn al-Najjār.

[38]For its use by Umayyads, 'Abbāsids and 'Alīds, see Sharon, "Legitimacy of Authority," 135–36.

[39]Ibn al-Ja'd 2/1046; Abū Nu'aym, *Akhbār Iṣbahān* 1/38.

phrase ... *fa-stawṣū bihim khayran*, "... so treat them well."[40] A third *ḥadīth* attributed to the Prophet the saying that Quraysh is God's choice from among the Arabs, and that the Persians are his choice from among the *'ajam*.[41]

Through Abū Hurayra we hear of a Prophetic statement to the effect that "the Persians are those who have the greatest desire in Islam" (*a'ẓamu l-nāsi ṣab'an fī l-islāmi ahlu fāris*).[42] Another, reflecting a similar notion, was attributed to the Prophet by Ma'mar (ibn Rāshid, d. 152–53/769–70) ← a colleague of his (*'an ṣāḥibin lahu*) in a *mursal* form. This describes the Persians as the happiest of all peoples, the Byzantines as the most miserable, and Banū Taghlib and the 'Ubbād[43] as the most miserable of all the Arabs as a result of the rise of Islam (*as'adu l-nāsi bi-l-islāmi l-fursu, wa-ashqā l-nāsi... al-rūmu, wa-ashqā l-'arabi... banū taghlib wa-l-'ubbād*).[44]

A notion similar to this last one, but limited to mentioning the 'Ubbād and Byzantines (or alternatively, the 'Ubbād from among the Byzantines), was also attributed to the Prophet on the authority of Mūsā ibn Abī 'Ā'isha (Kūfan, d. *ca.* 150/767), though this time in a full *isnād* through Salmān al-Fārisī.[45] This tradition is not the only one, however, but rather deploys a general literary convention allowing for ambivalent combination of praises and slanders of different peoples in a single tradition. Such is the above-noted *ḥadīth* that specifies the Arabs as accounting for nine tenths of all human jealousy; the Persians were noted by the same tradition for a similar portion of all human avarice, and the Berbers for quick anger, arrogance and disloyalty. This tradition was attributed to the Prophet through Anas on the authority of Ṭalḥa ibn Zayd (a Syrian who moved to Raqqa and was active there in the second half of the second/eighth century).[46] Similar traditions were

---

[40]Ibn 'Asākir 14/652.

[41]*Ibid.* 14/730.

[42]Daylamī 1/359.

[43]The 'Ubbād were a group of Christian Arabs in southern Iraq, specifically Kūfa, in early Islam.

[44]'Abd al-Razzāq, *Muṣannaf* 11/66.

[45]Ibn Ḥajar, *al-Maṭālib* 4/146, quoting the *Musnad* of al-Ḥārith ibn Abī Usāma; Munāwī 1/6, quoting Daylamī.

[46]Kinānī 1/177, quoting Dāraquṭnī's *Afrād*.

transmitted in *mursal* forms by Khālid ibn Ma'dān on the authority of Marwān ibn Sālim (a Syrian *mawlā* of Banū Umayya who was active in the second half of the second century AH) and Muḥammad ibn Muslim (either Zuhrī or Abū l-Zubayr al-Makkī) on the authority of Sayf ibn 'Amr (probably Sayf ibn 'Umar, Kūfan d. *ca.* 180/796).[47]

Various degrees of Berber viciousness (*khubth*) were cited in two Prophetic traditions through 'Uthmān ibn 'Affān and 'Uqba ibn 'Āmir. The exact portions of all human and demonic viciousness attributed to them by these traditions are 60 to 1 and 69 to 1, respectively.[48] A third tradition, by Abū Hurayra, says of the Berbers that belief does not pass beyond their throats (*al-barbarīyu lā yujāwizu īmānuhu tarāqīhi / inna l-īmāna lā yujāwizu ḥanājirahum*).[49] Finally, people were advised not to give alms if the only beneficiary from such an act would be a Berber.[50]

One tradition advises people to beware of Indians and blacks / var. Jews, even those with an ancestor from one of these groups seventy generations previously (*ittaqū l-sūd / l-yahūd wa-l-hunūd wa-law bi-sab'īna baṭnan*).[51] About the actual policy towards dark-skinned gypsies (al-Zuṭṭ) we do not know much. Only one report with a defective *isnād* says that 'Alī burned a group of them because they worshipped an idol.[52] From another one we learn about a belief current in the generation of Dāwūd ibn Abī Hind (d. 139/756) that the Angel of Death was a black figure of monstrous proportions "like those who are called al-Zuṭṭ."[53] Through Abū l-Dardā' we hear of a Prophetic tradition stating that beginning with the creation of Adam the colours white and black were destined by God for the people of Paradise and Hell,

[47] *Ibid.*, quoting Suyūṭī who, he says, cited them from the *Kitāb al-'Aẓama* by Abū l-Shaykh and al-Khaṭīb al-Baghdādī's *Bukhalā'*.

[48] Ibn Ḥajar, *al-Maṭālib*, quoting Ibn Abī 'Umar; Kinānī 1/177, quoting Ṭabarānī and Haythamī.

[49] Ibn Ḥanbal, *Musnad* 2/367; Ṭabarānī, *al-Mu'jam al-Awsaṭ* 1/146; Haythamī, *Majma'* 4/234.

[50] Muttaqī 6/16554.

[51] Fattanī 114, quoting al-Ṣaghānī; Shawkānī 417.

[52] This tradition is reported through the link Qatāda ← Anas, but Ibn Abī Ḥātim, in his *'Ilal* 1/449, believes that the correct *isnād* is a *maqṭū'* one by Qatāda ← 'Ikrima.

[53] Ibn 'Asākir 6/10.

respectively.[54] A tradition attributed to the Prophet through the *isnād* al-A'mash (Sulaymān ibn Mihrān) ← Abū Wā'il (Shaqīq ibn Salama), warns against Turks, Nabaṭ / Anbāṭ (a name usually referring to the Syriac-speaking mostly rural peasant population) and Khūzistānīs, and praises only the Persians. To the element concerning the Turks a separate reference will be made below. As for Anbāṭ, this tradition advises against taking them as neighbours (*wa-lā tujāwirū l-anbāṭ*), calls them "the bane of religion" (*fa-innahum āfatu l-dīn*), recommends that they be humiliated (*fa-adhillūhum*) when they pay *jizya* and expresses concern over their outward acceptance of Islām (*fa-idhā aẓharū l-islāma*), reading the Qur'ān, learning Arabic and being overly involved in Islamic social and religious life. To this, one variant adds the warning not to have marital relations with Khūzistānīs (*wa-lā tunākiḥu l-khūz*) because, it says, "they have an origin driving them to infidelity" (*fa-inna lahum aṣlan yad'ūhum ilā ghayri l-wafā'*). Finally, this tradition ends by praising the Persians via the well-known claim that they would take hold of religion even if it were hanging from the Pleiades.[55]

Two other traditions slandering the Nabaṭ were associated with the name of Abū Hurayra. The authority for one of these is 'Abd al-Raḥmān ibn Mālik ibn Mighwal, who took it from Sa'īd ibn Salama ← Sha'bī. This *ḥadīth* says that Abū Hurayra once saw a man whose appearance (*hay'a*) he liked; but when he learned that the man was one of the Nabaṭ he turned him away and recalled that he had heard the Prophet describe them as "killers of the prophets and helpers of the unjust" (*qatalatu l-anbiyā' wa-a'wānu l-ẓalama*) and order his Companions to flee should the Nabaṭ ever establish themselves and build houses (*fa-idhā ittakhadhū l-ribā'a wa-shayyadū l-bunyāna fa-l-harabu l-harab*).[56] The second tradition is similar in spirit and only lacks the element of urging people to flee. This was transmitted from Abū Hurayra by Zuhrī ← Sa'īd ibn al-Musayyib, and recommends caution toward the Anbāṭ when Islam becomes widespread among them and they acquire houses and become used to sitting in the gardens of

[54]Ibn 'Asākir 15/268–69.
[55]'Uqaylī 3/286–87; Ibn Ḥajar, *Lisān* 4/369.
[56]'Uqaylī 2/345–46; Suyūṭī, *La'ālī* 1/446; Kinānī 2/29; Shawkānī 416.

houses. Such an attitude, the tradition explains, should be adopted because the Anbāṭ are sources of corruption, rancour and communal strife.[57]

Another Prophetic tradition on the Nabaṭ was transmitted from Ibn ʻAbbās through a certain ʻImrān ibn Tammām ← Abū Hamza (possible ʻImrān ibn Abī ʻAṭā', death date unknown). It says that when the Nabaṭ become eloquent and acquire palaces in the provinces, then the overthrow of religion must be expected.[58] One may also note that a similar statement was reported from ʻUmar I in reply to an enquiry about the reason why he cried when he heard that the Nabīṭ of Iraq were converting to Islam.[59]

The popular sexual slur that the solicitude of a Nabaṭī is to protect his anus (*... anna ghaḍaba l-nabaṭīyi fī istihi*) while that of an Arab is to protect his head, is expressed in a report concerning a *mawlā* of Manṣūr who was beaten by the latter's governor of Baṣra, Salm ibn Qutayba.[60] From this tradition we also learn that such was the evaluation of Nabaṭ even though the *mawlā* in question held a high administrative position, a case that illustrates the fact that Arabizing the Nabaṭ was not a smooth process. Actually, as late as the mid-third/ninth century, the Egyptian ascetic figure Dhū l-Nūn warns, among other things, against trusting Nabaṭ who pretentiously act like Arabs (*iḥdharū... al-nabaṭa l-mustaʻribīn*).[61]

A few Arabic terms that originally denoted certain social strata eventually acquired ethnic or racial meanings. These terms are *khiṣyān*, lit. "eunuchs," *mamālīk*, i.e. "owned ones" and *ʻabīd*, meaning "slaves." As far as the last two are concerned, Lewis rightly notes that they eventually became synonymous to white and black slaves, respectively.[62] One should also add that because of the masses of white slaves, mainly of Turkish origin, the term *mamālīk* gradually came to be used with reference to Turkish ethnicity as well. As for the group of black peoples bordering the Muslim caliphate in Africa, or slaves brought from

---

[57]Ibn ʻAsākir 8/1008.
[58]Kinānī 2/29.
[59]Muttaqī 11/267 no. 31479, quoting the *Ḥujja* by Naṣr al-Maqdisī.
[60]Ibn ʻAsākir 2/835.
[61]Abū Nuʻaym, *Ḥilya* 9/367.
[62]Lewis, *Race and Color* 63–64. See also *Shorter Encyclopedia of Islam*, 325.

this continent, these were referred to as blacks (*sūd*, *sūdān*), Zanj and Ḥabash / Ḥabasha. One may also note that while the last term could denote Abyssinia (al-Ḥabasha) as the country of origin, other words derived from the same root also occur in Arabic texts in reference to bedouins, blacks, confederates, mercenaries and so forth.[63]

An outward warning against the potential danger of possessing *mamālīk* took the form of a Prophetic tradition associated with the name of Ibn ʿUmar, and was transmitted from him through the link Muḥammad ibn Ayyūb al-Riqāshī (possibly al-Raqqī, death date unknown) ← Maymūn ibn Mihrān (from Raqqa, d. 116–17/734–35). With a slight variation, it simply states that "the worst property / people at the end of times will be the *mamālīk*" (*sharru l-māli / l-nāsi fī ākhiri l-zamāni l-mamālīk*).[64] However, what seems to be an earlier tradition attributes to the Prophet the saying: "A *mamlūk* will receive a double recompense [for his good deeds], and no reckoning will be levied against him [on the Judgement Day]" (*al-mamlūku lahu ajrāni wa-lā ḥisāba ʿalayhi*). This is a *mursal* tradition by al-Bāqir and occurs already in the early work of al-Muʿāfā ibn ʿImrān.[65]

Eunuchs are targeted by a Prophetic tradition associated with the name of Ibn ʿAbbās and transmitted from him in the *isnād* Ibn Abī Najīh (d. 131/748) ← Mujāhid, on the authority of Isḥāq ibn Yaḥyā / ibn Abī Yaḥyā ibn al-Kaʿbī (possibly al-Kalbī, a Ḥimṣī whose death date is unknown). This *ḥadīth* says: "If God had known any merit in eunuchs, he would have brought forth from their loins descendants

---

[63]See J. Wansbrough, "Gentilics and Appellatives: Notes on ʿAḥābīsh Quraysh'," *BSOAS* 49 (1986), 203; W.M. Watt, art. "Ḥabash; Aḥābīsh" in *EI*^{2}, 3/7–8 and the sources cited therein. On Ḥabash Banī l-Mughīra, see below, 84. From Ibn ʿAsākir 17/195, we learn that Abū Salām al-Ḥabashī was so called because he belonged to a tribal branch of the Ḥimyar confederation called Ḥabash. On the allies of Quraysh, called Aḥābīsh, from Banū Kināna, Banū Khuzāʿa and Banū l-Hawn ibn Khuzayma both in pre-Islamic times and during the battles of Uḥud and al-Ḥudaybiya, see Balādhurī *Ansab* I, 52, 76, 101; Ibn Ḥabīb, *al-Muḥabbar* 246, 267; Ibn Hishām 2/16, 3/199; Wāqidī, *Maghāzī* 2/579–81, 595, 599–600; Wāḥidī 177.

[64]Abū Nuʿaym, *Ḥilya* 4/94; Daylamī 2/371; Ibn al-Jawzī, *al-Mawḍūʿāt* 2/236; Ibn Qayyim al-Jawzīya (d. 751/1350), *al-Manār al-Munīf*, Beirut 1970, 101; Suyūṭī, *al-Jāmiʿ al-Ṣaghīr* 2/40; Qārī 333, quoting Abū Yaʿlā; Albānī 2/165.

[65]Al-Muʿāfā ibn ʿImrān (d. 185/801), *Kitāb al-Zuhd*, Ms. Ẓāhirīya, *Ḥadīth* no. 359, 239.

who would worship Him" (*law 'alima l-lāhu fī l-khiṣyāni khayran l-akhraja min aṣlābihim dhurrīyatan ya'budūna l-lāh*).[66] One should also note a statement voicing a clear prejudice against delegating power to eunuchs. This was reported from Sufyān al-Thawrī by a certain Radhdhādh ibn al-Jarrāḥ and warns that the *umma* will perish if eunuchs should come to govern (*halāku hādhihi l-ummati idhā malaka l-khiṣyān*).[67]

One tradition of 'Umar I, but transmitted in a clearly *maqṭū'* line by Sa'īd ibn al-Musayyib, attributes to the Prophet the saying: "Whoever prides himself in [owning] slaves, God will humiliate him" (*man i'tazza bi-l-'abīdi adhallahu l-lāh*).[68] From Ibn Ḥazm we learn of a consensus (*ijmā'*) concerning the legal ruling that a slave (*'abd*) could take a maximum of two wives and not four, as the free Muslim was entitled to do.[69] In several Arabic poems, the words *'abīd* and *mawālī* occur in extremely slanderous contexts.[70]

The one specific group of slaves that occupied a most central place in this kind of traditional material was the black slaves, often designated as Zanj. From two statements that Aṣma'ī attributes to "the sages" (*qālat al-ḥukamā'*), we learn of two contradictory attitudes towards the Zanj that were current in his time. The first perceives them as the worst of creatures, and their physique as ruined by the heat of their homeland, which has caused them to be burned in the womb (*al-zanju shirāru l-khalqi wa-arda'uhum tarkīban li-anna bilādahum sakhanat fa-aḥraqathumu l-arḥām*). The second, on the other hand, identifies the

---

[66]Ibn al-Jawzī, *al-Mawḍū'āt* 2/235; Suyūṭī, *La'ālī* 1/445; Kinānī 2/29; Qārī 333; Ibn Qayyim 101.

[67]Abū Nu'aym, *Ḥilya* 7/44.

[68]*Ibid.* 2/174; Tirmidhī, *Kitāb al-Akyās wa-l-Mughtarrīn*, Ms. Ẓāhirīya, *Taṣawwuf* no. 104/1, 45–46.

[69]Ibn Ḥazm, *Marātib al-Ijmā'* 73.

[70]E.g. Jarīr's slander against Banū Hanīfa (cited by Mubarrad 442, and Muḥammad al-Ṣawī, *Sharḥ Dīwān Jarīr*, Maktabat al-Nūrī, Damascus and al-Sharika al-Lubnānīya, Beirut, 1353 AH, 1000): *ṣārat hanīfatu athlāthun fa-thulthuhumu // mina l-'abīdi wa-thulthun min mawālīhā*, "Banū Hanīfa has come to amount to three parts, one of which consists of slaves and another of *mawālī*." Another verse by Ibn Abī 'Uyayna (cited in Ibn Manẓūr, *Lisān al-'Arab* 20/252; Zabīdī, *Tāj* 10/417) slanders "the cowardly *mawālī* and slaves" (*wa-andhālu l-mawālī wa-l-'abīd*).

Zanj as having the best mouth odour, even though they do not clean their teeth (*aṭyabu l-umami afwāhan al-zanju wa-in lam tastann*).[71]

This compliment, however, is not recorded in the relevant *ḥadīth* material, which is overwhelmingly anti-Zanjī. A family tradition of Sulaymān ibn ʿAlī (d. 142/759) that goes back to his grandfather, Ibn ʿAbbās, advises people to purchase *raqīq* (slaves, mostly white ones of Byzantine origin), but warns them against the Zanj (*wa-iyyākum wa-l-zanj*). The latter, this tradition explains, have only a short life span and produce little income (*fa-innahum qaṣīratun aʿmāruhum qalīlatun arzāquhum*).[72]

The most widely circulated anti-Zanjī tradition is the one that claims: "When a Zanjī is hungry he steals, and when he is sated he fornicates" (*al-zanjīyu idhā jāʿa saraqa wa-idhā shabiʿa zanā*). Lewis, who noted this tradition, draws attention to the recurrence of the same statement in the form of a proverb. The main difference between the two forms is that the one current in *ḥadīth* has an additional element extolling the Zanj for two good qualities: "magnanimity and fortitude in adversity."[73]

In an attempt to follow the development of this tradition we may first note that in several sources its two component parts actually appear in a variant associated with the name of ʿĀʾisha.[74] Other sources cite only the first part, i.e. without mentioning the two positive qualities. As such, this variant is close to another tradition associated with the name of Abū Rāfiʿ, the only difference being that here the opening statement is: "The worst of slaves are the Zanj" (*sharru l-raqīqi l-zanj*).[75] The authority held responsible for circulating ʿĀʾisha's tradition is ʿAnbasa al-Baṣrī, who received it through the *isnād* ʿAmr ibn Maymūn (al-Jazarī, d. 147–48/764–65) ← Zuhrī ← ʿUrwa ← ʿĀʾisha ←

---

[71]Cited by Ibn Qutayba, *ʿUyūn al-Akhbār* 2/67.

[72]Ṭabarānī, *al-Muʿjam al-Awsaṭ* 2/13; Daylamī 1/387; Haythamī, *Majmaʿ* 4/235.

[73]Lewis, *Race and Color* 19 n. 31, citing the proverb from Maydānī (d. 518/1124), *Amthāl al-ʿArab*, ed. G. Freytag, Bonn 1839, 2/404.

[74]Qārī 332; Kinānī 2/32; Suyūṭī, *Laʾālī* 1/444; Ghumārī 55; Sakhāwī 111; Fattanī 114; Shawkānī 415; Albānī 2/158—all quoting Ibn ʿAdī for it. See also Ibn al-Jawzī, *al-Mawḍūʿāt* 2/233.

[75]Cf. Ibn al-Qayyim 101, with Suyūṭī, *al-Jāmiʿ al-Kabīr* 1/555; *idem*, *Laʾālī* 1/444–45; Sakhāwī 112; Kinānī 2/32. The sources citing the Abū Rāfiʿ tradition quote Abū Nuʿaym's *Ḥilya* and Daylamī for it.

the Prophet. The Abu Rāfi‘ tradition was circulated by his grandson ‘Abbād ibn ‘Ubayd Allāh ibn Abī Rāfi‘ in a family *isnād*.

A similar combination of almost the same two elements occurs in another Prophetic tradition transmitted from Ibn ‘Abbās through the chain Sufyān ibn ‘Uyayna ← ‘Amr ibn Dīnār (Meccan, d. 125–26/742–43) ← ‘Awsaja (a Meccan *mawlā* of Ibn ‘Abbās, death date unknown). Note that the opening sentence here replaces "Zanj" with "Ḥabasha," and that the statement as a whole is cited within a narrative context concerning a certain group named Ḥabash Banī l-Mughīra, who refrained from coming to the Prophet for fear of being turned away. From the comment made by al-Bazzār (d. 292/904) we learn that ‘Amr ibn Dīnār is the common link of this tradition, and that tradents other than Ibn ‘Uyayna transmitted it from him in a *mursal* form.[76]

Another tradition of Ibn ‘Abbās says that his father used to feed the Ḥabasha and provide them with clothing. The Prophet, however, advised him not to do so, for "when they are hungry they steal, and when they are sated they fornicate." Note that the element concerning their two good qualities does not appear in this variant. A close look at the *isnād* reveals that this version was reported only by a certain ‘Umar ibn Ḥafṣ al-Makkī via the link Ibn Jurayj ← ‘Aṭā’.[77] There is also a *mursal* tradition of a certain Hilāl, *mawlā* of Banū Hāshim,which opens with the introductory statement: "It has reached us that the Prophet said...." This was transmitted from Hilāl by Mahdī ibn Maymūn (d. 171/787–88) ← Wāṣil (al-Aḥdab?, d. 120–29/737–46), and the *Musnad* of Ḥumaydī (d. 219/834) was quoted for it. It says: "Some of your worst slaves are the blacks (*min sharri raqīqikumu l-sūdān*), for when they are hungry they steal, and when they are sated they fornicate."[78]

To sum up on this tradition, we may say that the core, which occurs in various traditional forms, was a slander directed against black slaves (*sūdān*), also referred to as Zanj and Ḥabash. Only in one traditional

---

[76]Cf. Haythamī, *Kashf* 3/316. For the *isnād* of this tradition see also Ibn ‘Adī 5/2020; Sakhāwī 111; Suyūṭī, *La’ālī* 1/444; Kinānī 2/31; Shawkānī 415; Albānī 2/158. Besides Bazzār, Ṭabarānī's *al-Mu‘jam al-Kabīr* is also quoted by some of these sources.

[77]Ibn al-Jawzī, *al-Mawḍū‘āt* 2/234; Ibn Qayyim 101; Suyūṭī, *La’ālī* 1/444; Kinānī 2/31; Qārī 332; Shawkānī 415, quoting Dāraquṭnī.

[78]Suyūṭī, *La’ālī* 1/444–45; Kinānī 2/32.

variant of 'Ā'isha, for which a certain 'Awsaja al-Baṣrī (probably active around the turn of the first/seventh century) was held responsible, does the additional element of conceding the two good qualities of Zanj occur. Otherwise, the original core slandering them was also current in the form of a proverb in southern Iraq in the second/eighth century.

From a unique story, cited in the name of Shāfi'ī (d. 204/819) in a work on his merits (*manāqib*) by Bayhaqī, we learn that this core was known already at his time as a *ḥadīth* concerning black slaves (*'abīd*).[79] As for the personal position of Shāfi'ī himself, the same source quotes him as saying that the prices for blacks are only low because of their feeble intelligence (*mā naqaṣa min athmāni l-sūdāni illā li-ḍa'fi 'uqūlihim*); otherwise, he concludes, black would certainly have been a colour appreciated and even preferred by some people.[80]

Another expression of prejudice against blacks was attributed to the Prophet by two traditions associated with the names of Ibn 'Abbās and Umm Ayman. They are identical in saying: "A black lives only for his belly and his genitals" (*innamā l-aswadu li-baṭnihi wa-farjih*). The only difference between the two is that the Ibn 'Abbās version opens with the phrase "relieve me of blacks" (*da'ūnī mina l-sūdān*). This was circulated through the link Yaḥyā ibn Sulaymān / ibn Abī Sulaymān al-Madīnī (death date unknown) ← 'Aṭā' (ibn Abī Rabāḥ).[81] As for the Umm Ayman variant, this was reported by Khālid ibn Muḥammad ibn Khālid al-Zubayrī / his father (death date unknown) and appears in a narrative form. "We went out," he says, "with 'Alī ibn al-Ḥusayn to meet al-Walīd ibn 'Abd al-Mālik. A Ḥabashī stood in the way of our caravan (*fa-'araḍa ḥabashīyun li-rikābinā*) and 'Alī ibn al-Ḥusayn then said that he heard Umm Ayman saying from the Prophet...," etc.[82]

---

[79]Cf. Sakhāwī 112.

[80]*Ibid.* 396; 'Ajlūnī 2/224.

[81]Ṭabarānī, *al-Mu'jam al-Kabīr* 11/191–92; Ibn 'Adī 7/2686; al-Khaṭīb al-Baghdādī 4/108; Ibn al-Jawzī, *Mawḍū'āt* 2/232; Ibn Qayyim 101; Sakhāwī 111–12; Suyūṭī, *La'ālī* 1/443, quoting al-Khaṭīb al-Baghdādī; *idem*, *al-Jāmi' al-Ṣaghīr* 2/16, quoting Ṭabarānī; Fattanī 114; Kinānī 2/31, quoting al-Khaṭīb al-Baghdādī; Qārī 332; Ghumārī 47; Shawkānī 414–15, quoting al-Khaṭīb Baghdādī; Albānī 2/157, quoting Ṭabarānī and al-Khaṭīb Baghdādī.

[82]'Uqaylī 2/14; Ibn Abī Ḥātim, *'Ilal* 2/292; Ṭabarānī, *al-Mu'jam al-Kabīr* 25/89; Ibn al-Jawzī, *Mawḍū'āt* 2/323; Sakhāwī 111–12; Suyūṭī, *La'ālī* 1/443–44, quoting Ṭabarānī and 'Uqaylī; Munāwī 1/74, quoting Abū Ya'lā; Kinānī 2/31, quoting

As noted above, certain variants of the traditions of 'Ā'isha and Anas relate to the question of worthiness in marriage (*al-kafā'a*) and advocate avoiding the Zanj because they are "disfigured" by their colour.[83] We may add here that the tradition of 'Ā'isha was transmitted by the chain Muḥammad ibn Marwān al-Suddī ← Hishām ibn 'Urwa ← his father, 'Urwa ibn al-Zubayr. However, as reported from Hishām, not by Suddī but by Ṣāliḥ al-Zubayrī, several sources cited only the part on avoiding the Zanj.[84] The Anas variant bearing the same element of warning against the Zanj was transmitted through the *isnād* Sufyān ibn 'Uyayna ← Ziyād ibn Sa'd ← Zuhrī.[85]

There are a few less-circulated statements expressing contempt towards blacks and Zanj. Of these, one may recall the aforementioned notion current in the second/eighth century to the effect that the colour of the Angel of Death who collects (*yaqbiḍ*) the souls of unbelievers (*kuffār*) is black.[86] An isolated tradition attributes to the Prophet the blunt statement that "a Zanjī is an ass" (*al-zanjīyu ḥimār*). This was transmitted from 'Ā'isha through the chain 'Amr ibn Maymūn ← Zuhrī ← 'Urwa.[87] Finally, though the present work does not aim at reviewing the actual role played by individual blacks or the socio-political history of the Zanj in early Islam, attention should be drawn to a Zanjī uprising as early as the year 76/695 in the area of Baṣra, and a major one that for a whole decade and a half, from 255/868 until 270/883, constituted a major threat to 'Abbāsid rule.[88]

The above-noted statement of Aṣma'ī complimenting the Zanj for their fresh breath is actually not an isolated one, but constitutes part of a whole corpus of traditions reflecting the integration of large numbers of blacks into Islam. This is clearly reflected in the central roles

---

'Uqaylī and Ibn Abī Ḥātim; Shawkānī 414–15, quoting 'Uqaylī; Ghumārī 30, quoting 'Uqaylī and Ṭabarānī.

[83]See above, 38.

[84]Ibn Ḥibbān, *al-Majrūḥīn* 2/281; Ibn al-Jawzī, *al-Mawḍū'āt* 2/233; Ibn Qayyim 101; Qārī 332; Albānī 2/160.

[85]Albānī 2/160, quoting *al-Aḥādīth al-Mukhtāra* by al-Ḍiyā' al-Maqdisī and Ibn 'Asākir's *Tārīkh*.

[86]See above, 78.

[87]Ibn al-Jawzī, *al-Mawḍū'āt* 2/233.

[88]See *Anonyme arabische Chronik* 304–305; Mas'ūdī, *Murūj al-Dhahab*, ed. C. Pellat, Beirut 1966, 2/439–46.

played by *mawālī* figures, some of them black or at least dark-skinned, in early Muslim scholarship. In statements alternatively attributed to Ibn Jurayj, Ja'far al-Ṣādiq and Ibn Ḥanbal there is a clear recognition of the role played by such personalities as Mujāhid, 'Aṭā' ibn Abī Rabāḥ, Yazīd ibn Abī Ḥabīb (d. 128/745), Makḥūl al-Shāmī and even Sa'īd ibn Jubayr who, as noted above, had "a very dark skin."[89] The report circulated by Khālid ibn Yazīd "from a group of Successors" (*'an jamā'atin mina l-tābi'īn*) on the conquest of Egypt, not only mentions the leadership role played by the black 'Ubāda ibn al-Ṣāmit, but also stresses the point that blackness was not considered a negative trait in early Islam (*wa-laysa yunkaru l-sawādu fīnā*).[90] Above all, there is Bilāl, the black freed slave of Abū Bakr and *mu'adhdhin* (public cryer for prayer) of the Prophet, who is so symbolic in representing his colour and race. Together with the above-noted traditions identifying Bilāl as "the forerunner of the Abyssinians" (*sābiqu l-ḥabasha*), such representation is evident in two Prophetic statements transmitted through Abū Hurayra and 'Utba ibn 'Abd al-Sulamī. Portraying the particular role played by certain groups and tribes in early Islam, these statements say that kingship (*mulk*) / the caliphate (*khilāfa*) pertains to Quraysh, judgeship (*qaḍā'*) / governorship (*ḥukm*) to the Anṣār, calling for prayer (*adhān* / *da'wa*) to the Ḥabasha, etc. The authority for the Abū Hurayra tradition is the Kūfan Zayd ibn al-Ḥabbāb (d. 203/818), who reported it from Mu'āwiya ibn Ṣāliḥ (Ḥimṣī, d. 181–82/797–98) ← Ḍamḍam ibn Zur'a (Ḥimṣī, death date unknown) ← Kuthayyir ibn Murra (Ḥimṣī, d. 70–80/689–99).[91]

The reference to the two positive qualities of blacks mentioned above also reappears in a tradition of Jābir ibn 'Abd Allāh, this time coupled with an exhortation to acquire black slaves and avail oneself of their services and professional abilities (*...fa-t-takhidhūhum wa-mtahinūhum*). It also stresses the notion that they are strong and a source of blessing (*yumn*). This *ḥadīth* was transmitted by 'Abd Allāh ibn 'Āmir ← Muḥammad ibn al-Munkadir on the authority of the Egyptian scribe

[89]Ibn 'Asākir 11/643, 15/422.

[90]Ibn 'Abd al-Ḥakam, *Futūḥ Miṣr*, ed. C.C. Torrey, New Haven 1922, 66; cf. also Lewis, *Race and Color* 10, and Rotter 92.

[91]Ibn Ḥanbal, *Musnad* 2/364, 4/185; cf. Haythamī, *Majma'* 4/192, who quotes Tirmidhī and Ṭabarānī; Daylamī 2/207; Haytamī 33/4.

of Mālik, Ḥabīb ibn Abī Ḥabīb ibn Zurayq.[92] Finally, there is the tradition of Ibn 'Umar on the authority of Khālid ibn Yazīd / ibn Mihrān al-Ḥadhdhā' al-Makkī / al-Baṣrī (d. 142/759?), which promises that blessedness / prosperity will enter the house of anyone who brings to it a male or female black slave (*al-ḥabasha*).[93]

One group of traditions that reflects the ambivalent attitude of Muslim scholarship towards non-Arabs, particularly blacks, is of the kind noted by Lewis as appearing in the form of a rhetorical device that he calls *trajectio ad absurdum*—i.e. one that produces a sense contrary to the one it apparently aims at, because it labours so much to assert it. One such tradition of extremely broad circulation commands the Muslim to "obey whoever happens to be in power, even if he be a crop-nosed Ethiopian (*ḥabashī*) slave."[94] Other modern scholars have noted a variant of this tradition associated with the name of the Companion Abū Dharr, and have raised the possibility of assigning a Khārijite origin to it, since it mirrors the latter's opposition to dynastic claims.[95] Goitein, however, expressed serious doubts about this and noted that the tradition in question was used by the early Abū Yūsuf as "a prime argument in defence of blind submission to authority," and hence was included in a volume dedicated to the caliph.[96]

A quick glance at the wide range of traditional sources cited for this tradition reveals that apart from the version transmitted from Abū Dharr, similar versions were attributed to the Prophet through Anas, Umm al-Ḥuṣayn, Irbāḍ ibn Sāriya and 'Alī ibn Abī Ṭālib.[97] We also

---

[92]Ibn 'Adī 2/820; Ibn al-Jawzī, *al-Mawḍū'āt* 2/234; Suyūṭī, *La'ālī* 1/443; Kinānī 2/20; Shawkānī 414.

[93]Daylamī 3/572; Kinānī 2/37; Fattanī 113; Sakhāwī 296; 'Ajlūnī 2/224 (the last two sources quote also a work by Ibn al-Jawzī entitled *Tanwīr al-Ghabash Fī Faḍl al-Sūdān wa-l-Ḥabash*).

[94]Noted and translated by Lewis, *Race and Color* 19–22.

[95]I. Goldziher, *Vorlesungen über den Islam*, Heidelberg 1910, 205; cf. S.D. Goitein, *Studies in Islamic History and Institutions*, Leiden 1966, 204 n. 2; von Grunebaum, *Medieval Islam* 209.

[96]Goitein, *Studies* 204 n. 2, referring to Abū Yūsuf, *Kitāb al-Kharāj* 10.

[97]Ṭayālisī 230, 280; Ibn al-Ja'd 1/623; Ibn Sa'd 2/184–85; Ibn Ḥanbal, *Musnad* 3/114, 6/402–403; Bukhārī, *Ṣaḥīḥ* 8/105; Muslim 6/14–15; Basawī 2/344; Ibn Abī 'Āṣim, *Sunna* 2/29, 459, 488, 491–92, 505–506; Muḥammad ibn Naṣr al-Marwazī, *Sunna*, Beirut 1988, 26–27; Nasā'ī, *Sunan* 7/154; Ibn al-Khallāl (d. 311/923), *al-*

notice that certain elements of it, occurring within a variety of textual formulations, were reported in a *mawqūf* form from ʿUmar, a *maqṭūʿ* one through him, as a *mursal* of Ibn Sīrīn (d. 110/728) and even as Shaʿbī's own statement.[98]

To begin with, the most widely circulated variant of Abū Dharr's tradition was reported by Shuʿba ibn al-Ḥajjāj (d. 160/776) from the chain Abū ʿImrān al-Jawnī (Baṣran, d. 123–28/740–45) ← ʿUbāda ibn al-Ṣāmit; as noted above, ʿUbāda was himself black. According to this version, Abū Dharr says that "his friend" (*khalīlī*), i.e. the Prophet, admonished him to obey even a chop-limbed slave (*wa-in kāna ʿabdan mujaddaʿa l-aṭrāf*). It is only in a few variants of the tradition reported from Shuʿba that the attribute *ḥabashīyan*, "Abyssinian" or "black," occurs after *ʿabdan*, "slave." In others there is no mention of the phrase "even a slave" at all, and the advice simply enjoins obedience to those in authority.[99]

Other less-circulated variants of Abū Dharr's *ḥadīth* were transmitted via the links Bahz ibn Ḥakīm ibn Muʿāwiya ← his father, Qatāda ← ʿAlqama al-Shaybānī, ʿĀṣim ibn Kulayb ← Salama ibn Nubāta, Iyās ibn Salama ← his father Salama ibn al-Akwaʿ and Kahmas ibn al-Ḥasan ← Abū l-Sulayl. There are similar statements occurring within different narrative contexts: e.g. that such advice was given to Abū Dharr when the Prophet found him asleep in the mosque, that he advised him to move to Syria, that Abū Dharr recalled the whole story when, being in exile, he was led by a black slave in prayer, etc. The terms *ʿabd*, *ḥabashī* and *aswad* do occur in these versions, but because of their limited circulation, and hence, the lack of variants and chains of transmission for them, it is impossible to follow their development

---

Sunna, Riyadh 1989, 107–108, 110–11; Ibn Abī Ḥātim, *ʿIlal* 2/417; Ibn Ḥibbān, *Ṣaḥīḥ* 7/46; al-Ājurrī (d. 360/970), *al-Sharīʿa*, Cairo 1950, 40; Ṭabarānī, *al-Muʿjam al-Awsaṭ* 2/97; Ḥākim 4/75–76; al-Khaṭīb al-Baghdādī 4/125; Bayhaqī, *Shuʿab* 6/4–5; *idem*, *Sunan* 3/88, 8/155, 185, 10/114; Daylamī 1/70; Ibn ʿAsākir 1/41, 65–67, 18/186; Sakhāwī 58–59; Suyūṭī, *Durr* 2/176–77; Haytamī 33; Muttaqī 6/nos. 14795, 14799, 14816, 15/no. 43297.

[98]Ibn al-Khallāl, *Sunna* 107–108, 110–11; Ājurrī, *Sharīʿa* 40; Suyūṭī, *Durr* 2/176–77; Ibn ʿAsākir 5/344, 8/702.

[99]See Muslim 6/14; Ibn Abī ʿĀṣim 2/488; Bayhaqī, *Shuʿab* 6/4–5; *idem*, *Sunan* 3/88, 8/155, 185.

any further.[100] We should also note that none of these terms occur in the variant circulated by Dāwūd ibn Abī Hind ← Abū Ḥarb ibn Abī l-Aswad al-Daylī (al-Du'alī). Instead, the whole tradition is cited in the context of the rebellion (*fitna*) against 'Uthmān.[101]

The *mursal* tradition of Ibn Sīrīn, which includes the element of the "crop-nosed Ḥabashī slave" (*'abd ḥabashī mujadda'*), is interesting because it was reported from him through the link Wakī' ← Yazīd ibn Ibrāhīm (al-Tustarī al-Baṣrī, d. 162–63/778–79).[102] In a certain variant of another tradition, that of Umm al-Ḥuṣayn, whose commonest link is Shu'ba, Wakī' seems again to be responsible for introducing the same element.[103] This does not necessarily mean that this element is only Wakī''s responsibility, or that that of Shu'ba was the only link of Umm al-Ḥuṣayn's tradition. However, notice must be taken of the fact that when Wakī' transmits the Umm al-Ḥuṣayn tradition (from Yūnus ibn 'Amr / var. ibn Abī Isḥāq), as also when he transmits 'Umar's *mawqūf* one, then the same element reemerges.[104] Again, Wakī' is not the only one responsible for introducing this element, for it occurs in other variants of 'Umar's *mawqūf* tradition reported by some of Wakī''s contemporaries, like Layth (ibn Sa'd) and Mūsā ibn A'yan.[105]

To return to Umm al-Ḥuṣayn's tradition, we notice that it specifies the Farewell Pilgrimage as the context for the Prophet's statement and adds the notion that obedience to the ruler in power is conditional upon his acting according to the Book of God. Concerning our investigation, we also notice that when this tradition is reported from Shu'ba by Muḥammad ibn Ja'far (Ghundar, d. 192–94/807–809) or a certain Khālid, it uses the term "slave" (*'abd*), though without identifying him as a Ḥabashī. Now when the report is transmitted by 'Abd al-Raḥmān ibn Mahdī (d. 198/813), Ṭayālisī (d. 204/819) and Wakī', then the full title, *'abd ḥabashī mujadda' / aswad*, occurs. One must immediately

---

[100] See Ibn Abī 'Āṣim 2/459, 487; Ibn Abī Ḥātim, *'Ilal* 2/417; Ibn 'Asākir 1/41, 67.

[101] Ibn 'Asākir 1/65–66.

[102] Ibn al-Khallāl 107–108.

[103] Muslim 6/15; Ibn al-Khallāl 110; Ibn Abī 'Āṣim, *Sunna* 2/505–506.

[104] Ibn al-Khallāl 110–11; Ibn Abī 'Āṣim, *Sunna* 2/506. Compare also with Suyūṭī, *Durr*, 2/176, quoting Ibn Abī Shayba.

[105] Ājurrī 40.

add, however, that this full title occurs also in variants reported from transmitters other than Shu'ba.[106]

The link Shu'ba ← Abū l-Tayyāḥ is the only one that bears Anas' tradition enjoining obedience "even to a Ḥabashī whose head is like a raisin" (*wa-law li-ḥabashīyin ka-anna ra'sahu zabība*). From Shu'ba it was reported by both Yaḥyā ibn Sa'īd (al-Qaṭṭān, d. 198/813) and Tayālisī, the latter adding that the Prophet gave the same order to Abū Dharr.[107]

The traditions of al-'Irbāḍ ibn Sāriya and 'Alī include the element of obedience to an *'abd ḥabashī / mujadda'*, but cite it in contexts that prophesy future adversities (lit. "whoever shall live from among you will see much dissension," *man ya'ishu minkum sa-yarā ikhtilāfan kathīran*). In such circumstances, people are advised to adhere to the principle that Imāms should come from Quraysh (*al-a'immatu min quraysh*), as well as to the *sunna* of the Prophet and the Rāshidūn caliphs after him (*fa-'alaykum bi-sunnatī wa-sunnati l-khulafā'i l-rāshidīna min ba'dī*).[108] Not much can be learned from the *isnād* of the tradition of 'Alī. As for al-Irbāḍ's, it is worth noting that Khālid ibn Ma'dān constitutes an important link in its chain of transmission. This fact gains more weight when it is realized that Khālid's name occurs also in a line attributing to the Prophet, albeit in a *maqṭū'* form through 'Umar I, a unique tradition that couples the two elements of enjoining obedience to a *'abd ḥabashī* and warning one against becoming a Khārijite (*wa-sma' wa-aṭi' 'abdan ḥabashīyan wa-lā takun khārijīyan*).[109]

The other sects against which this tradition warns are the Rāfiḍa, the Murji'a and the Qadarīya, which held divergent views on various points of theology. However, one cannot but notice the existence of four similar variants reported as the personal statements of Sha'bī, who was

---

[106]See Muslim 6/14–15; Ṭayālisī 230; Ibn Sa'd 2/184–85; Ibn Ḥanbal, *Musnad* 6/402–403; Ibn Abī 'Āṣim, *Sunna* 2/491–492; Nasā'ī 7/154; Ibn Ḥibbān, *Ṣaḥīḥ* 7/46; Ṭabarānī, *al-Mu'jam al-Awsaṭ* 2/97; Bayhaqī, *Sunan* 8/155; Suyūṭī, *Durr* 2/177.

[107]Ṭayālisī 280; Ibn al-Ja'd 1/623; Ibn Ḥanbal, *Musnad* 3/114; Bukhārī, *Ṣaḥīḥ* 8/105; Ājurrī 38–39; al-Khaṭīb al-Baghdādī 4/125; Bayhaqī, *Sunan* 3/88, 8/155; *idem*, *Shu'ab* 6/4; Daylamī 1/70; Sakhāwī 58–59; Suyūṭī, *Durr* 2/176.

[108]Basawī 2/344; Ibn Abī 'Āṣim, *Sunna* 19, 29, 482–84; Marwazī, *Sunna* 26–27; Ḥākim 4/75–76; Bayhaqī, *Sunan* 10/114; Haytamī 33.

[109]Ibn 'Asākir 5/344.

a contemporary of Khālid ibn Ma'dān. Still, only one of them, reported from Sha'bī by Ḍamra ← Sufyān al-Thawrī, gives, like Khālid's, the epithet of "Khārijite" to one who does not obey "an Abyssinian slave."[110]

As far as I know, these are the only traditional instances that suggest a possible Khārijite connection with the injunction to obey an Abyssinian slave. Moreover, the *isnād* review conducted above shows that this connection belongs to the second half of the second/eighth century, which is also the time when the *qāḍī* Abū Yūsuf was active. Goitein was right to express reservations regarding the idea that the order to obey an Abyssinian slave expressed a Khārijite doctrine. One may also note that this widely circulated traditional complex was usually included by *ḥadīth* compilers in chapters the main theme of which was the obligation to obey those in religious authority (*wujūb ṭā'at al-imām*).

The phrase "even if an Abyssinian slave" is used in much the same way by a statement cited in the name of the early third/ninth-century scholar Aṣma'ī. According to this account, he reported al-Ḥasan ibn al-Ḥasan ibn 'Alī (sic.) as saying to him: "O Aṣma'ī, God created Paradise for whoever obeys Him, even if an Abyssinian slave, and created Hell for whoever disobeys Him, even if born of Quraysh."[111]

Another tradition noted by Lewis as representing the rhetorical device mentioned above[112] is one in which the Prophet expresses his preference for a pious (*dhātu dīnin*) / fertile (*walūdun*) woman even though she be black (*sawdā'*) / stupid (*kharqā'*) / deranged (*kharmā'*) / mangy (*jarbā'*), over a beautiful woman (*ḥasnā'*) who is impious / barren. These variants were associated with the name of Ibn 'Amr, or else with a family line extending back from Bahz ibn Ḥakīm.[113]

Though blacks are comforted by a tradition guaranteeing their eligibility for Paradise, they are reminded, albeit in the form of an assurance, that their colour there will become white.[114] This tradition is associated with the names of Ibn 'Abbās and Ibn 'Umar, though

[110] Ibn 'Asākir 8/702.

[111] Ibn 'Asākir 12/28–29.

[112] Lewis, *Race and Color* 20, referring also to Rotter 132.

[113] See Sa'īd ibn Manṣūr 1/142; Bayhaqī, *Sunan* 7/80; Ibn 'Asākir 4/661.

[114] Also noted by Lewis, *Race and Color* 21–22, referring to Rotter 103 and Goldziher, *Muslim Studies* 1/75.

one notices that in both cases the link responsible for circulating it is Ayyūb ibn 'Utba (Abū Yaḥyā al-Yamānī, d. 160/776) ← 'Aṭā'. Here we are told that the Prophet was approached by a man from among the Ḥabasha who recognized that they were inferior to the Arabs "in colour, appearance and [possession of] prophecy," and asked whether, in spite of all this, he would join the Prophet in Paradise if he believed in him and followed his example. To this the Prophet replied in the affirmative, assuring the man that blacks would appear white in Paradise from within a walking distance of one thousand years.[115]

One tradition conveying a similar notion bears the name of Anas through the link Ḥammād ← Thābit al-Bunānī. According to this, the man who came to the Prophet was black and identified himself as one "with a stinking smell, an ugly face and no money." He asked where he would go if he were to be killed fighting for the Prophet, and the latter assured him that he would go to Paradise. We are also told that when the man died the Prophet said: "God has whitened your face, perfumed your smell and multiplied your wealth" (*qad bayyaḍa l-lāhu wajhaka wa-ṭayyaba l-lāhu rīḥaka wa-akthara l-lāhu mālak*).[116] One may add that a similar tradition was reported by Ibn Zayd ('Abd al-Raḥmān, Medinese, d. 182/798) in a *mursal* form that did not, however, gain wide circulation.[117] From two reports cited in the name of the mid-third/ninth century Egyptian ascetic Dhū l-Nūn, we learn of his testimony that, while in the Wilderness of Sinai, he saw a black / Zanjī with peppered hair (*mufalfalu l-sha'r*), whose face turned white whenever he mentioned the name of God.[118]

---

[115]Ibn Ḥibbān, *al-Majrūḥīn* 1/169–70; Abū Nu'aym, *Dalā'il al-Nubuwwa* 3/319; Ibn al-Jawzī, *al-Mawḍū'at* 2/231; Sakhāwī 207, quoting Ṭabarānī; Kinānī 2/32–33; Shawkānī 417; Muttaqī 14/no. 39352. See also Qārī 119–20, who notes the view of both Manūfī and Ibn Hajar that black believers do not enter Paradise except as whites (*inna mu'minī l-sūdān lā yadkhulūna l-jannat illā bīḍan*).

[116]Ḥākim 2/93–94; Kīnānī 2/32–33, quoting Bayhaqī's *Shu'ab*. A *double entendre* is also involved here, as the phrase *bayyaḍu l-lāhu wajhaka* would normally bear the meaning: "God has granted you felicity."

[117]I could find only one late source, Kinānī 2/32–33, that cited it.

[118]Abū Nu'aym, *Ḥilya* 9/368, 391.

CHAPTER V

APOCALYPTIC INSECURITIES

ON A FEW OCCASIONS ABOVE we have encountered statements that indirectly refer to the position of Arabs towards the end of times, namely those references to the adoption of bedouin life during the *fitna* (*al-ta'arrub fī l-fitna*), the Prophet's intercession (*shafā'a*) being granted to the Arabs, their closeness to his banner on the Day of Judgement, and so forth. Likewise, we have touched upon certain traditions expressive of Arab insecurities *vis-à-vis* other nations in apocalyptic forms, namely those warning that Iraq, Syria and Egypt will be lost to Arab rule, that nations will swarm over the Arabs like hungry eaters do over a bowl of food, etc. In what follows more material will be reviewed in order to examine fresh aspects of Arab insecurity concomitant with their emergence as a nation, and the way in which this insecurity was perpetuated in Muslim faith.

An important *ḥadīth* combining a sense of historical insecurity with the newly acquired role of the Arabs as bearers of a new faith was circulated by Sulaymān ibn Ḥarb (d. 224/838). The *isnād* available for this tradition shows that it was reported around the mid-second/eighth century by Muḥammad ibn Abī Razīn in a family line from his mother Umm Razīn, from a certain woman named Umm al-Ḥarīr. The latter, we are told, used to take the death of any Arab very badly. When she was asked about this, she testified hearing from her master, Ṭalḥa ibn Mālik, a Prophetic tradition that claimed: "The destruction of the

Arabs is a sign that the Hour has drawn nigh" (*min iqtirābi l-sā'ati halāku l-'arab*).[1]

From another Prophetic tradition, this time by Umm Sharīk, we basically learn that the Arabs will be but few when, towards the end of times, the Antichrist (*al-dajjāl*) will appear and all people will seek refuge in mountainous areas. This was transmitted from her through two Companions: Jābir ibn 'Abd Allāh (by either Wahb ibn Munabbih, d. 110/728, or Abū l-Zubayr Muḥammad ibn Muslim al-Makkī, d. 126/743) and Abū Umāma al-Bāhilī (by Abū Zur'a Yaḥyā ibn Abī 'Amr al-Saybānī, Ḥimṣī, d. 148–50/765–67). We also notice that this latter Syrian line places the location of the few remaining Arabs in those days in Jerusalem.[2]

Sporadic references to what will happen to the Arabs during these last days are made by a few traditions. From 'Abd Allāh ibn 'Amr, for example, we hear of a warning against a *fitna* that will wipe out the Arabs and result in those warriors who are killed going to Hell.[3] 'Amr ibn al-Ḥamq al-Khuzā'ī, in turn, speaks about a *fitna* in which the best / safest of all will be the Arab army / district (*al-jund al-'arabī*).[4] A *ḥadīth* transmitted on the authority of Abū Hurayra, however, says that the vanguard of the Antichrist (*muqaddimatu l-dajjāl*) will number 12,000 from among the Arab hypocrites, who will wear crowns (*min munāfiqī l-'arabi 'alayhimu l-tījān*).[5] Similarly, the sale of girls and the attainment of puberty by the sons of Persian women (i.e. by Arab youths whose mothers were Persian) were considered by the traditions of Abū Hurayra and 'Umar I as other signs of the Hour or of the impending destruction of the Arabs, respectively.[6]

---

[1]Ibn Abī Shayba 12/195; Basawī 1/276–77; Tirmidhī 5/724; Ṭabarānī, *al-Mu'jam al-Kabīr* 8/370; *idem*, *al-Mu'jam al-Awsaṭ* 3/264–65; 'Irāqī 5–6; Haytamī 23; Muttaqī 12/no. 38471; al-Barzanjī (d. 1103/1691), *al-Ishā'a li-Ashrāt al-Sā'a*, Cairo 1393/1973, 48; Mar'ī al-Ḥanbalī, *Bahjat al-Nāẓirīn*, Ms. Jerusalem, al-Maktaba al-Khālidīya, Ar. no. 21, 72r (I am indebted to Dr. Lawrence Conrad for drawing my attention to this source).

[2]Ibn Māja 2/1361; Ibn Ḥanbal, *Musnad* 6/462; Muslim 8/207; Tirmidhī 5/724; Ṭabarānī, *al-Mu'jam al-Kabīr* 25/96–97; 'Irāqī 6; Haytamī 24.

[3]Ibn Māja 2/1312.

[4]Basawī 2/483.

[5]Abū Ḥayyān, *Ḥadīth*, Ms. Ẓāhirīya, *Majmū'* no. 93, 36.

[6]Ibn Abī Shayba 12/192–93; Ibn 'Asākir 1/179.

But the one apocalyptic current that expressed the insecurity of Arabian Islam in its most acute form was the speculation that towards the end of times the Ḥabasha / a Ḥabashī will violate the sanctity of the Ka'ba and effect its complete destruction. One tradition of this kind, prominently associated with the name of Abū Hurayra, warns the Arabs that they will perish if they violate the sanctity of their House (i.e. the Ka'ba); it ends with prophesying that when this happens, the Ḥabasha will come, effect its final destruction and dig out its treasure.[7] To the other element occurring in this tradition, concerning a man to whom allegience will be given in Mecca in these circumstances,[8] we shall return later.

Apocalyptic speculations about the destruction of the Ka'ba by a Ḥabashī occur in different traditions attributed to the Prophet, as well as to a few Companions, within various textual formulations. One Prophetic *ḥadīth* transmitted on the authority of Abū Hurayra by several late first/seventh, early second/eighth-century tradents warns that a man with two thin legs (*dhū l-suwayqatayn*) from al-Ḥabasha will destroy the Ka'ba / the House of God. It is worth noting that, as transmitted by Abū l-Ghayth, this tradition occurs in a *mawqūf* form, while when transmitted by Sa'īd ibn al-Musayyib and Abū Salama ibn 'Abd al-Raḥmān, both on the authority of Zuhrī, it acquires a *marfū'*, Prophetic one.[9] Note also that as transmitted by an unnamed "*shaykh* from the people of Medina" (reported from him by the mid-second/eighth century Egyptian, Yazīd ibn 'Amr al-Ma'āfirī), Abū Hurayra is quoted for a substantially different statement, namely the description of a bald man with a dislocated ankle joint, whose legs are wide apart (*aṣla', ufayda', ufayḥaj*), who will climb onto the roof of

[7]Ṭayālisī 312–13; Ibn al-Ja'd 2/1005; al-Fākihī, *Tārīkh Makka*, Ms. Leiden, Or. 463, 317v; Azraqī, *Akhbār Makka*, ed. F. Wüstenfeld, Göttingen 1868, 194–95; Qurṭubī, *Tadhkira* 2/332. Compare also with Nu'aym ibn Ḥammād, *Kitāb al-Fitan*, fol. 188r.

[8]Madelung regards this as belonging to a traditional complex originating during Ibn al-Zubayr's rebellion in 63–72/682–91; see his "'Abd Allāh ibn al-Zubayr and the Mahdī," *JNES* 40 (1981), 291–306.

[9]See Ḥumaydī 2/485; Azraqī 193; Nu'aym ibn Ḥammād 187v–188r; Fākihī 316v; Bukhārī, *Ṣaḥīḥ* 2/158; Muslim 8/183; Ibn Ḥibbān, *Ṣaḥīḥ* 8/265; Ḥākim 4/453; Bayhaqī, *Sunan* 4/340; Qurṭubī, *Tadhkira* 2/331; Ibn Kathīr, *Nihāya* 1/205, quoting Bazzār.

the Ka'ba and strike it with a certain tool called a *karzana*.[10] We shall soon see that this descriptive element belongs to traditions usually associated with the names of other Companions, which suggests that its attribution to Abū Hurayra was possibly the work of al-Ma'āfirī, who also disguised the identity of his source (the *shaykh*).

Ibn Jurayj reported from Ṣāliḥ ibn Abī Ṣāliḥ (Mihrān al-Kūfī) that he had heard a *mawqūf* tradition from Abū Hurayra that combines the original core of Abū Hurayra's *marfū'* tradition, noted above, with the introductory statement: "Avoid the Ḥabasha as long as they avoid you" (*utrukū l-ḥabasha mā tarakūkum*).[11] The same combination of these two elements occurs in another Prophetic tradition, transmitted by Abū Umāma As'ad ibn Sahl ibn Ḥunayf (d. 100/718) from an unnamed Companion (*'an rajulin min aṣḥābi l-nabī*) who is identified by some sources as either Ibn 'Amr or Ibn 'Umar.[12] Finally, from a unique *mursal* tradition of Sa'īd ibn al-Musayyib we learn that the Prophet said to "avoid the Ḥabasha as long as they avoid you" in the context of his exchange of letters with the Negus of Abyssinia upon receiving news of the latter's good treatment of Muslim emigrants in his country.[13]

Associated with the name of Anas are two traditions: one transmitted by Qatāda and the other by Abū 'Iqāl (Hilāl ibn Zayd, Baṣran, death date uncertain). The first is a *mawqūf* one according to which Anas, while circumambulating the Ka'ba, addressed the monument and said: "Verily, the Ḥabasha will conquer you" (*la-taghlibanna 'alayki l-ḥabasha*). The second has the Prophet imagining that already before him stood the Ḥabashī (*ka-annī bihi*) with two thin legs who would violate the Ka'ba (*yahtiku l-bayt*).[14]

From the caliphs 'Alī ibn Abī Ṭālib and 'Umar ibn al-Khaṭṭāb we hear of traditions urging people to accomplish their duty of *ḥajj* / *hijra*

---

[10]Nu'aym ibn Ḥammād 188r.

[11]Fākihī 317v.

[12]Cf. Azraqī 194; Abū Dāwūd 4/114; Ibn Ḥanbal, *Musnad* 5/371; Ḥākim 4/453; al-Khaṭīb al-Baghdādī 12/403; Bayhaqī, *Sunan* 9/176; Ibn Kathīr, *Nihāya* 1/205; Haythamī, *Majma'* 5/303–304; Suyūṭī, *al-Jāmi' al-Kabīr* 1/15; *idem*, *al-Jāmi' al-Ṣaghīr* 1/8; Qārī 333; Sakhāwī 214; al-Ḥūt al-Bayrūtī 16; Muttaqī 4/no. 10935; Albānī, *Silsilat al-Aḥādīth al-Ṣaḥīḥa*, al-Maktab al-Islāmī, Beirut 1979, 2/415.

[13]Sa'īd ibn Manṣūr 2/189–90.

[14]Cf. Fākihī 317v, and al-Khaṭīb al-Baghdādī 3/335, respectively.

quickly because of an imminent attack expected against the Ka'ba by a Ḥabashī / the Ḥabasha. The tradition of 'Umar describes such an attack as "one of the two darknesses" (*iḥdā l-ẓalmatayn*). That of 'Alī goes into a detailed description of the Ḥabashī who will destroy the Ka'ba as a man with small ears (*aṣma'*), a dislocated ankle joint (*afda'*), a small head (*aṣ'al*) and two thin legs (*ḥamishu l-sāqayn*). According to this *ḥadīth*, he will be sitting on the Ka'ba with a mattock (*mi'wal*), destroying it stone by stone. The *isnād* information on 'Umar's tradition shows that it is a *maqṭū'* one attributed to him by Arṭāt ibn al-Mundhīr (Ḥimṣī, d. 162–63/778–79) ← 'Abd al-Raḥmān ibn Jubayr ibn Nufayr (d. 118/736). 'Alī's tradition, on the other hand, was transmitted in two lines: one in a *mawqūf* form by Ḥafṣa bint Sīrīn (Baṣran, d. 101–10/719–28) ← Abū l-'Āliya, and the other in a *marfū'* one by Ibrāhīm al-Taymī (Kūfan, d. 92–94/710–12) ← al-Ḥārith ibn Suwayd. We also notice that this latter variant ends with a question by al-Ḥārith to 'Alī as to whether this was his opinion or something that he heard from the Prophet, an element that clearly reflects later suspicions that this was actually a *mawqūf* tradition, in spite of 'Alī's reported assurances to the contrary.[15]

A similar speculation concerning a black bald-headed man who will tear down the Ka'ba stone by stone is given in a tradition of Ibn 'Abbās transmitted from him exclusively by Ibn Abī Mulayka ('Abd Allāh ibn 'Ubayd Allāh, d. 117–18/735–36). We notice, however, that this tradition does not explicitly say that this man will be a Ḥabashī.[16] In later sources the same descriptive elements are cited in the form of a tradition attributed to the Prophet by Ḥudhayfa al-Ṭawīl, though here a host of new details have been added. We learn, for instance, that in addition to all that has been said, the man in question will also have

[15]For both 'Umar's and 'Alī's traditions, see Abū 'Ubayd, *Gharīb al-Ḥadīth* 3/454–55 (where he cites Aṣma'ī's interpretation of *aṣ'al* and *aṣma'*); Nu'aym ibn Ḥammād 187v–188r; Fākihī 316v–317r; Ibn 'Adī 2/804; Ḥākim 1/448–49; Abū Nu'aym, *Hilya* 4/131–32; Bayhaqī, *Sunan* 4/340 (where he also cites a tradition of Abū Hurayra that says that danger to the *ḥajj* would come from the bedouins, not the Ḥabasha); Qurṭubī, *Tadhkira* 2/331–32; Suyūṭī, *al-Jāmi' al-Ṣaghīr* 1/147; Samhūdī 97; Albānī, *Ḍa'īfa* 2/23–24.

[16]Ibn Ḥumayd 235; Bukhārī, *Ṣaḥīḥ* 2/159; Fākihī 316r–v; Ibn Ḥibbān, *Ṣaḥīḥ* 8/265; Ṭabarānī, *al-Mu'jam al-Kabīr* 11/121; Abū Nu'aym, *Ḥilya* 8/387; Bayhaqī, *Sunan* 4/340–41; Qurṭubī, *Tadhkira* 2/331; Ibn Kathīr, *Nihāya* 1/205.

blue (shining, diabolical) eyes, a flat nose and a big belly; he will not only tear the Ka'ba down stone by stone, but will also cast it into the sea.[17]

By far the richest and most diversified traditions on this issue are the ones associated with the name of 'Abd Allāh ibn 'Amr ibn al-'Āṣ. One, circulated in a family line back from 'Amr ibn Yaḥyā ibn Sa'īd ibn 'Amr ibn al-'Āṣ (fl. late second/eighth c.), attributes to Ibn 'Amr a *mawqūf* tradition similar to the one by 'Umar I cited above. This *ḥadīth* urges the people of Mecca to leave the city before the occurrence of one of the two darknesses (*iḥdā al-ẓalmatayn* / var. *al-ṣaylamayn*, the "two deadly wars"). When asked about these, he describes one as a black wind that will destroy everything in its path, and the second as a massive raid by blacks who will come up from the sea and destroy the Ka'ba. The tradition then goes on to say that their leader will be bald (*afḥaj*) and bow-legged (*aṣla'*), as described "in the Book of God."[18]

As transmitted by Mujāhid, another tradition of Ibn 'Amr may contain certain historical elements. It attributes to Ibn 'Amr the specification of the main speculative attributes of the Ḥabashī mentioned above, with one variant adding that he will strip the Ka'ba of its covering (*kiswa*) and then destroy it. However, after Mujāhid, this tradition splits from the point of view of both *isnād* and content. The core of it, concerning the attributes of the Ḥabashī, was transmitted from Muhāhid only through the links Abū Mu'āwiya ← al-A'mash and Ibn Isḥāq ← Ibn Abī Najīḥ.[19] We may also note that with Ibn Isḥāq the tradition looses its *mawqūf* form and acquires a *marfū'*, Prophetic one. And to this are added the elements of stripping the coverings and looting the decorations (*ḥilā*) of the Ka'ba.

A third line of transmission, by Sufyān (al-Thawrī?) ← Ibn Abī Najīḥ, adds another noteworthy element in reporting from Mujāhid: "When Ibn al-Zubayr pulled down the Ka'ba, I came to look for the description that 'Abd Allāh [ibn 'Amr] gave [of the Ḥabashī who will destroy it, etc.], but did not see him."[20] The same variant was also

[17]Qurṭubī, *Tadhkira* 2/331, quoting Ibn al-Jawzī.

[18]Azraqī 193; Fākihī 316v.

[19]Nu'aym ibn Ḥammād 188r–189r; Fākihī 316v; Ibn Kathīr, *Nihāya* 1/204, quoting Ibn Ḥanbal.

[20]Nu'aym 187v; Fākihī 316v; Azraqī 194.

transmitted from Mujāhid by Ibn Jurayj and was cited by Azraqī as part of an account of the first siege of Mecca by the Umayyads in the year 62–63/681–82, the burning of the Ka'ba and Ibn al-Zubayr's reconstruction of it. Note especially that this narrative ends with the report that Ibn al-Zubayr sent Ḥabashī slaves up onto the roof and ordered them to destroy it, hoping to see the fulfillment of the Prophet's statement concerning the Ḥabashī man with the two thin legs.[21]

An indication of some Ḥabashī military presence in Mecca during the conflict between Ibn al-Zubayr and the Umayyads is given by several sources.[22] There are also traditional reports about a coastal attack by al-Ḥabasha against Jidda during the time of the Prophet,[23] and before that, Abraha's famous campaign against Mecca in pre-Islamic times. An enquiry into the actual historical basis for the existence of a local Meccan apocalyptic tradition and speculative fears about the Ḥabasha, or even who these were or where they came from, would be a tangential undertaking in the present context. The fact of the matter is that such a local tradition did exist in the first/seventh century. It is quite plausible to suggest that when Mecca was eventually established as Islam's cultic center, this local tradition also assumed a central role in Muslim apocalyptic discourse, a suggestion that may explain the disproportion obtaining between Muslim apocalyptic speculations, on the one hand, and any real threat posed by Abyssinia against the world of Islam, on the other.

In a few traditions associated with the names of Ibn 'Amr and Ka'b al-Aḥbār, the element of an attack by *al-ḥabasha / dhū l-suwayqatayn* was connected with the Muslim belief in the second coming of Christ ('Īsā ibn Maryam) towards the end of times and his struggle against both the Ḥabasha and Gog and Magog.[24] From a variant of the tradition of Ka'b, circulated by the Ḥimṣī Ṣafwān ibn 'Amr (d. 100–108/718–26), one can easily discern a current of apocalyptic speculation favouring the role that the Syrians would play in saving the Ka'ba from the Ḥabasha, possibly drawing on their role during Ibn al-Zubayr's

[21]Azraqī 138–42.

[22]Balādhurī, *Ansāb* IVB, 51, 58; Ibn 'Asākir, Damascus 1981, 479.

[23]Ibn Sayyid al-Nās 2/207.

[24]See Nu'aym ibn Ḥammād 188r–189r; Abū Nu'aym, *Ḥilya* 6/24; Ibn Kathīr, *Nihāya* 1/202; Qurṭubī, *Tadhkira* 2/332, quoting Ḥalīmī.

rebellion.[25] In any case, the Ḥabashī apocalyptic menace continued to live on and seems to have been very deeply rooted in Meccan memory. During the Carmathian attack on the Ka'ba and their sacking and removal of the holy Black Stone to Kūfa in the year 317/929, some of the inhabitants of Mecca went out to see if it would be cast down by a black man from the seventh arch of its mosque, as one tradition of 'Alī prophesied.[26]

The historical insecurity of the Arabs is the main theme of another set of widely circulated traditions attributed to the Prophet through Abū Hurayra and Zaynab bint Jaḥsh. The core of these warn the Arabs against "an evil that has drawn nigh" (*waylun li-l-'arab min sharrin qad iqtarab*). However, through different *isnāds* variant comments and elaborations were added, and the core itself stands alone only in one rare transmission from Abū Hurayra.[27]

In an implicit reference to internal Arab discords (*fitan*) in the future as the evil intended by this *ḥadīth*, another transmission from Abū Hurayra advises people to restrain themselves (*aflaḥa man kaffa yadahu*). This exegesis was provided through the chain Sufyān al-Thawrī ← al-A'mash ← Abū Ṣāliḥ (Bādhām, d. 101/719).[28] Another variant, transmitted on the authority of Ibn Lahī'a ← a certain Abū Yūnus, describes these troubles as "parts of a dark night" (*fitanun ka-qiṭa'i l-layli l-muẓlim*). People are also warned that in these circumstances belief will be rare and difficult to maintain, that a man will arise in the morning as a believer and retire at night as an unbeliever and so forth.[29]

Though it does not mention *fitan* in this context, one variant by a certain Yazīd / Zayd ibn Qays says that "evil" in this tradition means

---

[25] Fākihī 316v; Nu'aym ibn Ḥammād 188r.

[26] Ibn 'Asākir 4/584. On this attack in 317/929, see al-Nahrawālī, *al-I'lām bi-A'lām Bayt Allah al-Ḥarām*, ed. F. Wüstenfeld, Leipzig 1857, 165.

[27] By 'Aṭīya (ibn Sa'd al-'Awfī?, Kūfan, d. 111–27/729–44) and a certain Hishām ← Muḥammad. See Quḍā'ī 1/197 and al-Khaṭīb al-Baghdādī 4/317, respectively.

[28] Al-Fazārī (d. 186/802), *Kitāb al-Siyar*, ed. Fārūq Ḥamāda, Mu'assasat al-Risāla, Beirut 1987, 311; Abū Dāwūd 4/97; Abū Nu'aym, *Ḥilya* 8/265; Daylamī 4/395; Suyūṭī, *al-Jāmi' al-Ṣaghīr* 2/197; Ibn Ḥanbal, *Musnad* 2/441; Munāwī 2/147–48.

[29] Ibn Ḥanbal, *Musnad* 2/390–91; Daylamī 4/395; Ibn 'Asākir 19/501–502.

a decrease in scholarship and an increase in *harj*, which is interpreted as "killing."[30] From Abū Salama ibn ʿAbd al-Raḥmān we hear of advice to people even to seek death in these circumstances.[31] Another, by Saʿīd ibn Kathīr (Meccan or Kūfan, death date unknown) ← his father, anticipates that at this time "one will go to the grave of his father or brother and wish to be buried in his place" (saying literally: *laytanī kuntu makānak*, "Would that I were in your place").[32] Abū l-Ghayth describes the evil mentioned in this tradition as "a deaf and dumb *fitna*" (*fitna ṣammāʾ bakmāʾ*), saying that during this time it will be far better to remain passive (lit. "the one who sits during it will be better than the one who stands," *al-qāʿidu fīhā khayrun mina l-qāʾim*).[33] A certain hint that the Arabs' own leaders will drive them to such evil is offered by the variant of Saʿīd al-Maqburī, which warns that those who disobey will be killed and those who obey will be cast into Hell.[34]

Two variants contain references to specific circumstances and dates in which the evil will be inflicted. One, transmitted by a certain Saʿīd, warns that at the turn of AH 60 (*ʿalā raʾsi l-sittīn*), ordinances like trust (*amāna*), charity (*ṣadaqa*), testimony (*shahāda*) and judgement (*ḥukm*) will not be rightly fulfilled.[35] Another, circulated by a certain Ḥamza ibn al-Mundhir and ʿAbd al-Raḥmān ibn Hilāl (Kūfan Successor, death date unknown), contain a clear reference to the Umayyad caliph Walīd II, who was killed during the civil war marking the beginning of the collapse of Umayyad rule in 126/744. For the phrase "an evil that has drawn nigh," this variant substitutes an explicit warning against things that will happen "after the year 125" (*waylun li-l-ʿarab min baʿdi l-khams wa-l-ʿishrīn wa-l-māʾa*). It also calls Walīd II "the Manichaean heretic (*zindīq*) of Quraysh and the Arabs."[36] We notice, however, that some of the motifs deployed in this variant to describe

---

[30]Ibn Ḥanbal, *Musnad* 2/541; Abū Yaʿlā 11/523.

[31]Ḥākim 4/439–40.

[32]Al-Khaṭīb al-Baghdādī 4/251.

[33]Ibn Ḥibbān, *Ṣaḥīḥ* 8/249.

[34]Ibn Abī Ḥātim, *ʿIlal* 2/413.

[35]Ḥākim 4/483.

[36]Al-Azdī (d. 334/945), *Tārīkh al-Mawṣil*, ed. ʿAlī Ḥabība, al-Majlis al-Aʿlā li-l-Shuʾūn al-Islāmīya, Cairo 1967, 59; Ibn ʿAsākir 15/202.

these developments (e.g. *mawtun sarīʿ*, "rapid death;" *qatlun dharīʿ*, "widespread killing," etc.) also occur in a tradition of Muʿādh ibn Jabal that attributes to the Prophet a long apocalyptic account of the future. From this *ḥadīth* we learn that the anticipated evil, of rapid death and widespread killing, etc., of Arabs will come to pass after the year 120 (*waylun li-l-ʿarab min baʿdi l-ʿishrīn wa-miʾa min mawtin sarīʿ wa-qatlin dharīʿ*). We may also note that one of the things warned against is that "the property of the Arabs' fathers, meaning their slaves, will inherit their world" (*wa-yarithu dunyāhā mulku ābāʾihā, yaʿnī ʿabīdahā*). Then, we are told, a man from among the children of ʿAbbās will oppressively rule over them (*fa-ʿinda halākihim sulliṭa ʿalayhim rajulun min wuldi l-ʿabbās*).[37]

One variant of Abū Hurayra's tradition (transmitted by Wuhayb ibn Khālid al-Bāhilī, Baṣran d. 165–69/781–85 ← ʿAbd Allāh ibn Ṭāwūs, d. 131–32/748–49 ← his father) does not open with the standard warning against an evil that has drawn nigh, but rather substitutes for it the statement: "Today the Wall of Gog and Magog has been breached" (*futiḥa l-yawma min radmi yaʾjūja wa-maʾjūj*).[38] However, this latter statement is overwhelmingly linked with the former warning in a tradition prominently associated with the name of the Prophet's wife Zaynab.[39] The common link in the *isnād* of this tradition is Zuhrī ← ʿUrwa, from which it was reported by several mid-second/eighth-century tradents, usually with the addition of an explanatory gesture with their fingers to illustrate their point (lit. "and he circled his two fingers like this," *wa-ḥallaqa iṣbaʿayhi mithla hādhihi*). The deep sense of urgency and insecurity conveyed by this descriptive element is also expressed by a tradition in which Zaynab asks the Prophet: "Are we to perish even though righteous men reside amongst us?" (*a-nahlaku wa-fīnā l-ṣāliḥūn?*). To this, we are told, the Prophet answered:

---

[37]Suyūṭī, *Laʾālī* 1/454–56, quoting Ṭabarānī and the *Fitan* of Abū l-Shaykh for the *isnād* Ibn Lahīʿa ← Abū Qabīl al-Maʿāfirī (Ḥayy ibn Hāniʾ, Baṣran, d. 127–28/744–45) ← Ibn ʿAmr ← Muʿādh ← the Prophet.

[38]Abū Nuʿaym, *Ḥilya* 4/21–22.

[39]Compare, however, with Ṭabarānī, *al-Muʿjam al Kabīr* 23/416, where according to the *isnād* al-Ḥakam ibn ʿAbd Allāh ibn Saʿd al-Aylī (death date unknown) ← al-Qāsim ibn Muḥammad (d. 101–12/719–30), the same was attributed to the Prophet in an *isnād* leading back to ʿĀʾisha and Umm Salam.

"Yes, if scum becomes abundant [amongst us]" (*na'am, idhā kathura l-khabath*).[40]

Belief in the imminent breaching of the Wall of Gog and Magog was eventually connected in the traditional lore of the second/eighth century with the rising menace of the Turks in the East. Previously, we have encountered traditional examples in which both the Turks and the legendary Gog and Magog were identified as children to the same ancestor, Noah's son Japheth. A tradition of Suddī (d. 127/744) says that the Turks were one of 22 tribes of Gog and Magog who were left outside the wall because they were out on a raid when it was erected.[41]

We have also seen instances representing the opposite current, identifying the Turks as the progeny of Keturah, wife of Abraham. One may add here that Jāḥiẓ is probably one of the earliest sources where such identification was made and which recorded the traditional lore advising people to "avoid the Turks so long as they avoid you" (*wa-fī l-ma'thūri mina l-khabari / fa-innahu qad qīl: tārikū l-turka mā tarakūkum*). It is also of some interest to note that such statements were recorded by Jāḥiẓ in the name of a certain Sa'īd ibn 'Uqba ← his father, 'Uqba ibn Salam al-Hannā'ī, in the context of a report on a military encounter between the Turks and the Khārijites, i.e. definitely not as a Prophetic statement.[42] On the other hand, there is a Prophetic tradition associated with the name of Ibn Mas'ūd where the advice to avoid Turks is associated with the warning that the Sons of Keturah will be the first ones to plunder the *umma* of whatever God has bestowed upon it (*utrukū l-turka mā tarakūkum fa-inna awwala man yaslibu ummatī mā khawwalahumu l-lāhu banū qanṭūrā'*). This *ḥadīth* was transmitted from Ibn Mas'ūd by both Shaqīq ibn Salama (Kūfan, d. 82–101/701–19) and Zayd ibn Wahb (Kūfan, d. 82–96/701–14) and was reported

40 'Abd al-Razzāq, *Muṣannaf* 11/363; Ḥumaydī 1/147–48; Bukhārī, *Ṣaḥīḥ* 4/109, 8/88, 104; Muslim 8/165–66; Ibn Māja 2/1305; Basawī 2/722; Abū Ya'lā 13/82, 88; Ibn Ḥibbān, *Ṣaḥīḥ* 1/272, 2/28–29, 3/249, 293–94; Ṭabarānī, *al-Mu'jam al-Kabīr* 24/51–56; Bayhaqī, *Sunan* 10/93; Ibn 'Asākir 2/438, 19/406; Ibn Kathīr, *Nihāya* 1/196; Suyūṭī, *Khaṣā'iṣ* 2/100.

41 Sakhāwī 17, quoting Ḍiyā' al-Dīn al-Maqdisī; 'Ajlūnī 1/38, quoting Ibn Mardawayh.

42 Jāḥiẓ, *Manāqib al-Turk* 48–51.

from them through the chain Marwān ibn Sālim (a Syrian *mawlā* of Banū Umayya, death date unknown) ← al-A'mash.[43]

To other variants of Ibn Mas'ūd's tradition we shall return in the following paragraphs. Here, however, we may recall that avoiding the Turks was sometimes connected with similar advice to avoid the Ḥabasha.[44] Such a connection is also evident in the form of a Prophetic tradition, albeit with vague *isnāds*. This *ḥadīth* was transmitted by Abū Sukayna (Ḥimṣī, death date unknown), who is described as "one of the freed men" (*rajulun mina l-muḥarrarīn*) and is said to have transmitted it from an anonymous Companion (*'an rajulin min aṣḥābi l-nabī*). It advises people to avoid both the Turks and the Ḥabasha (*da'ū l-ḥabasha mā wada'ūkum wa-trukū l-turka mā tarakūkum*); in one *ḥadīth* compilation such advice is placed in the context of the Prophet's digging of the Ditch in Medina prior to the Meccans' attack on the city.[45]

In the variant attributed to Ibn Mas'ūd by the chain 'Ammār / var. 'Utba ibn Ghaylān (unidentified) ← al-A'mash ← Abū Wā'il (probably the same Shaqīq ibn Salama noted above), the advice to avoid the Turks stands alone, i.e. without the identification of them as the Sons of Keturah.[46] This suggests that the identification may have been made one generation after al-A'mash. This conclusion is supported by a

[43]Ṭabarānī, *al-Mu'jam al-Kabīr* 10/223–24; Haythamī, *Majma'* 5/304, 7/317, quoting Ṭabarānī's *al-Mu'jam al-Kabīr* and *al-Mu'jam al-Awsaṭ*; Sakhāwī 17; Suyūṭī, *al-Jāmi' al-Kabīr* 1/15; *idem*, *al-Jāmi' al-Ṣaghīr* 1/8; *idem*, *La'ālī* 1/446; *idem*, *Khaṣā'iṣ* 2/120; Kinānī 2/32; Qārī 333–34; 'Ajlūnī 1/38.

[44]Goldziher, in *Muslim Studies* 1/245, expresses the view that *utrukū l-ḥabasha* was an earlier tradition and that *utrukū l-turk* was formulated along the same lines, utilizing the Arabic verb *taraka* as meaning "departed."

[45]Nasā'ī, *Sunan* 6/43–44; but compare with Abū Dāwūd 4/112; Bayhaqī, *Sunan* 9/176; Suyūṭī, *al-Jāmi' al-Ṣaghīr* 2/16; *idem*, *La'ālī* 1/446; Kinānī 2/32; 'Ajlūnī 1/38; Ibn Ḥajar, *Tahdhīb* 12/114.

[46]Suyūṭī, *La'ālī* 1/445; Kinānī 2/32, quoting the *Fitan* of Abū l-Shaykh; Fattanī 114 (wrongly attributing it to Ibn 'Abbās); Ibn al-Jawzī, *Mawḍū'āt* 2/235; Shawkānī 416. There is also a variant reported from Abū Wā'il by a certain 'Amr ibn 'Abd al-Ghaffār ← al-A'mash, which combines the statement *utrukū l-turka mā tarakūkum* with advice not to take the Anbat as neighbours and not to have marital relations with the people of Khūzistān (*wa-lā tunākiḥū l-khūz*), and ends by praising the Persians for reaching out for religion even were it to be suspended from the Pleiades. See 'Uqaylī 3/286–87; Ibn Ḥajar, *Lisān* 4/369.

variant of another tradition, this time Mu'āwiya's, which, as circulated by Ibn Lahī'a, actually makes no such identification at all.[47]

More suggestive, due to the historical information they convey, are the other traditions associated with the names of Ibn Mas'ūd and Mu'āwiya, as well as one by 'Umar. 'Umar's position is cited by Jāḥiẓ in a *maqṭu'* report transmitted concerning him around the mid-second/eighth century by Yazīd ibn Qatāda ibn Di'āma (death date unknown). According to this tradition, 'Umar described the Turks as "an enemy difficult to pursue and yielding little booty" (*'aduwwun shadīdun ṭalabuhu qalīlun salabuh*). It is worth noting that this description was cited in support of the view that one should avoid engaging in war against a tough enemy.[48]

Another warning to the Muslims attributed to 'Umar (*wa-kāna 'umaru yaqūlu li-l-muslimīn*) includes the statement: "And hence, avoid them so long as they avoid you" (*fa-trukūhum mā tarakūkum*). On this occasion, we are told, 'Umar described the Turks as having shield-shaped (*ka-l-daraq*) faces and eyes like seashell (*ka-l-wada'*).[49] However, a warning similar to this one was also attributed to the Prophet through Abū l-Dardā', though here it was placed in the context of an exhortation to fight the Byzantines (lit. "the yellow ones," *banū l-aṣfar*), not the Turks.[50]

Through Ibn Sīrīn we hear of a *mawqūf* tradition of Ibn Mas'ūd that expresses a speculative warning that the Turks will come riding upon slit-eared war ponies (*'alā barādhīna mukharramati l-ādhān*) that they will tether on the banks of the Euphrates.[51] The tradition of Mu'āwiya ibn Abī Sufyān, usually transmitted by Mu'āwiya ibn Ḥudayj, describes the reaction of the caliph upon receiving news from one of his governors saying that the latter had fought and looted the Turks. Mu'āwiya ordered him to stop and to avoid fighting them in the future, we are

---

[47]Haythamī, *Majma'* 5/304; Sakhāwī 17; Suyūṭī, *al-Jāmi' al-Kabīr* 1/15; *idem*, *La'ālī* 1/446; Kinānī 2/32; 'Ajlūnī 1/38.

[48]Jāḥiẓ, *Manāqib al-Turk* 49.

[49]Nu'aym ibn Ḥammād 191r–v.

[50]Daylamī 1/108–109.

[51]Nu'aym ibn Ḥammād 191v; Ḥākim 4/475; Haythamī, *Majma'* 7/312 (quoting Ṭabarānī but implicitly expressing doubts that Ibn Sīrin had ever heard from Ibn Mas'ūd). Compare also with Suyūṭī, *Khasā'iṣ* 2/121.

told, for the caliph had heard the Prophet saying that the Turks would overcome the Arabs and drive them to the desert (lit. "to the lands where wormwood and pyrenthium grow," *ilā manābiti l-shīḥi wa-l-qayṣūm*).[52]

The scene of horrifying Turks / Sons of Keturah who will drive the Arabs out of Iraq and back into Arabia reappears in other Prophetic traditions associated with the names of Burayda al-Aslamī, Abū Bakra and Abū Qulāba. We are alternatively told that the Turks are people with small eyes and broad faces that look like balls of dried porridge (*juḥuf*). They will camp on the Tigris and attack Baṣra / var. Ubulla. The Muslims will eventually split into three groups: one will withdraw to Arabia (*al-bādiya / ta'khudhu adhnāba l-ibili / l-baqari / talḥaqu bi-manābiti l-shīḥi wa-l-qayṣūm*), another will run / move to Syria, and only one third will fight / stay.[53]

Similar elements also occur in traditions attributed to ʿAbd Allāh ibn ʿAmr,[54] Abū Hurayra, Kaʿb, Ḥudhayfa, Muʿāwiya and possibly others as well—all in a *mawqūf* form. One should also note that similar apocalyptic speculations about the Arabs being driven back to the desert are expressed in traditions relating to Arab–Byzantine wars in Syria,[55] a fact that confirms the feelings of deep historical insecurity among the Arabs in early Islam. As for the Turks, some of the relevant variants include new descriptive and vivid elements, such as driving out the peoples of Khurāsān and Sijistān, attacking Adharbayjān, Āmid and the Jazīra, and even joining with Burjān, Slavs and Byzantines in their wars against the Arabs. One notices, however, that the transmitters of some of these traditions are the same second/eighth-century

[52]Abū Yaʿlā 13/366–67; cf. also Haythamī, *Majmaʿ* 5/304, 7/311–12; Suyūṭī, *Khaṣāʾiṣ* 2/120; Ibn Ḥajar, *al-Maṭālib al-ʿĀliya* 4/337. Compare, however, with Nuʿaym ibn Ḥammād 191v, where the same is reported in the name of Ibn Dhī l-Kilāʿ rather than Ibn Ḥudayj. It is also worth noting that the latter tradition is a family one reported by Isḥāq ibn Ibrāhīm ibn al-Ghamr, *mawlā* of Samūk ← his father ← grandfather, while the transmitter of the former one is Ibn Lahīʿa.

[53]For these variants, see Nuʿaym ibn Ḥammād 190r–v; Ṭayālisī 117; Ibn Ḥibbān, *Ṣaḥīḥ* 8/264; Ḥākim 4/474; Qurṭubī, *Tadhkira* 2/319–21, 324; Abū Dāwūd 4/113; Suyūṭī, *Khaṣāʾiṣ* 2/120.

[54]He is once wrongly identified as ʿAmr ibn al-ʿĀṣ, the father, and in another instance as Ibn ʿUmar.

[55]Bashear, "Apocalyptic and Other Materials."

tradents who appear in the *isnāds* of either the Prophetic traditions or those attributed to Ibn Mas'ūd, reviewed above.[56] We also notice that the early source of Nu'aym cites the Prophetic tradition on the two campaigns (*kharjatān*) by the Turks against Adharbayjān and the Jazīra in a *mursal* form from Makḥūl.[57]

The description of the Sons of Keturah as pug-nosed with small eyes and faces that look like flattened shields (*khunsu l-unūfi, ṣighāru l-a'yuni, ka-anna wujūhuhumu l-mijānnu l-muṭarraqa*), which occurs in one *mawqūf* variant by Ibn 'Amr,[58] reappears with slight changes in several variants of widely circulated traditions attributed to the Prophet through Abū Hurayra, Abū Sa'īd al-Khudrī and 'Amr ibn Taghlib. The common denominator of this group of traditions is that all of them present the Muslim–Turkish future struggles within an eschatological context, the key statement being: "The Hour shall not come until you / the Muslims fight the Turks" (*lā taqūmu l-sā'atu ḥattā tuqātilū / yuqātilu l-muslimūna l-turk*). Another common feature is the reiteration of certain descriptive elements with ethnic and racial undertones. We read, for example, that the enemy will have flat noses (*fuṭsu / dhulfu l-unūf*), small eyes (*ṣighāru l-a'yuni / ka-anna 'uyūnahum ḥadaqu l-jarād*) and red / broad faces (*ḥumru / 'irāḍu l-wujūh*) like flattened shields (*ka-l-mijānni l-muṭarraqa*). They will use shields (*daraq*), tie their horses to palm trees and wear hairy boots (*ni'āluhumu l-sha'ru / yanta'ilūna l-sha'r*).

Beyond this, there are some nuances worth noting. Above all, the traditions of Abū Sa'īd al-Khudrī and 'Amr ibn Taghlib are not explicit about the identity of this eschatological enemy, although they adduce most of the features and attributes mentioned above.[59] The

[56]Of such names, mention may be made of 'Ubayd Allāh ibn Burayda (death date unknown), 'Abd al-Raḥmān ibn Abī Bakra (Baṣran, d. 96/714) and Ibn Sīrin. See Nu'aym ibn Ḥammād 189v–191r; Ḥākim 4/474–75, 534–35; Ibn al-Athīr, *al-Nihāya* 3/314–15. In one source, Nu'aym ibn Ḥammād 190v–191r, a statement in the name of Mu'āwiya calls for avoidance of the Khazars, who are described as al-Rābiḍa, "those who kneel down."

[57]Nu'aym ibn Ḥammād 190r, 191v.

[58]Ḥākim 4/534–35.

[59]Ṭayālisī 161; Bukhārī 3/232–33; Ibn Māja 2/1372; Ibn Ḥibbān, *Ṣaḥīḥ* 8/263; al-Khaṭīb al-Baghdādī 4/284; Bayhaqī, *Sunan* 9/176; Qurṭubī, *Tadhkira* 2/321; Ibn Kathīr, *Nihāya* 1/20.

same can be noted about the tradition of Abū Hurayra when transmitted by Sa'īd ibn al-Musayyib and Qays ibn Abī Ḥāzim (Kūfan, d. 84–98/703–16).[60] The variant transmissions from Abū Hurayra by al-A'raj ('Abd al-Raḥmān ibn Hurmuz, Medinan, d. 110/728) are also worth noting, for only when they are reported from him by Abū Ṣāliḥ 'Abd Allāh ibn al-Faḍl (Medinan, d. *ca.* 120/737) and Ja'far ibn Rabī'a (Egyptian, d. 136/753) are the Turks mentioned by name.[61] On the other hand, when the report is transmitted through the link Zuhrī ← al-A'raj, then no such reference of the name appears.[62] And the link Abū l-Zinād ('Abd Allāh ibn Dhakwān, Medinan, d. 130–32/747–49) ← al-A'raj, is even more suggestive because it splits during the generation that reported from Abū l-Zinād. Note specifically that Abū l-Yamān, Shu'ayb and Warqā' report from him variants mentioning the Turks by name, while the one reported by Sufyān ibn 'Uyayna does not.[63] But before one jumps to the conclusion that Ibn 'Uyayna was probably the one responsible for mentioning the Turks by name, it is worth noting that when he reports from the *isnāds* of Zuhrī ← Ibn al-Musayyib and Zuhrī ← al-A'raj, no such reference to the Turks appears. Moreover, from a note made by Bukhārī on Ibn 'Uyayna's report from Zuhrī ← al-A'raj, we learn that the descriptive phrase "small-eyed, flat-nosed, with faces like flattened shields" was actually an addition made by Abū l-Zinād when reporting the tradition of al-A'raj.[64] To this, one may add the comment made by Muḥammad ibn 'Abbād (d. 234/848) when reporting the Ibn 'Uyayna ← Abū l-Zinād

[60]Ḥumaydī 2/269; Nu'aym ibn Ḥammād 192r; Bukhārī, *Ṣaḥīḥ* 3/233; Muslim 8/184; Abū Dāwūd 4/112; Ibn Māja 2/1371; Basawī 3/161–62; Ibn Ḥibbān, *Ṣaḥīḥ* 8/263; Bayhaqī, *Sunan* 9/175; Qurṭubī, *Tadhkira* 2/319. See also Nu'aym ibn Ḥammād 191r–v, for one isolated variant of al-Faḍl ibn 'Amr ibn Umayya al-Ḍamrī and another attributed to Abū Hurayra by Zuhrī in a *maqṭū'* form, where similar descriptive elements are cited, but without explicitly saying that those referred to are the Turks.

[61]Bukhārī, *Ṣaḥīḥ* 3/233; Muslim 8/184; Abū Dāwūd 4/112; Ibn Ḥibbān, *Ṣaḥīḥ* 8/263; Nasā'ī, *Sunan* 6/44–45; Ḥākim 4/475–76; Hammām ibn Munabbih (d. 132/749), *Ṣaḥīfa*, ed. Rif'at 'Abd al-Muṭṭalib, Maktabat al-Khānjī, Cairo 1985, the margin of 632.

[62]Ṭabarānī, *al-Mu'jam al-Awsaṭ* 1/60; Ibn 'Asākir 19/145.

[63]See Abū Nu'aym, *Dalā'il* 475; Ibn Kathīr, *Nihāya* 1/19, quoting Bukhārī.

[64]Bukhārī, *Ṣaḥīḥ* 3/233.

← al-A'raj variant: "It has reached me," he says, "that the followers of Bābak had hairy boots" (*balaghanī anna aṣḥāba bābak kānat ni'āluhumu l-sha'r*).[65]

Other less-circulated variants and traditions are also worth noting. As transmitted by Hammām ibn Munabbih (d. 132/749), the Abū Hurayra tradition mentions, instead of the Turks, both "Khūz and Kirmān from among the *a'ājim*."[66] Fighting against the Turks is mentioned in an isolated tradition attributed to 'Umar, not the Prophet, and as such was cited in the context of an account of an actual Muslim war against them on the eastern front during 'Umar's time.[67] There is also one tradition, attributed to the Prophet in a *mursal* form by al-Ḥasan al-Baṣrī, that contains an interesting comment identifying people with faces like flattened shields as Turks, and those who wear hairy boots as Kurds.[68]

Unclear in formulation, but vivid and rich in details, these traditions reflect, above all, certain cross-currents and ambivalences in the complex process of absorbing a strong neighbour and an enemy into Islam, and the rise, from the second/eighth century on, of the Turkish element in the life of the Muslim state. The task of giving a full account of the appearance of the Turks on the scene and the relations between them and the early caliphate lies beyond the scope of this study. From a few scattered reports at hand, we learn of a Turkish raid on Adharbayjān and an order by 'Umar II to fight them in the year 99/717.[69] During Hishām's reign and throughout the years 108–14/726–32, fierce fighting was continuously conducted against them in Farghāna and Samarqand.[70] In the year 117/735 we hear about a major attack by Turks on Khurāsān.[71] Other engagements with them

---

[65]Bayhaqī, *Sunan* 9/176. On the uprising of Bābak al-Khurramī in the year 221/836, see Mas'ūdī, *Murūj* 2/350–52.

[66]This was reported by 'Abd al-Razzāq ← Ma'mar. See Ibn Ḥibbān, *Ṣaḥīḥ* 8/262; Ḥākim 4/476; Bayhaqī, *Dalā'il* 6/336; *idem*, *Sunan* 9/176; Qurṭubī, *Tadhkira* 2/319; Suyūṭī, *Khaṣā'iṣ* 2/112, quoting Bukhārī.

[67]Abū Nu'aym, *Dalā'il* 475–76.

[68]Nu'aym ibn Ḥammād 192r.

[69]Ibn 'Asākir 10/349, quoting Khalīfa ibn Khayyāṭ.

[70]*Ibid.* 4/45, 16/444, 447.

[71]*Ibid.* 2/800, quoting Khalīfa.

were recorded for the years 142–43/759–60 and 147/764.[72] And the recognition of their rising military power seems to have stood behind the decision of the early ʿAbbāsid caliphs Manṣūr and Mahdī to recruit them for the struggle against the Khārijites.[73] From that time on, their importance as a military force consistently continued to rise and reached a new peak during the reign of al-Mutawakkil (d. 247/861),[74] which was also the background for Jāḥiẓ' essay on their merits, cited above. Though the author's purpose was explicitly stated as one of harmonization, not preference, he could not but say that fighting was as characteristic of the Turks as wisdom was of the Greeks, manufacturing for the Chinese, poetry and rhetoric for the Arabs, and so forth. In this respect, Jāḥiẓ also cited Ḥamīd ibn ʿAbd al-Ḥamīd's answer to the caliph Ma'mūn, saying that granted the choice to fight Turks or Khārijites, he would certainly choose the latter.[75]

During certain periods of Muslim history, the role of Islamized Turkish dynasties, like the Seljuks and Ottomans, became predominant. This naturally provided favourable ground for promoting Turkish merits. However, this could not have been done since it would have undermined the position of the Arabs, whose precedence had by that time established deep roots; it was, after all, the Arabs who had given Islam its scriptures, its prophethood, its caliphate, and so forth. In the words of several scholars who lived during and immediately after the rise of the Ottomans to power in the early tenth century AH, to say: "Rather the injustice of the Turks than the justice of the Arabs" (*jawru l-turki wa-lā ʿadlu l-ʿarab*) was not only "vile talk" (*kalām sāqiṭ*), but also "manifest unbelief" (*kufr ṣarīḥ*).[76]

[72]Basawī 1/127, 132.

[73]ʿAskarī 184, quoting Jāḥiẓ. Concerning Manṣūr's policy in this respect, compare also with the Syriac source in Chabot, ed. and trans., *Chronique de Denys de Tell-Maḥre*, 84/72; cf. P. Crone, *Slaves on Horses*, Cambridge 1980, 16.

[74]Cf. Goldziher, *Muslim Studies* 1/140.

[75]Jāḥiẓ, *Manāqib al-Turk* 17, 25–35, 45–47.

[76]Samhūdī 93; al-Qārī, *al-Maṣnūʿ Fī Maʿrifat al-Ḥadīth al-Mawḍūʿ*, ed. ʿAbd al-Fattāḥ Abū Ghudda, Maktabat al-Maṭbūʿāt al-Islāmīya, Aleppo 1969, 69. This saying was briefly noted by Goldziher, *Muslim Studies*, 1/246 as a proverb "which probably came into being in later times."

CHAPTER VI

SUMMARY DISCUSSION AND CONCLUDING NOTES

THE PRESENT WORK was initially stimulated by the feeling that the way modern scholarship has dealt with the issues concerning the relations between Arabs and non-Arabs in early Islam has left both major and minor gaps to be filled. In particular, research thus far has focused primarily on the evidence of historical texts, and has paid only slight attention to the rich and varied materials in *ḥadīth* and *tafsīr*. One must of course concede that this material is basically anachronistic, representing retrojections of later controversies, but the fact that almost all currents are represented in it adds to rather than detracts from its value for historical research.

As the present work has implicitly shown, the methodological problems facing modern scholarship on such matters are also of a conceptual nature. Failure to deal with the relations between Arabs and non-Arabs beyond the paradigm of conquerors and converted from among the conquered has been a major factor behind the inability of contemporary research to come to terms with the sharp discrepancies in the relevant material. To all intents, an *a priori* acceptance of the notion that the Arab polity and Islam coincided right from the outset, i.e. that Islam, in more or less the classical form that has reached us, was from the beginning the religious project of whatever political entity the Arabs had in the seventh century AD, is not sustained by Muslim tradition itself if the latter is subjected to critical scrutiny. Moreover, it must be recognized that in order to move such a scheme from the domain of chimera to that of historical reality, one must presume the operation of certain material and physical factors. But that is in itself problematic. The proposition that Arabia could have constituted the source of the vast material power required to effect such changes in world affairs within so short a span of time is, to say the least, a thesis calling for proof and substantiation rather than a secure foundation upon which one can build. One may observe, for example, that in spite of all its twentieth-century oil wealth, Arabia still does not possess such material and spiritual might. And at least as extraordinary is the disappearance of most past legacies in a wide area of the utmost diversity in languages, ethnicities, cultures, and religions. One of the most important developments in contemporary scholarship is the mounting evidence that these were not simply and suddenly swallowed up by Arabian Islam in the early seventh century, but this is precisely the picture that the Arabic historical sources of the third/ninth century present.

True, mainstream traditional Islam from the late second/eighth century on pulled constantly towards the classical scheme of the relationship between Arabism and Islam. To give a full assessment of the objective historical factors behind this development has not been the aim of the present work, which has rather sought to examine the literary process that reflects this steady but gradual shift, in as much as the issues under discussion here are concerned. By applying a method of *isnād* analysis as well as a thematic investigation into the material at hand, we have arrived at certain conclusions concerning not only the dates and historical circumstances in which Arab particularism and Islamic religious universalism were fused, but also concerning such realities as may have prevailed prior to this fusion.

As implied on several occasions throughout this work, its conclusions are not offered as discoveries of currents and themes previously unknown to modern scholarship; many of these have been familiar since the time of Goldziher and Wellhausen. Rather, an attempt has been made here to reset these within a new paradigm based on the profuse and valuable evidence of Muslim tradition in the fields of *ḥadīth* and *tafsīr*; in doing do, our aim has been to provide a more comprehensive framework for analysis and comparison and a better understanding of questions hitherto overlooked or underestimated.

Above all, there is the fact already noted by some scholars that while the Qur'ān reveals a clear consciousness of difference, it actually expresses no ethnic or racial prejudice at all. Furthermore, it reveals no explicit awareness of the Arabs as a separate nation and does not identify Muḥammad along ethnic lines, much less express preference for the Arabs as his people. At the same time, the bedouins (*a'rāb*) are often referred to in contexts of blasphemy, hypocrisy, unbelief, unwillingness to fight for the cause of Islam and so forth. It is only from Qatāda that one can detect any attempt to diffuse the sting of Qur'ānic deprecation by saying that the verses concerned refer only to individual tribes and not to all the bedouins.

The Qur'ānic current that predominantly demeans bedouins finds clear support in numerous *ḥadīth* statements portraying bedouins in very dark colours and contrasting bedouin life, habits and so forth, to the *hijra* of believing Muslims. One notices that these statements are very old as, to use one of Schacht's dating criteria, they were attributed to the Prophet in *mursal* forms by transmitters who lived in the early second/eighth century. Similar attitudes were also attributed to the caliph 'Umar I and were reported as the personal positions of the early second/eighth-century figures Sha'bī and Ḥasan al-Baṣrī, who, it seems, were considered authorities solid enough to be invoked.

The Qur'ānic term *umma* initially seems not to have denoted a national or ethnic entity. At least, this is how it was understood and presented by most exegetical figures down to the mid-second/eighth century, including Sa'īd ibn Jubayr, 'Ikrima, al-Ḍaḥḥāk ibn Muzāḥim, Mujāhid, Suddī, Yazīd al-Naḥawī, 'Aṭā' al-Khurāsānī, 'Aṭīya al-'Awfī and Ibn Jurayj. These either interpreted the term as referring to individual Companions of the Prophet or said that it generally referred to "the best of people." A current of clear Shī'ī colouring, represented by a tradition of al-Bāqir, interpreted it as referring to the Prophet's relatives. The earliest attempt to interpret *umma* along ethnic lines, albeit only in an implicit way, is connected with the name of al-Rabī' ibn Anas alone, though later attempts were recorded to "improve" the *isnād*, to use Schacht's term, by extending it from Rabī' backwards to the generation of the Companions.

The same should be noted for the traditional current that comments on certain Qur'ānic statements by saying that the Prophet was sent to all mankind, i.e. not particularly to the Arabs. Here, the same traditions that were attributed by Mujāhid to the Prophet in *mursal* forms later acquired full *isnāds*, providing another example of what Schacht terms as the tendency of the *isnāds* of later traditions to grow backwards and to assume finer and more polished forms.

The notion that the Prophet was not sent just to the Arabs gains further support from the self-identifying epithet "master of all mankind" (*sayyidu wuldi ādam*) attributed to him. We also notice that this was the main current, and that the epithet "master of the Arabs" was variously connected with ʻAlī, Abū Bakr, ʻAbbās and other figures all the way down to the early ʻAbbāsid era. On the other hand, there is a clear early second/eighth-century attempt, associated with the name of Ḥasan al-Baṣrī, to boost the ethnic identity of the Prophet by giving him the epithet "forerunner (*sābiq*) of the Arabs," while his three non-Arab Companions Salmān, Ṣuhayb and Bilāl receive parallel epithets through which each represents his own people (Persians, Byzantines and Abyssinians). The implicit references to such non-Arab Companions and their peoples, especially the Persians, should in all probability be seen as representative of a major exegetical current on several Qur'ānic verses. Of these, a special note has been made of Sūrat al-Ḥujurāt (49), v. 13, to which a Prophetic statement was attached in the first half of the second/eighth century, warning explicitly against preference for Arabs over non-Arabs.

Both the Qur'ān itself and Qur'ānic exegesis of the early to mid-second/eighth century are thus completely silent concerning the ethnic character of the message of the Prophet. Anywhere that the bedouins or bedouin life are referred to as a group or a category in either Qur'ānic exegesis or *ḥadīth* literature, it is by way of demeaning and in terms of contempt that this is done. At the same time, there is a strong current in both genres that makes direct reference to non-Arab individuals and ethnic groups who were either active during Muḥammad's lifetime or to whom his message was also directed—with a strong emphasis on the universalist and egalitarian character of this message.

To all intents, such a state of affairs stands in clear contrast to the traditional current that attributes to the Prophet statements of pure nationalistic character *vis-à-vis* the Persians and Byzantines. However, a close examination of the *isnād* information on such statements clearly shows that these were the creations of tradents who lived around the mid-second/eighth century, a period in which we believe the great fusion between Arabism and Islam reached its culmination.

Though the present work has not aimed at a thorough investigation of the early Muslim conquests, note has been made of several instances in *futūḥ* reports where "the Arab forces" are separately identified. That the Arabs politically benefited from the collapse of Persian and Byzantine rule in the area and played a role in these developments is of course not to be denied. What cannot be accepted on face value is the assumption that such a role was part of a religious project of the Arabs right from the outset. The main thesis forwarded in the course of this study is that the first/seventh century witnessed two parallel, albeit initially separate processes: the rise of the Arab polity on the one hand, and the beginnings of a religious movement that eventually crystallized into Islam. It was only in the beginning of the second/eighth century and throughout it, and for reasons that have yet to be explained, that the two processes were fused, resulting in the birth of Arabian Islam as we know it, i.e. in the Islamization of the Arab polity and the Arabization of the new religion.

Our traditional sources of the second/eighth century are, in a sense, mostly the literary expression of the discussions and debates that culminated in this fusion. To demonstrate this proposition, several examples have been given of discrimination between Arabs and non-Arabs within the framework of the Arab polity that was emerging in the first/seventh-century; these include discussions of the possibility of enslaving Arabs, exempting Arabs from the payment of tithes, and permitting mixed marriages with non-Arabs. These cases stimulated no explanation—let alone religious justification—by scholars throughout the second/eighth century. Similar queries may be raised concerning the reports on issues of discriminatory treatment of Arab tribes that persisted in rejecting conversion to Islam, like Banū Taghlib. Here, it has been highly suggestive to note that the second/eighth and early third/ninth-century authorities Thawrī, Abū Ḥanīfa, Shāfiʿī and Ibn Ḥanbal held such a discriminatory position, relying on a Kūfan tradition that attributed this position to ʿUmar I. The issue of discriminating between non-Muslim Arabs and non-Arabs in the field of payment of *jizya* was also a matter of hot controversy between Mālik ibn Anas, Shāfiʿī, Abū ʿUbayd and other contemporaries of theirs. And beyond the general question of what sort of Islam there was in the second/eighth century, there is the fact that behind ʿUmar I's policy towards Banū Taghlib lie mainly political and military, not religious considerations. As for the traditional lore concerning the issue that only Muslims could live in Arabia, a close examination of this reveals that the attribution of such policies to ʿUmar I and others, concerning the Jews of Khaybar and the Christians of Najrān, was the work of the generation of Zuhrī, Ḥasan al-Baṣrī and ʿUmar II. There is also the unique information occasionally cited by Ibn ʿAsākir that during the reigns of ʿAbd al-Malik and Hishām, separate registers (*dawāwīn*) were kept for Arabs and non-Arabs.

It is only within this new scheme that one can understand the policies attributed to ʿUmar I to distinguish between Arabs and non-Arabs in the fields of settlement, occupation, etc., and his order to refrain from imitating *ʿajam* in speech, dress fashions and habits. As one would expect, some traditional attempts to connect the same policies and attitudes with the name of the Prophet were also recorded, though reports stating that he conceded certain non-Arab practices were also not lacking. A thorough examination of the relevant material shows, however, that such attempts belong only to the second/eighth century. And in the case of the Prophet's reported prohibition of imitating *aʿājim* in kissing the hands of their kings, one cannot but notice the existence of information to the contrary concerning not only the Prophet, but also the caliphs ʿUmar I and ʿAbd al-Malik. In fact, the only caliphs who reportedly did not allow people to kiss their hands were the second/eighth-century rulers Hishām, Mahdī and Ma'mūn. As for another reported injunction by the Prophet, the prohibition of the *aʿjamī* practice of mentioning the name of the addressee at the beginning of a letter, note should be made that such a Prophetic sanction was not known to a scholar as late as Shaybānī, who instead relied on the reports concerning practices during the times of Muʿāwiya and ʿAbd al-Malik for ruling that there is no objection to writing in this way.

Other first/seventh century figures like ʿAlī ibn Abī Ṭālib, ʿAbd Allāh ibn ʿAmr and Ziyād ibn Abī Sufyan were reported to have differentiated between Arabs and non-Arabs in terms of occupation. And the case of the people of Kūfa rejecting the appointment of Saʿīd ibn

Jubayr to a judgeship during the time of Ḥajjāj, on the ground that he was a *mawlā*, is one in point. But probably the most important field in which discrimination was reported was the issue of worthiness (*kafā'a*) in marriage, and specifically, mixed marriages between Arabs and non-Arabs. The statements attributed to non-Arab Companions like Salmān al-Fārisī and the actual cases of his and the black-skinned Bilāl's attempts to marry Arab women are important ones in this respect. One also cannot ignore the reports that 'Umar I, Mu'āwiya, 'Umar II, Ḥasan al-Baṣrī, Zuhrī, and even personalities as late as Ibn Jurayj and Thawrī, stood strongly against mixed marriages. Other reports do not fail to note that to be the offspring of a mixed marriage (*hajīn*) was not an easy position for even the Umayyad princes, sons and grandsons of the caliph 'Abd al-Malik. And on the whole, the policies of Mu'āwiya, 'Abd al-Malik, Sulaymān ibn 'Abd al-Malik and 'Umar II are reported to have been pro-Arab. As for the 'Abbāsid movement (*da'wa*) and early state, recent research has clearly shown that in spite of the fact that non-Arabs took an active part in them, both remained basically Arab in leadership and political aspiration. To be of non-Arab descent was difficult for a person as eminent as Abū Ḥanīfa and other prominent figures of the nascent legal school based on the doctrine of independent legal reasoning (*aṣḥāb al-ra'y*), just as it had been for Umayyad *hajīn* princes half a century earlier. And as the case of Ibn Ḥanbal shows, not to boast of one's pure Arab descent was considered a great merit even in the first half of the third/ninth century.

As against what we believe to have been initially a non-national character of the new religion, the impact of the rising Arab polity on it is clearly reflected in the attempts to stress the national Arabian identity of the prophet of Islam and of Arabic as the divine tool of revelation. Concerning the Prophet, these attempts centred around interpretation of the Qur'ānic adjectives *ummī* and *ummīyūn*. Though the available traditional material is not totally conclusive, we can discern an early phase of a passage from interpretation of the terms as denoting those who are other than "People of the Book" to identifying those who do not have / recite a scripture, i.e. the Arab polytheists. This step was connected with the name of Ibn 'Abbās by the mid-second/eighth century Ibn Jurayj, albeit on unspecified authority. The second phase was to drop polytheism and illiteracy and to assert simply that *ummī* and *ummīyūn* denote an Arab prophet and Arabs, respectively. This was traditionally connected with the names of the contemporaries of Ibn Jurayj, Sa'īd ibn Abī 'Arūba, Asbāṭ and al-Rabī' ibn Anas.

We have sufficient grounds for believing that this development in Qur'ānic exegesis was part of a general process, during the early to mid-second/eighth century, which marked the assertion of the national character of the Prophet and his message to the Arabs. For we also notice that the same traditions that attributed to Muḥammad statements or deeds promoting his Arab attributes or those of the Arabs in general, were reported either in *mursal* forms by the early second/eighth-century Khālid ibn Ma'dān or as the personal statements of his younger contemporary, Zuhrī.

Certainly, clear support for this current was provided by several Qur'ānic passages in which the Qur'ān is described as a scripture in Arabic. The notion, however, that Arabic was a divine tool of revelation seems clearly to have risen around the turn of the first/seventh century. It is prominently connected with the name of Muḥammad al-Bāqir, who in several cases transmitted Prophetic traditions to that effect in *mursal* forms, while later formulations add to the chain of transmitters the link of the Companion Jābir between Muḥammad al-Bāqir and the Prophet. Al-Bāqir's contemporaries, Wahb ibn Munabbih and Zuhrī, are cited as saying themselves that Arabic was God's choice for the divine language of Paradise. But the case of Zuhrī is another example where the tendency of *isnāds* to grow backwards can clearly be seen. Only one generation after Zuhrī the same notion was attributed in a full *isnād* through him to the Prophet.

Towards the late second/eighth–early third/ninth century, a supplementary element was attached to this original core that demeaned non-Arabic languages, especially Persian, and prohibited people from learning or speaking them; not unexpectedly, this notion also provoked an opposing counter-current. However, reviewing the earlier material that cites first/seventh century figures as urging the spread of the learning of Arabic, one clearly notices the absence of any religious motives behind the policies of 'Umar I, Mu'āwiya and 'Abd al-Malik, whose explicitly stated aims were to increase manliness (*muruwwa*) and to facilitate the governing of the Arabs, etc., and who often urged the learning of astronomy and genealogy as well. We also notice that in the case of ʿUmar I, some early to mid-second/eighth century attempts were made to rehabilitate his motives by attributing to him the line of reasoning that learning Arabic was necessary for knowledge of the scriptures. This was pursued in a tradition of ʿAṭā' ibn Abī Rabāḥ and two *mursal* reports by Ḥasan al-Baṣrī and Ghālib al-Qaṭṭān. The case of ʿAṭā' is especially interesting because he also attributed almost the same claim to the Prophet in a tradition whose full *isnād* goes back through Abū Hurayra.

In any case, the rise of the position of Arabic as the language of scripture and the assertion of the Arabian attributes of the Prophet and his people from the early second/eighth century on was simultaneous with the rehabilitation of the image of bedouins as the core of the emerging national Arabian identity. Again, our available *isnād* information points to the generation between ʿUmar II, Zuhrī and Ṣāliḥ ibn Kaysān as most active in this field—whether by teaching the bedouins (i.e. spreading religion among them), circulating a Prophetic saying that those from among them who are converted to Islam must not be treated as bedouins, and even referring in a very curious way to the message of Muḥammad as "the religion of the bedouin" (*dīn al-aʿrābī*). The passage from bedouinism to Arabism was expressed by another contemporary of this group, the poet Jarīr, who says that the name *aʿrāb* is only a pejorative one given by non-Arabs, and that the proper name to be used is "Arabs."

The improvement in the position of Arabs as a result of these developments was tremendous. From the two mid-second/eighth century authorities Ibn Jurayj and ʿAwf al-Aʿrābī we hear of traditions that say that being an Arab whose tongue is not *aʿjamī* is an important condition for the recitation of the Qur'ān and leading Muslims in prayer. To the position of Arabic as a sacred language was soon added the Arabian ethnicity of Muḥammad as the second focal point around which traditions extolling the merits of Arabs revolved. These traditions urge love of the Arabs for these two reasons: thus, for example, they connect loving and hating them with loving and hating the Prophet, promote the notion that Arabs are actually God's choice from among all peoples and creatures, establish their leading position together with that of Quraysh, warn against cheating or slandering Arabs, urge the safeguarding of their well being, and assert that their survival is light in Islam. An investigation into the *isnāds* of such traditions shows that they were usually circulated by mid-second/eighth century authorities who reported them from the generation of Thābit al-Bunānī, ʻAmr ibn Dīnār, ʻAṭā' ibn Abī Maymūna, ʻAlī ibn Zayd ibn Judʻān, al-ʻAlā' ibn ʻAbd al-Raḥmān and others.

Needless to say, this is not meant to imply that such a great fusion was an easy or a smooth one. After all, Arabian Islam eventually developed into a faith that engulfed other ethnicities and races. And though Islam retained and still retains highly important features from the crucial period of its fusion with Arabism, its far-ranging spread ensured that its initial universalist and egalitarian elements would not be completely vitiated, and in certain cases this diffusion even imparted to these elements a new impetus. On the level of inter-ethnic and interracial relations, the traditional material reveals the high complexity not only of keeping alive these early universalist features within the framework of Arabian Islam, but also of engulfing other ethnicities, cultures, and races that converted, came under the rule of the caliphate, or lived in neighbouring regions. The ambivalences of universalist acceptance and particularistic rejection, as well as the contempt and fear of Muslim Arabs towards non-Arabs in daily life and in the form of eschatological speculations, reflect, after all, the historical sensitivity and insecurity of the Arabs in an area that has constituted from time immemorial what may be termed as the path of world empires, where a rich mosaic of cultures, religions and other legacies, together with political and economic cross-interests and pressures, makes its presence felt.

It is within this framework of a highly sensitive balance between inter-dependence and particularism that the attitudes that Arabian Islam developed towards other ethnicities must be considered. As such, the scheme of tribal genealogical relations that in the Old Testament reflect the relations between the Israelites and other nations was also applied by Arabian Islam. Here, the case of relating not only Judaism to Islam but also the Jews to the Arabs was repeated in varying degrees in the cases of Persians, Copts, Abyssinians, Byzantines, Turks and possibly others as well. Clearly, the initial position of Islam as a universal heir and continuator of previous messages of prophets and saintly figures, both Judeo-Christians and those of other peoples too, facilitated their acceptance within the above-mentioned scheme. However, the degree of such acceptance varied from one case to another in a way that corresponded to the actual facts on the ground, e.g. the degree of receptivity or resistance of each of these peoples to Arabization and Islamization, and other circumstantial factors. Hence the Persians, for example, were accepted by one major current as sons of Isaac and cousins to the Arabs, the sons of Ishmael. The fact of their support for the ʿAbbāsid movement and early state gave rise to other traditions that described them as supporters of the people of the house of the Prophet or even as God's army upon earth, promoted certain groups of pious Muslims from among them to the rank of Quraysh, and so forth.

The same can be noted in the way in which the Copts of Egypt were related to Arabian Islam through the marital relations of both Abraham and Muḥammad with them. The case of the Copts proves to be the easiest historically because, after a continuous chain of almost yearly uprisings throughout the second/eighth and early third/ninth centuries, Egypt was eventually Islamized and Arabized. The conclusive *isnād* information on the traditions recommending good treatment of the Copts on account of this scheme of marital relations shows that they were the product of the generation of Zuhrī, Makhūl and al-Bāqir, and constitutes a clear—albeit indirect—proof that this was the period when perceptions of Islam as an Arabian religion began to crystallize.

More problematic was the attempt to include the Turks within this scheme of genealogical relationship to the Arabs. The ambivalent attitude towards the Turks that one encounters in early *ḥadīth* and *tafsīr* must be explained against the background that they were historically a strong neighbouring nation that constituted a genuine military threat to the caliphate prior to their conversion and rise to a high administrative and military position from the third/ninth century on. With this transition, the old statements that viewed this eastern enemy as descendants of the eschatological Gog and Magog, whose overpowering of the Arabs was in some quarters anticipated as one of the signs for the end of times, and with whom clashes should therefore be avoided, gave way to a new approach that found a proper place for the Turks within the scheme of genealogical relationship to the Arabs. Our investigation has led us to the conclusion that such a shift of attitude was effected around the beginning of the third/ninth century, with al-Haytham ibn ʻAdī being one of the names associated with it.

The deep sense of historical insecurity within Arabian Islam cannot be fully appreciated without taking into consideration the prolonged enmity of the Byzantines on its northern frontier. An investigation that we have conducted on a previous occasion completes the picture of the deep insecurity that the emerging Arabian Islam felt, and that in both *ḥadīth* and *tafsīr* was expressed in apocalyptic speculations concerning the imminent threat of a reconquest of Syria by the whole Christian world under Byzantine leadership. There, it has been shown that such speculations, which were also predominantly seen as events preceding the end of times, were actually portrayed along lines similar to the ones drawn for the Arabs' occupation of Syria.

Of an even more complicated nature are the attitudes of Arabian Islam towards blacks. As clearly reflected in the traditional material reviewed above, complex attitudes arose from a number of factors. One of these was an old local Meccan tradition involving eschatological speculations about an expected Abyssinian attack upon and destruction of the Kaʻba—an anxiety entirely disproportionate to any real threat that Abyssinia ever posed to Islam, its hostility to the new faith notwithstanding. Hence, the cause for the intensity of such anxiety must be sought in the absorption into traditional Islam of a local tradition that probably reflects the fearful impressions of an Abyssinian campaign in pre-Islamic times and a possible military presence of forces from Abyssinia in Arabia sometime in the first/seventh century. As for the approximate period in which such absorption was achieved, our investigation points clearly to the generation of those who reported it from Mujāhid's main Meccan transmitter, Ibn Abī Najīh, i.e. tradents active in the second quarter of the second/eighth century, especially Ibn Isḥāq, Ibn Jurayj and Sufyān al-Thawrī.

Another factor influencing the negative attitude towards blacks was clearly the existence of a substantial number of black slaves (known as the Zanj) concentrated in southern Iraq, especially around Baṣra. This community constituted a hotbed of social unrest as early as the late first/seventh century, and in the mid-third/ninth century this culminated in a general uprising that lasted for fifteen years and posed a major threat to the caliphate. Our investigation points clearly to the emergence in that area of a popular slogan that demeaned blacks as folk who "steal when they are hungry and fornicate when they are sated" and warned against acquiring them for service. We could also identify certain Baṣran figures, like ʿAnbasa al-Baṣrī, who in the second half of the second/eighth century circulated this slogan in the form of a statement by the Prophet.

Blacks were recognized within the scheme of relationship to the Arabs (as the sons of Ham); but according to one exegetical tradition, their colour was a punishment from God because Ham saw his father Noah naked. And indeed, in one variant of a tradition on worthiness for marriage sharp warning was made against black colour as "a trait of disfigurement."

As against this anti-Zanjī current, certain attempts were also made to diffuse the sting by pointing to the good qualities of blacks. Traditionally, these attempts relied upon a third factor that determined the attitude of Arabian Islam to blacks, namely the existence of a group of pious figures in early Islam like Bilāl, the Negus and Mihjaʿ, or the saintly black Luqmān, who was recognized in the Qur'ān. Indeed, reference to these figures as "masters of the people of Paradise" is made by some traditions that extol the merits of black slaves (*sūdān*) and urge people to acquire them, saying that they bring blessedness, etc. One may even add that the saying "obey even a black slave," which Lewis rightly noted as a rhetoric device, and which our investigation has confirmed as an attempt to promote absolute obedience to authority, still carries within it a grain of early Muslim egalitarianism.

Beyond this category of peoples that occupied the main attention of Arabian Islam, occasional references to other ethnic or racial groups were also made. Of these, mention may be made of Nabaṭ (remnants of the Aramaean peasantry population), ʿUbbād (Christians of Kūfa), Zuṭṭ (possibly the gypsies), Kurds, Berbers, Khazars (or Khūz), Kirmān, Indians and Slavs (*ṣaqāliba*). The scarcity of statements concerning some of these, like Indians, Slavs or even Berbers, may be explained by the fact that they were far away from the central scene of the caliphate and their presence was not closely felt. Note that the Slavs were still incorporated into the scheme of relationship to the Arabs through their identification as sons of Japheth, though it was immediately added that "no good resides amongst them." Others, like the Khūz, Kirmān, and Kurds, were occasionally incorporated into the traditional lore warning against the Turks. Prejudice against the Zuṭṭ was expressed by presenting them as resembling the Angel of Death on account of their dark skin and huge physical proportions. And the 'Ubbād were noted only as being most unfortunate because of the rise of Islam (*ashqā l-nāsi bi-l-islām*)—possibly a comment on their refusal to convert.

Indeed, out of this group, only the Nabaṭ or Anbāṭ gained a substantial representation in the tradition of Arabian Islam. From the contents of the relevant statements reviewed above, it becomes clear that this group, which was the quickest to dissolve culturally and linguistically into the emerging Arab ethnicity, was despised rather from a social and occupational standpoint, a fact that gives support to von Grunebaum's observation that the "nationalistic ideal" that the town dwellers in the Near East adopted with the rise of Arabian Islam was that of a "bedouin nation."

GENERAL BIBLIOGRAPHY

The following list includes only the sources cited in the course of the present work. In the alphabetical order followed here, the Arabic definite article *al-*, as well as diacritical marks and variations in transliteration, have been disregarded. The works included in this list appear under the name by which the author was best known, whether personal, professional, *kunya*, *nisba*, etc.

ʿAbd ibn Ḥumayd al-Kissī, Abū Muḥammad (d. 249/861), *al-Muntakhab Min al-Musnad*, ed. Ṣubḥī al-Sāmarrāʾī and Maḥmūd al-Ṣaʿīdī, Maktabat al-Sunna, Cairo 1988.

ʿAbd al-Razzāq ibn Hammām al-Ṣanʿānī, Abū Bakr (d. 211/826), *al-Muṣannaf*, ed. Ḥabīb al-Raḥmān al-Aʿẓamī, al-Maktab al-Islāmī, Beirut 1983.

———, *Tafsīr*, Ms. Cairo, Dār al-Kutub, *Tafsīr* no. 242.

al-ʿAbdī, Abū ʿAlī, *Ḥadīth*, Ms. Damascus, Ẓāhirīya, *Majmūʿ* no. 22.

Abū l-ʿArab Muḥammad ibn Aḥmad al-Tamīmī (d. 333/944), *Kitāb al-Miḥan*, ed. Yaḥyā al-Jabbūrī, Dār al-Gharb al-Islāmī, Qaṭar 1983.

Abū l-Baqāʾ Hibat Allāh al-Ḥillī (d. early sixth/twelfth c.), *al-Manāqib al-Mazyadīya*, ed. Ṣāliḥ Darādka and Muḥammad Khraysāt, Maktabat al-Risāla al-Ḥadītha, Amman 1984.

Abū Dāwūd Sulaymān ibn al-Ashʿath al-Sijistānī (d. 275/888), *Sunan*, Dār al-Kutub al-ʿIlmīya, Beirut n.d.

Abū Ḥayyān al-Tawḥīdī, ʿAlī ibn Muḥammad ibn al-ʿAbbās (d. 444/1052), *al-Baṣāʾir wa-l-Dhakhāʾir*, ed. Wadād al-Qāḍī, Beirut 1988.

Abū Nuʿaym Aḥmad ibn ʿAbd Allāh al-Iṣbahānī (d. 430/1038), *Dalāʾil al-Nubuwwa*, Hyderabad 1950.

———, *Dhikr Akhbār Iṣbahān*, ed. S. Dedering, Leiden 1934.

———, *Ḥilyat al-Awliyāʾ*, Maktabat al-Khānjī and Maṭbaʿat al-Saʿāda, Cairo 1938.

Abū l-Shaykh, Abū Muḥammad ʿAbd Allāh ibn Muḥammad ibn Jaʿfar ibn Ḥayyān (d. 369/979), *Ṣifat al-Janna*, Dār al-Maʾmūn, Damascus 1987.

———, *al-Tawbīkh wa-l-Tanbīh*, ed. Ḥasan ibn al-Mandūḥ, Maktabat al-Tawʿiya al-Islāmīya, Cairo 1408/1987.

Abū Tammān Ḥabīb ibn Aws al-Ṭā'ī (d. 236/850), *Kitab Ash'ār al-Ḥamāsa*, ed. G. Freytag, Bonn 1828–47.

Abū 'Ubayd al-Bakrī al-Awnabī, 'Abd Allāh ibn 'Abd al-'Azīz (d. 487/1094), *Simṭ al-La'ālī, al-La'ālī Fī Sharḥ Amālī l-Qālī*, ed. 'Abd al-'Azīz al-Maymanī, Maṭba'at Lajnat al-Ta'līf wa-l-Tarjama wa-l-Nashr, Cairo 1354/1935.

Abū 'Ubayd al-Qāsim ibn Sallām al-Harawī (d. 224/838), *Gharīb al-Ḥadīth*, ed. Muḥammad 'Abd al-Mu'īd Khān, Hyderabad 1966.

———, *Kitāb al-Amwāl*, ed. Muḥammad Ḥāmid al-Fiqī, al-Maktaba al-Tijārīya al-Kubrā, Cairo 1353/1934.

Abū 'Ubayda Ma'mar ibn al-Muthannā al-Taymī (d. 210/825), *Majāz al-Qur'ān*, ed. F. Sezgin, Maktabat al-Khānjī, Cairo 1954.

Abū l-'Umaythil al-A'rābī, *Mā Ittafaqa Lafẓuhu wa-Ikhtalafa Ma'nāhu*, Ms. Damascus, Ẓāhirīya, *Majmū'* no. 104.

Abū Ya'lā Aḥmad ibn 'Alī ibn al-Muthannā al-Tamīmī al-Mawṣilī (d. 307/919), *al-Mafārīd*, ed. 'Abd Allāh al-Juday', Maktabat Dār al-Aqṣā, Medina 1985.

———, *al-Musnad*, ed. Ḥusayn Asad, Dār al-Ma'mūn li-l-Turāth, Damascus 1984.

Abū Yūsuf Ya'qūb ibn Ibrāhīm al-Anṣārī (d. 182/798), *Kitāb al-Kharāj*, al-Maṭba'a al-Salafīya, Cairo 1352/1933.

al-'Ajlūnī, Ismā'īl ibn Muḥammad al-Jarrāḥī (d. 1162/1748), *Kashf al-Khafā' wa-Muzīl al-Ilbāl 'Ammā Ishtahara Min al-Ḥadīth 'Alā Alsinat al-Nās*, ed. Muḥammad al-Qallāsh, Maktabat al-Turāth, Aleppo, and Dār Iḥyā' al-Turāth al-'Arabī, Beirut, n.d.

al-Ājurrī, Abū Bakr Muḥammad ibn al-Ḥusayn (d. 360/370), *al-Sharī'a*, Cairo 1950.

al-Akhfash, Aḥmad ibn 'Imrān ibn Salāma (d. 207/822), *Ma'ānī l-Qur'ān*, ed. 'Abd al-Amīr al-Ward, 'Ālam al-Kutub, Beirut 1406/1985.

al-Albānī, Muḥammad Nāṣir al-Dīn, *Silsilat al-Aḥādīth al-Ḍa'īfa wa-Atharuhā al-Sayyi' Fī l-Umma*, al-Maktab al-Islāmī, Beirut 1384/1964.

———, *Silsilat al-Aḥādīth al-Ṣaḥīḥa*, al-Maktab al-Islāmī, Beirut 1979.

al-'Allāf, Abū Bakr, *Amālī*, Ms. Damascus, Ẓāhirīya, *Majmū'* no. 67.

Anonyme Arabische Chronik (possibly Balādhurī's *Ansāb al-Ashrāf*, vol. XI), ed. W. Ahlwardt, Greifswald 1883.

Arberry, A.J., *The Koran Interpreted*, London 1955.

al-Aṣamm, Abū l-'Abbās, *Ḥadīth*, Ms. Damascus, Ẓāhirīya, *Majmū'* no. 31.

al-ʻAskarī, Abū Hilāl al-Ḥasan ibn ʻAbd Allāh ibn Sahl (d. 395/1004), *Kitāb al-Awā'il*, Dār al-Kutub al-ʻIlmīya, Beirut 1987.

al-Azdī, Abū Ismāʻīl Muḥammad ibn ʻAbd Allāh al-Baṣrī (d. 178/794), *Futūḥ al-Shām*, ed. W.N. Lees, Calcutta 1854.

al-Azdī, Abū Zakarīyā Yazīd ibn Muḥammad (d. 334/945), *Tārīkh al-Mawṣil*, ed. ʻAlī Ḥabība, al-Majlis al-Aʻlā li-l-Shu'ūn al-Islāmīya, Lajnat Iḥyā' al-Turāth al-Islāmī, Cairo 1967.

al-Azraqī, Abū l-Walīd Muḥammad ibn ʻAbd Allāh ibn Aḥmad (d. 212–25/827–39), *Akhbār Makka*, ed. F. Wüstenfeld, Göttingen 1285/1868.

al-Baʻalbakī, Muḥyī l-Dīn, *Mashyakha*, Ms. Damascus, Ẓāhirīya, *Majmūʻ* no. 25.

al-Baghawī, Abū Muḥammad al-Ḥusayn ibn Masʻūd al-Farrā' (d. 510/1116), *Maʻālim al-Tanzīl*, Bombay 1273/1856.

al-Baghawī, Abū l-Qāsim, *Mukhtaṣar al-Muʻjam*, Ms. Damascus, Ẓāhirīya, *Majmūʻ* no. 94.

al-Balādhurī, Abū l-Ḥasan Aḥmad ibn Yaḥyā ibn Jābir (d. 279/892), *Ansāb al-Ashraf* vol. I, ed. Muḥammad Ḥamīd Allāh, Dār al-Maʻārif, Cairo 1959.

________, *Ansāb al-Ashrāf*, vol. IVA, ed. Max Schloessinger and M.J. Kister, Jerusalem 1971.

________, *Ansāb al-Ashrāf*, vol. IVB, ed. Max Schloessinger, Jerusalem 1938.

________, *Ansāb al-Ashrāf*, vol. V, ed. S.D. Goitein, Jerusalem 1936.

________, *Futūḥ al-Buldān*, ed. Riḍwān Riḍwān, Dār al-Kutub al-ʻIlmīya, Beirut 1978.

al-Barzanjī, Muḥammad ibn ʻAbd al-Rasūl (d. 1103/1691), *al-Ishāʻa li-Ashrāṭ al-Sāʻa*, Cairo 1393/1973.

al-Barqī, Abū Jaʻfar Aḥmad ibn Muḥammad, *Kitāb al-Maḥāsin*, ed. Muḥammad Ṣādiq Baḥr al-ʻUlūm, al-Maṭbaʻa al-Ḥaydarīya wa-Maktabatuhā, Najaf 1384/1964.

al-Basawī, Abū Yūsuf Yaʻqūb ibn Sufyān (d. 277/890), *al-Maʻrifa wa-l-Tārīkh*, ed. Akram Diyā' al-ʻUmarī, Beirut 1981.

Bashear, S., "Apocalyptic and Other Materials on Early Muslim–Byzantine Wars: a Review of Arabic Sources," *JRAS*, Third Series, 1 (1991), 173–207.

________, "The Mission of Diḥya al-Kalbī and the Situation in Syria," *JSAI* 14 (1991), 84–114.

al-Bayhaqī, Abū Bakr Aḥmad ibn al-Ḥusayn (d. 458/1065), *Dalā'il al-Nubuwwa*, ed. ʻAbd al-Muʻṭī Qalʻajī, Dār al-Kutub al-ʻIlmīya, Beirut 1985.

———, *Shu'ab al-Īmān*, ed. Muḥammad Basyūnī Zaghlūl, Dār al-Kutub al-'Ilmīya, Beirut 1990.

———, *al-Sunan al-Kubrā*, Dār al-Ma'rifa, Beirut 1987.

al-Bazzār, Abū Bakr Aḥmad ibn 'Amr (d. 292/904), *al-Baḥr al-Zakkār Musnad al-Bazzār*, ed. Maḥfūẓ Zayn Allāh, Maktabat al-'Ulūm wa-l-Ḥikam, Medina and Mu'assasat 'Ulūm al-Qur'ān, Beirut 1988.

al-Bazzār, Abū l-Ḥasan, *Faḍā'il Banī Hāshim*, Ms. Damascus, Ẓāhirīya, *Majmū'* no. 103.

Bībī bint 'Abd al-Ṣamad (d. 447/1084), *Juz'*, ed. 'Abd al-Raḥmān al-Faryawā'ī, Dār al-Khulafā' li-l-Kitāb al-Islāmī, Kuwait 1986.

al-Bisṭāmī, Bāyazīd, *Risāla Fī Mas'alat al-Qaḍā' wa-l-Qadar*, Ms. Damascus, Ẓāhirīya no. 4690.

Brock, S.P., "Syriac Views of Emergent Islam," in G.H.A. Juynboll, ed., *Studies on the First Century of Islam*, Carbondale 1982, 14–21.

al-Bukhārī, Abū 'Abd Allāh Muḥammad ibn Ismā'īl (d. 255/868), *al-Adab al-Mufrad*, Maktabat al-Ādāb, Cairo 1979.

———, *Ṣaḥīḥ*, Dār al-Fikr, Beirut 1981.

———, *al-Tārīkh al-Kabīr*, Hyderabad 1380/1960.

Conrad, L.I., "Al-Azdī's History of the Arab Conquests in Bilād al-Shām: Some Historiographical Observations," in Muḥammad 'Adnān al-Bakhīt, ed., *The Fourth International Conference on the History of Bilād al-Shām*, Amman 1987, 28–62.

Crone, P., *Slaves on Horses*, Cambridge 1980.

al-Dāraquṭnī, Abū l-Ḥasan 'Alī ibn 'Umar (d. 385/995), *al-'Ilal al-Wārida Fī l-Aḥādīth al-Nabawīya*, ed. Maḥfūẓ al-Salafī, Dār Ṭayba, Riyadh 1985.

———, *Sunan*, ed. 'Abd Allāh Hāshim Yamānī al-Madīnī, Medina 1966.

al-Daylamī, Abū Shujā' Shīrawayh ibn Shahradār (d. 509/1115), *al-Firdaws bi-Ma'thūr al-Khiṭāb*, ed. Sa'īd Zaghlūl, Dār al-Kutub al-'Ilmīya, Beirut 1986.

al-Dhahabī, Shams al-Dīn Abū 'Abd Allāh Muḥammad ibn Aḥmād ibn 'Uthmān (d. 748/1347), *Mīzān al-I'tidāl Fī Naqd al-Rijāl*, ed. 'Alī al-Bijāwī, Dār al-Ma'rifa, Beirut 1963.

———, *Tārīkh al-Islām*, ed. 'Umar Tadmurī, Dār al-Kitāb al-'Arabī, Beirut 1987–proceeding.

al-Dhakwānī, *Amālī*, Ms. Damascus, Ẓāhirīya, *Majmū'* no. 63.

al-Dhuhalī, Abū Ṭāhir, *Fawā'id*, Ms. in private possession.

Donner, F.M., *The Early Muslim Conquests*, Princeton 1983.

Duri, A.A., *The Historical Formation of the Arab Nation*, trans. L.I. Conrad, London 1987.

al-Fākihī, Abū ʻAbd Allāh Muḥammad ibn Isḥāq ibn al-ʻAbbās (d. *ca.* 272/885), *Tārīkh Makka*, Ms. Leiden, Or. no. 463.

al-Farrā', Abū Zakarīyā Yaḥyā ibn Ziyād (d. 207/822), *Ma'ānī l-Qur'ān*, ed. Aḥmad Najātī and Muḥammad al-Najjār, al-Hay'a al-Miṣrīya al-ʻĀmma li-l-Kitāb, Cairo 1980.

al-Fattanī (d. 986/1578), *Ma'rifat Tadhkirat al-Mawḍū'āt*, Bombay 1342/1923.

al-Fīrūzābādī, Abū Ṭāhir Muḥammad ibn Ya'qūb (d. 817/1414), *Tanwīr al-Miqbās Min Tafsīr Ibn 'Abbās*, Dār al-Jīl, Beirut n.d.

al-Fazārī, Abū Isḥāq Ibrāhīm ibn Muḥammad (d. 186/802), *Kitāb al-Siyar*, ed. Fārūq Ḥamāda, Mu'assasat al-Risāla, Beirut 1987.

Fueck, J., "The Originality of the Arabian Prophet," trans. M. Swartz in his *Studies on Islam*, Oxford 1981, 87–97.

al-Ghumārī, Ibn al-Ṣiddīq, *al-Mughīr 'Alā Ḍa'īf al-Jāmi' al-Ṣaghīr*, Cairo n.d.

Gibb, H.A.R., *Islam*, Oxford 1980.

————, *Studies on the Civilization of Islam*, ed. S.J. Shaw and W.R. Polk, Cambridge, Mass. 1962.

Goitein, S.D., *Studies in Islamic History and Institutions*, Leiden 1966.

Goldziher, I., *Muslim Studies*, ed. and trans. C.R. Barber and S.M. Stern, London 1967–71.

————, *Vorlesungen über den Islam*, Heidelberg 1910.

von Grunebaum, G.E., *Medieval Islam*, Chicago 1953.

————, "The Nature of Arab Unity Before Islam," *Arabica* 10 (1963), 5–23.

Guillaume, A., *Islam*, Edinburgh 1954.

al-Ḥākim al-Nīsābūrī , Abū 'Abd Allāh Muḥammad ibn 'Abd Allāh (d. 405/ 1014), *Ma'rifat 'Ulūm al-Ḥadīth*, Dār al-Kutub al-'Ilmīya, Medina 1977.

————, *al-Mustadrak 'Alā l-Ṣaḥīḥayn*, Dār al-Ma'rifa, Beirut 1986.

al-Ḥakīm al-Tirmidhī, Abū 'Abd Allāh Muḥammad ibn 'Alī *Kitāb al-Akyās wa-l-Mughtarrīn*, Ms. Damascus, Ẓāhirīya, *Taṣawwuf* no. 104/1.

al-Ḥalīmī, Abū 'Abd Allāh al-Ḥusayn ibn al-Ḥasan (d. 402/1011), *al-Minhāj Fī Shu'ab al-Īmān*, Dār al-Fikr, Beirut 1979.

Hammām ibn Munabbih al-Ṣan'ānī, Abū 'Uqba (d. 132/749), *Ṣaḥīfa*, ed. Rif'at 'Abd al-Muṭṭalib, Maktabat al-Khānjī, Cairo 1985.

Hannād ibn al-Sarī ibn Muṣ'ab al-Dārimī al-Kūfī (d. 243/857), *Kitāb al-Zuhd*, Dār al-Khulafā', Kuwait 1985.

al-Ḥarbī, Ibrāhīm ibn Isḥāq (d. 285/898), *Gharīb al-Ḥadīth*, ed. Sulaymān al-'Āyid, Kullīyat al-Sharī'a, Mecca 1985.

Hartman, S.S., "Secrets for Muslims in Parsi Scriptures," in G.L. Tikku, ed., *Islam and its Cultural Divergence*, Chicago 1971, 63–75.

Hārūn, 'Abd al-Salām, ed., *Nawādir al-Makhṭūṭāt*, Maṭba'at Lajnat al-Ta'līf wa-l-Tarjama wa-l-Nashr, Cairo 1954.

Hasson, I., "The Penetration of Arab Tribes in Palestine During the First Century of the Hijra," *Cathedra* 32 (1984), 54–65 (in Hebrew).

Hawting, G.R., *The First Dynasty of Islam*, London and Sydney 1986.

al-Haytamī, Ibn Ḥajar, Abū l-'Abbās Aḥmad ibn Muḥammad (d. 973/1565), *Fakhr al-'Arab*, ed. Majdī al-Sayyid Ibrāhīm, Maktabat al-Qur'ān, Cairo 1987.

al-Haythamī, Nūr al-Dīn Abū l-Ḥasan 'Alī ibn Abī Bakr (d. 807/1404), *Kashf al-Astār 'An Zawā'id Musnad al-Bazzār*, Mu'assasat al-Risāla, Beirut 1983.

———, *Majma' al-Zawā'id wa-Manba' al-Fawā'id*, Dār al-Rayyān li-l-Turāth, Cairo, and Dār al-Kitāb al-'Arabī, Beirut 1987.

al-Ḥāzimī, Abū Bakr Muḥammad ibn Mūsā (d. 584/1188), *al-I'tibār Fī l-Nāsikh wa-l-Mansūkh Min al-Āthār*, ed. 'Abd al-Mu'ṭī Qal'ajī, Dār al-Wa'y, Aleppo 1982.

al-Ḥirafī, Abū l-Qāsim, *Fawā'id*, Ms. Damascus, Ẓāhirīya, *Majmū'* no. 87.

al-Ḥumaydī, Abū Bakr 'Abd Allāh ibn al-Zubayr (d. 219/834), *Musnad*, ed. Ḥabīb al-Raḥmān al-A'ẓamī, 'Ālam al-Kutub, Beirut 1383/1963.

al-Ḥunaṭī, *al-Risāla al-Wāḍiḥa*, Ms. Damascus, Ẓāhirīya, *Majmū'* no. 18.

al-Ḥūt, Muḥammad ibn Darwīsh al-Bayrūtī, *Asnā l-Maṭālib Fī Ma'rifat Aḥādīth Mukhtalifat al-Marātib*, Beirut 1319/1901.

Ibn 'Abd al-Barr, Abū 'Umar Yūsuf ibn 'Abd Allāh (d. 463/1070), *al-Durar Fī Ikhtiṣār al-Maghāzī wa-l-Siyar*, Dār al-Kutub al-'Ilmīya, Beirut 1984.

———, *al-Tamhīd li-Mā Fī l-Muwaṭṭa' Min al-Ma'ānī wa-l-Asānīd*, ed. Muṣṭafā al-'Alawī and Muḥammad al-Bakrī, al-Markaz al-'Ilmī li-l-Ṭibā'a, Rabat 1981.

Ibn 'Abd al-Ḥakam, Abū l-Qāsim 'Abd al-Raḥmān ibn 'Abd Allāh (d. 257/870), *Futūḥ Miṣr*, ed. C.C. Torrey, New Haven 1922.

Ibn ʿAbd Rabbihi, Shihāb al-Dīn Abū ʿUmar Aḥmad ibn Muḥammad (d. 328/939), *al-ʿIqd al-Farīd*, ed. Aḥmad Amīn, Aḥmad al-Zayn and Ibrahim al-Abyārī, Maṭbaʿat Lajnat al-Taʾlīf wa-l-Tarjama wa-l-Nashr, Cairo 1940–53.

Ibn Abī ʿĀṣim, Abū Bakr Aḥmad ibn ʿAmr ibn al-Ḍaḥḥāk al-Shaybānī (d. 287/900), *al-Awāʾil*, ed. Muḥammad Saʿīd Zaghlūl, Dār al-Kutub al-ʿIlmīya, Beirut 1987.

________, *al-Sunna*, ed. Nāṣir al-Dīn al-Albānī, al-Maktab al-Islāmī, Beirut 1985.

Ibn Abī Ḥātim, Abū Muḥammad ʿAbd al-Raḥmān al-Rāzī (d. 327/938), *ʿIlal al-Ḥadīth*, Dār al-Maʿrifa, Beirut 1985.

________, *al-Marāsīl*, ed. Aḥmad ʿIṣām al-Kātib, Dār al-Kutub al-ʿIlmīya, Beirut 1983.

________, *Tafsīr*, ed. Aḥmad al-Zahrānī, Dār Ṭayba, Riyadh 1408/1987.

Ibn ʿAdī al-Jurjānī, Abū Aḥmad ʿAbd Allāh (d. 365/975), *al-Kāmil Fī Ḍuʿafāʾ al-Rijāl*, Dār al-Fikr, Beirut 1984.

Ibn al-Athīr, Abū l-Saʿādāt Majd al-Dīn al-Mubārak ibn Muḥammad (d. 606/1209), *al-Nihāya Fī Gharīb al-Ḥadīth wa-l-Athar*, Maṭbaʿat al-Khashshāb, Cairo 1318/1900.

Ibn ʿAsākir, Abū l-Qāsim ʿAlī ibn al-Ḥasan ibn Hibat Allāh (d. 571/1175), *Tārīkh Madīnat Dimashq*, facs. ed., Dār al-Bashīr, Amman 1988.

Ibn Badrān, ʿAbd al-Qādir (d. 1346/1927), *Tahdhīb Tārīkh Ibn ʿAsākir*, Maṭbaʿat Rawḍat al-Shām, Damascus 1331/1912.

Ibn Duqmāq, Ṣārim al-Dīn Ibrāhīm ibn Muḥammad (d. 809/1406, *al-Intiṣār li-Wāsiṭat ʿIqd al-Amṣār*, al-Maṭbaʿa al-Kubrā, Būlāq, Cairo 1893.

Ibn Ḥabīb, Abū Jaʿfar Muḥammad al-Baghdādī (d. 245/859), *al-Muḥabbar*, ed. Ilse Lichtenstädter, Dār al-Āfāq al-Jadīda, Beirut n.d.

________, *al-Munammaq Fī Akhbār Quraysh*, ed. Khurshīd Aḥmad Fāriq, Hyderabad 1964.

Ibn Ḥajar al-ʿAsqalānī, Shihāb al-Dīn Abū l-Faḍl Aḥmad ibn ʿAlī (d. 852/1448), *Lisān al-Mīzān*, Hyderabad 1330/1911.

________, *al-Maṭālib al-ʿĀliya Fī Zawaʾid al-Masānīd al-Thamāniya*, ed. Ḥabīb al-Raḥmān al-Aʿẓamī, Dār al-Maʿrifa, Beirut 1392/1972.

________, *Tahdhīb al-Tahdhīb*, Hyderabad 1325–27/1907–1909.

Ibn Ḥanbal, Abū ʿAbd Allāh Aḥmad ibn Muḥammad (d. 241/855), *Faḍaʾil al-Ṣaḥāba*, ed. Waṣī Allāh ʿAbbās, Muʾassasat al-Risāla, Beirut 1983.

________, *Kitāb al-ʿIlal wa-Maʿrifat al-Rijāl*, ed. Waṣī Allāh ʿAbbās, al-Maktab al-Islāmī, Beirut, and Dār al-Khānī, Riyadh 1988.

———, *Musnad*, Bulaq, Cairo 1313/1895.

Ibn Ḥanbal, Abū ʻAbd al-Raḥmān ʻAbd Allāh ibn Aḥmad (d. 290/902), *Masā'il al-Imām Aḥmad ibn Ḥanbal*, ed. Zuhayr al-Shāwīsh, al-Maktab al-Islāmī, Beirut 1988.

Ibn Ḥayyān, *Ḥadīth*, Ms. Damascus, Ẓāhirīya, *Majmūʻ* no. 93.

Ibn Ḥazm, Abū Muḥammad ʻAlī ibn Aḥmad ibn Saʻīd (d. 456/1063), *Marātib al-Ijmāʻ Fī l-ʻIbādāt wa-l-Muʻāmalāt wa-l-Muʻāqadāt*, Dār al-Āfāq al-Jadīda, Beirut 1978.

Ibn Ḥibbān al-Bustī, Abū Ḥātim Muḥammad (d. 354/965), *Kitāb al-Majrūḥīn*, ed. Maḥmūd Zāyid, Dār al-Waʻy, Aleppo 1402/1981.

———, *Ṣaḥīḥ*, ed. Kamāl al-Ḥūt, Dār al-Kutub al-ʻIlmīya, Beirut 1987.

———, *al-Sīra al-Nabawīya wa-Akhbār al-Khulafā'*, ed. Sayyid ʻAzīz Bek, Dār al-Fikr, Beirut 1987.

Ibn Hishām, Abū Muḥammad ʻAbd al-Malik al-Muʻāfirī (d. 213/828), *al-Sīra al-Nabawīya*, ed. ʻAbd al-Ra'ūf Saʻd, Dār al-Jīl, Beirut 1975.

Ibn al-ʻIbrī/Bar Hebraeus, Gregorius Abū l-Faraj (d. 685/1286), *Tārīkh Mukhtaṣar al-Duwal*, Beirut 1985.

Ibn Isḥāq, ʻAbd Allāh ʻMuḥammad ... ibn Yasār al-Muṭṭalibī (d. 150/767), *Kitāb al-Siyar wa-l-Maghāzī*, ed. Suhayl Zakkār, Dār al-Fikr, Beirut 1978.

Ibn al-Jaʻd, Abū l-Ḥasan ʻAlī ... ibn ʻUbayd al-Jawharī (d. 230/844), *Musnad*, ed. ʻAbd al-Mahdī ibn ʻAbd al-Hādī, Maktabat al-Falāḥ, Kuwait 1985.

Ibn al-Jārūd, Abū Muḥammad ʻAbd Allāh ibn ʻAlī al-Naysābūrī (d. 307/909), *al-Muntaqā Min al-Sunan*, Dār al-Qalam, Beirut 1987.

Ibn al-Jawzī, Abū l-Faraj ʻAbd al-Raḥmān ibn ʻAlī (d. 597/1200), *Gharīb al-Ḥadīth*, ed. ʻAbd al-Muʻṭī Qalʻajī, Dār al-Kutub al-ʻIlmīya, Beirut 1985.

———, *al-Mawḍūʻāt*, ed. ʻAbd al-Raḥmān ʻUthmān, al-Maktaba al-Salafīya, Medina 1966.

———, *Sīra wa-Manāqib ʻUmar ibn ʻAbd al-ʻAzīz*, ed. Naʻīm Zarzūr, Dār al-Kutub al-ʻIlmīya, Beirut 1984.

———, *al-Tabṣira*, Dār al-Kutub al-ʻIlmīya, Beirut 1986.

Ibn Jumayʻ al-Ṣaydāwī, Abū l-Ḥusayn Muḥammad ibn Aḥmad (d. 402/1011), *Muʻjam al-Shuyūkh*, ed. ʻUmar Tadmurī, Dār al-Īmān, Tripoli, and Mu'assasat al-Risāla, Beirut 1987.

Ibn Kathīr, ʻImād al-Dīn Abū l-Fidā' Ismāʻīl ibn ʻUmar (d. 774/1372), *al-Bidāya wa-l-Nihāya*, Maṭbaʻat al-Saʻāda, Cairo 1932.

———, *al-Nihāya Fī l-Fitan wa-l-Malāḥim*, ed. Aḥmad 'Abd al-'Azīz, al-Maktab al-Thaqāfī, Cairo 1986.

Ibn Khaldūn, 'Imād al-Dīn Abū Zayd 'Abd al-Raḥmān ibn Muḥammad (d. 808/1405), *Tārīkh* (*Kitāb al-'Ibar*), ed. 'Alāl al-Fāsī, 'Abd al-'Azīz ibn Idrīs and Muḥammad al-Mahdī al-Jabbā'ī, Fez 1936.

Ibn al-Khallāl, Abū Bakr Aḥmad ibn Muḥammad (d. 311/923), *al-Sunna*, ed. 'Aṭīya al-Zahrānī, Dār al-Rāya, Riyadh 1989.

Ibn Māja, Abū 'Abd Allāh Muḥammad ibn Yazīd al-Qazwīnī (d. 275/888), *Sunan*, ed. Muḥammad 'Abd al-Bāqī, Dār al-Ḥadīth, Cairo n.d.

Ibn Manẓūr, Jamāl al-Dīn Abū l-Faḍl Muḥammad ibn Mukarram (d. 711/1311), *Lisān al-'Arab*, Būlāq, Cairo 1308/1890.

Ibn al-Mubārak, Abū 'Abd al-Raḥmān 'Abd Allāh ibn Wāḍiḥ al-Marwazī (d. 181/797), *Kitāb al-Zuhd*, ed. Ḥabīb al-Raḥmān al-A'ẓamī, Dār al-Kutub al-'Ilmīya, Beirut 1386/1966.

Ibn Mukarram al-Qāḍī, *Fawā'id*, Ms. Damascus, Ẓāhirīya, *Majmū'* no. 63.

Ibn al-Mundhir, Abū Bakr Muḥammad ibn Ibrāhīm al-Naysābūrī (d. 318/930), *al-Ijtimā'*, ed. 'Abd Allāh al-Bārūdī, Dār al-Jinān, Beirut 1986.

Ibn al-Muqri', Abū Bakr al-Iṣbahānī, *Fawā'id*, Ms. Damascus, Ẓāhirīya, *Majmū'* no. 105.

Ibn al-Murajjā, Abū l-Ma'ālī al-Musharraf ... ibn Ibrāhīm al-Maqdisī (d. 492/1098), *Faḍā'il Bayt al-Maqdis*, Ms. Tübingen, no. 27.

Ibn al-Nadīm, Abū Ya'qūb Muḥammad ibn Isḥāq (d. 380/990), *The Fihrist of al-Nadīm*, trans. B. Dodge, New York, 1970.

Ibn al-Qaysarānī, Abū l-Faḍl Muḥammad ibn Ṭāhir al-Maqdisī (d. 507/1113, *Ma'rifat al-Tadhkira* ed. 'Imād al-Dīn Ḥaydar, Mu'assasat al-Kutub al-Thaqāfīya, Beirut 1985.

Ibn Qayyim al-Jawzīya, Shams al-Dīn Abū 'Abd Allāh Muḥammad ibn Abī Bakr (d. 751/1350), *al-Manār al-Munīf Fī l-Ṣaḥīḥ wa-l-Ḍa'īf*, Maktab al-Maṭbū'āt al-Islāmīya, Aleppo 1970.

Ibn Qutayba, Abū Muḥammad 'Abd Allāh ibn Muslim (d. 276/889), *al-Shi'r wa-l-Shu'arā'*, ed. M.J. de Goeje, Leiden 1902.

———, *Tafsīr Gharīb al-Qur'ān*, ed. Aḥmad Ṣaqr, Dār al-Kutub al-'Ilmīya, Beirut 1978.

———, *'Uyūn al-Akhbār*, al-Hay'a al-Miṣrīya al-'Āmma li-l-Kitāb, Cairo 1973.

Ibn Sa'd, Abū 'Abd Allāh Muḥammad ibn Manī' al-Baṣrī (d. 230/844), *al-Ṭabaqāt al-Kubrā*, Dār Ṣādir and Dār Beirut, Beirut 1957.

Ibn al-Sammāk, Abū 'Amr, *Ḥadīth*, Ms. Damascus, Ẓāhirīya, *Majmū'* no. 103.

Ibn al-Ṣawwāf, *Ḥadīth*, Ms. Damascus, Ẓāhirīya, *Majmū'* no. 105.

Ibn Sayyid al-Nās, Fatḥ al-Dīn Abū l-Fatḥ Muḥammad ibn Muḥammad al-Ishbīlī (d. 734/1333), *'Uyūn al-Athar Fī Funūn al-Maghāzī wa-l-Shamā'il wa-l-Siyar*, Dār al-Jīl, Beirut 1356/1945.

Ibn Shāhīn, Abū Ḥafṣ, *Ḥadīth*, Ms. Damascus, Ẓāhirīya, *Majmū'* no. 83.

Ibn al-Shajarī, Hibat Allāh ibn 'Alī (d. 542/1147), *Kitāb al-Ḥamāsa*, Hyderabad 1345/1926.

Ibn Ṭāwūs, Raḍī l-Dīn Abū l-Qāsim'Alī ibn Mūsā (d. 664/1265), *al-Malāḥim wa-l-Fitan*, Najaf 1963.

Ibn Taymīya, Abū l-'Abbās Aḥmad ibn 'Abd al-Ḥalīm (d. 728/1327), *Aḥādīth al-Quṣṣāṣ*, Beirut 1972.

Ibn 'Ubayd, Yūnus, *Ḥadīth*, Ms. Damascus, Ẓāhirīya, *Majmū'* no. 103.

Ibn 'Uyayna, Sufyān ... ibn Maymūn al-Hilālī, *Ḥadīth*, Ms. Damascus, Ẓāhirīya, *Majmū'* no. 22.

Ibn al-Yazīdī, Abū 'Abd al-Raḥmān 'Abd Allāh ibn Yaḥyā (d. 237/851), *Gharīb al-Qur'ān wa-Tafsīruhu*, ed. 'Abd al-Razzāq Ḥusayn, Mu'assasat al-Risāla, Beirut 1987.

Ibn Zanjawayh, Abū Aḥmad Ḥumayd ibn Makhlad ... al-Azdī (d. 251/865), *Kitāb al-Amwāl*, Riyadh 1986.

al-'Irāqī, Zayn al-Dīn 'Abd al-Raḥīm ibn al-Ḥusayn (d. 806/1403), *al-Qurab Fī Maḥabbat al-'Arab*, Bombay 1303/1885.

al-Iṣfahānī, Abū l-Faraj 'Alī ibn al-Ḥusayn (d. 356/966), *Kitāb al-Aghānī*, Dār al-Kutub al-Miṣrīya, Cairo 1950.

al-Jāḥiẓ, Abū 'Uthmān 'Amr ibn Baḥr (d. 255/868), *al-Bayān wa-l-Tabyīn*, Dār al-Fikr li-l-Jamī', Beirut 1968.

________, *Fakhr al-Sūdān 'Alā l-Bīḍān*, ed. G. van Vloten in his *Tria Opuscula*, Leiden 1903, 57–85.

________, *Rasā'il*, ed. 'Abd al-Salām Hārūn, Maktabat al-Khānjī, Cairo 1964–65.

________, *Risāla Ilā l-Fatḥ ibn Khāqān Fī Manāqib al-Turk*, ed. G. van Vloten in his *Tria Opuscula*, Leiden 1903, 1–56.

Jarīr ibn 'Aṭīya al-Khaṭafī (d. 110–11/728–29), *Sharḥ Dīwān Jarīr*, ed. Muḥammad Ismā'īl 'Abd Allāh al-Ṣāwī, Maktabat Muḥammad al-Nūrī, Damascus, and al-Sharika al-Lubnānīya li-l-Kitāb, Beirūt 1353/1934.

al-Jawraqānī (d. 543/1148), *al-Abāṭīl wa-l-Manākīr*, Varanasi 1983.

Juynboll, G.H.A., *Muslim Tradition*, Cambridge 1985.

al-Khaṭīb al-Baghdādī, Abū Bakr Aḥmad ibn ʿAlī (d. 463/1070), *Tārīkh Baghdād*, ed. Muḥammad Saʿīd al-ʿUrfī and Muḥammad Ḥāmid al-Fiqī, Maktabat al-Khānjī, Cairo, and al-Maktaba al-ʿArabīya, Baghdād, 1931.

al-Khuttalī, Abū l-Ḥasan al-Sukkarī, *Ḥadīth*, Ms. Damascus, Ẓāhirīya, *Majmūʿ* no. 118.

al-Kinānī, Abū l-Ḥasan ʿAlī ibn Muḥammad ibn ʿIrāq (d. 963/1555), *Tanzīh al-Sharīʿa al-Marfūʿa ʿAn al-Aḥādīth al-Mawḍūʿa*, ed. ʿAbd al-Wahhāb ʿAbd al-Laṭīf and ʿAbd Allāh al-Ṣiddīq, Dār al-Kutub al-ʿIlmīya, Beirut 1979.

Levy, R., *The Social Structure of Islam*, Cambridge 1969.

Lewis, B., *The Arabs in History*, London 1980.

———, *Race and Color in Islam*, London 1971.

Madelung, W., "ʿAbd Allāh ibn al-Zubayr and the Mahdī," *JNES* 40 (1981), 291–306.

Mālik ibn Anas, Abū ʿAbd Allāh (d. 179/795), *al-Muwaṭṭaʾ*, in the recension of al-Shaybānī (d. 189/804), ed. ʿAbd al-Wahhāb ʿAbd al-Laṭīf, Dār al-Qalam, Beirut n.d.

al-Maqrīzī, Abū l-ʿAbbās Aḥmad ibn ʿAlī (d. 854/1450), *al-Mawāʿiẓ wa-l-Iʿtibār bi-Dhikr al-Khiṭaṭ wa-l-Āthār*, Maṭbaʿat al-Nīl, Cairo 1324/1906.

Marʿī ibn Yūsuf ibn Abī Bakr al-Karmī al-Ḥanbalī, (d. 1033/1624), *Bahjat al-Nāẓirīn*, Ms. Jerusalem, al-Maktaba al-Khālidīya, Ar. no. 21.

al-Marwazī, Abū Bakr, *Akhbār al-Shuyūkh*, Ms. Damascus, Ẓāhirīya, *Majmūʿ* no. 120.

al-Marwazī, Muḥammad ibn Naṣr (d. 394/1003), *al-Sunna*, ed. Sālim al-Salafī, Muʾassasat al-Kutub al-Thaqāfīya, Beirut 1988.

———, *Taʿẓīm Qadr al-Ṣalāt*, ed. ʿAbd al-Raḥmān al-Faryawāʾī, Maktabat al-Dār, Medina 1406/1985.

al-Masʿūdī, Abū l-Ḥasan ʿAlī ibn al-Ḥusayn (d. 345/956), *Murūj al-Dhahab wa-Maʿādin al-Jawhar*, ed. C. Pellat, Manshūrāt al-Jāmiʿa al-Lubnānīya, Beirut 1966.

———, *al-Tanbīh wa-l-Ishrāf*, Maktabat Khayyāṭ, Beirut 1985.

al-Māwardī, Abū l-Ḥasan ibn Muḥammad ibn Ḥabīb (d. 450/1058), *al-Aḥkām al-Sulṭānīya*, Dār al-Kutub al-ʿIlmīya, Beirut 1978.

al-Maydānī, Abū l-Faḍl Aḥmad ibn Muḥammad al-Naysābūrī (d. 518/1124), *Amthāl al-ʿArab*, ed. G. Freytag, Bonn 1839.

Mottahedeh, R., "The Shu'ūbiyah and the Social History of Early Islamic Iran," *IJMES* 7 (1976), 161–82.

al-Mu'āfā ibn 'Imrān ibn Nufayl al-Mawṣilī (d. 185/801), *Kitāb al-Zuhd*, Ms. Damascus, Ẓāhirīya, *Ḥadīth* no. 359.

al-Mubarrad, Abū l-'Abbās Muḥammad ibn Yazīd (d. 286/899), *al-Kāmil Fī l-Lugha wa-l-Adab*, ed. W. Wright, Leipzig 1864.

Mughulṭāy, Nāṣir al-Dīn Abū 'Abd Allāh ... ibn Qilij, *al-Zahr al-Bāsim*, Ms. Leiden, Or. no. 370.

Mujāhid ibn Jabr al-Makhzūmī al-Makkī, Abū l-Ḥajjāj (d. 102–103/720–21), *Tafsīr*, ed. 'Abd al-Raḥmān al-Sawartī, al-Manshūrāt al-'Ilmīya, Beirut n.d.

al-Munāwī, 'Abd al-Ra'ūf Muḥammad ibn Tāj al-'Ārifīn (d. 1031/1621), *Kunūz al-Ḥaqā'iq*, on the margin of al-Suyūṭī, *al-Jāmi' al-Ṣaghīr*, Dār al-Kutub al-'Ilmīya, Beirut n.d.

al-Mundhirī, Zakī l-Dīn 'Abd al-'Aẓīm ibn 'Abd al-Qawī (d. 656/1258), *al-Targhīb wa-l-Tarhīb*, Dār al-Ḥadīth, Cairo n.d.

Muqātil ibn Sulaymān al-Azdī, Abū l-Ḥasan (d. 150/767), *Tafsīr*, Ms. Istanbūl, Ahmet III, no. 74/1–2.

Muslim, Abū l-Ḥusayn ibn al-Ḥajjāj al-Qushayrī al-Naysābūrī (d. 261/874), *al-Jāmi' al-Ṣaḥīḥ*, Dār al-Fikr, Beirut n.d.

al-Muttaqī al-Hindī, 'Alā' al-Dīn 'Alī ibn 'Abd al-Malik (d. 975/1567), *Kanz al-'Ummāl*, ed. Bakrī Ḥayyānī and Ṣafwat al-Saqqā, Mu'assasat al-Risāla, Beirut 1979.

Nagel, H.M.T., "The Authority of the Caliphate," in G.H.A. Juynboll, ed., *Studies on the First Century of Islam*, Carbondale 1982, 177–97.

al-Nahrawālī, Quṭb al-Dīn Muḥammad ibn Aḥmad (d. 990/1582), *al-I'lām bi-A'lām Bayt Allāh al-Ḥarām*, ed. F. Wüstenfeld, Leipzig 1857.

al-Naqqāsh, Abū Sa'īd al-Iṣbahānī, *Amālī*, Ms. Damascus, Ẓāhirīya, *Majmū'* no. 20.

al-Nasā'ī, Abū 'Abd al-Raḥmān ibn Shu'ayb (d. 303/915), *Faḍā'il al-Ṣaḥāba*, ed. Fārūq Ḥamāda, Dār al-Thaqāfa, al-Dār al-Bayḍa 1981.

———, *Sunan*, Dār al-Ḥadīth, Cairo 1987.

———, *Tafsīr*, ed. Sayyid al-Jalīmī and Ṣabrī al-Shāfi'ī, Maktabat al-Sunna, Cairo 1990.

Nu'aym ibn Ḥammād al-Marwazī, Abū 'Abd Allāh (d. 227/841), *Kitāb al-Fitan*, Ms. British Museum, Or. no. 9449.

———, *Ziyādāt al-Zuhd*, on the margin of Ibn al-Mubārak, *Kitāb al-Zuhd*.

Paret, R., art. "Umma" in *EI* [1], 4/1015–16.

Pipes, D., *Slave Soldiers and Islam*, New Haven and London 1981.

al-Qārī, al-Mullā 'Alī (d. 1014/1605), *al-Asrār al-Marfū'a Fī l-Akhbār al-Mawḍū'a* ed. Muḥammad Sa'īd Zaghlūl, Dār al-Kutub al-'Ilmīya, Beirut 1985.

———, *al-Maṣnū' Fī Ma'rifat al-Ḥadīth al-Mawḍū'*, ed. 'Abd al-Fattāḥ Abū Ghudda, Maktabat al-Maṭbū'āt al-'Ilmīya, Aleppo 1969.

al-Qaṭṭān, Abū 'Abd Allāh, *Ḥadīth*, Ms. Damascus, Ẓāhirīya, *Majmū'* no. 31.

al-Qaṭṭān, Abū Muḥammad, *Fawā'id*, Ms. Damascus, Ẓāhirīya, *Majmū'* no. 40.

al-Quḍā'ī, al-Qāḍī Abū 'Abd Allāh Muḥammad ibn Salāma (d. 454/1062), *Musnad*, ed. Ḥamdī al-Salafī, Mu'assasat al-Risāla, Beirut 1985.

al-Qummī, Abū l-Ḥasan 'Alī ibn Ibrāhīm (d. 307/919), *Tafsīr*, ed. al-Sayyid Ṭayyib al-Mūsawī al-Jazā'irī, Manshūrāt Maktabat al-Hudā, Maṭba'at al-Najaf, Najaf 1386/ 1966.

al-Qurṭubī, Shams al-Dīn Abū 'Abd Allāh Muḥammad ibn Aḥmad (d. 671/1272), *al-Jāmi' li-Aḥkām al-Qur'ān*, Dār al-Sha'b, Cairo n.d.

———, *al-Tadhkira Fī Aḥwāl al-Mawtā wa-Umūr al-Ākhira*, ed. Aḥmad al-Saqqā, Maktabat al-Kullīyāt al-Azharīya, Cairo 1985.

al-Rāmhurmuzī, al-Qāḍī Abū l-Ḥasan ibn 'Abd al-Raḥmān ibn Khallād, *Amthāl al-Ḥadīth*, ed. Aḥmad 'Abd al-Fattāḥ Tammām, Mu'assasat al-Kutub al-Thaqāfīya, Beirut 1988.

al-Razī, Abū l-Qāsim Tammām ibn Muḥammad al-Dimashqī (d. 414/1023), *Fawā'id*, ed. Jāsim al-Dawsarī, Dār al-Bashā'ir al-Islāmīya, Beirut 1989.

Rotter, G., *Die Stellung des Negres in der Islamisch-arabischen Gesellschaft bis zum XVI Jahrhundert*, Bonn 1967.

Sadan, J., "An Admirable and Ridiculous Hero," in *Poetics Today* 10 (1989), 471–92.

al-Ṣaffār, Ismā'īl ibn Muḥammad, *Ḥadīth*, Ms. Damascus, Ẓāhirīya, *Majmū'* no. 31.

Sa'īd ibn Manṣūr ibn Shu'ba al-Khurāsānī al-Makkī, Abū 'Uthmān (d. 227/841), *Sunan*, ed. Ḥabīb al-Raḥmān al-A'ẓamī, Dār al-Kutub al-'Ilmīya, Beirut 1985.

al-Sakhāwī, Shams al-Dīn Abū l-Khayr Muḥammad ibn 'Abd al-Raḥmān (d. 902/ 1496), *al-Maqāṣid al-Ḥasana Fī Bayān Kathīr Min al-Aḥādīth al-Mushtahira 'Alā l-Alsina*, ed. 'Abd Allāh Muḥammad al-Ṣiddīq and 'Abd al-Wahhāb 'Abd al-Laṭīf, Maktabat al-Khānjī, Cairo 1956.

al-Sam'ānī, 'Abd al-Karīm ibn Muḥammad (d. 562/1166), *Kitāb al-Ansāb*, facs. ed. D.S. Margoliouth, London 1912.

al-Samarqandī, Abū l-Layth Naṣr ibn Muḥammad (d. 373/983), *Tanbīh al-Ghāfilīn*, Dār al-Fikr, Beirut n.d.

al-Samarqandī, *Ḥadīth*, Ms. Damascus, Ẓāhirīya, *Majmū'* no. 40.

al-Samhūdī, Nūr al-Dīn Abū l-Ḥasan 'Alī ibn 'Abd Allāh (d. 911/1505), *al-Ghummāz 'Alā l-Lummāz*, ed. Muḥammad 'Aṭā, Dār al-Kutub al-'Ilmīya, Beirut 1986.

Schacht, J., *The Origins of Muhammedan Jurisprudence* Oxford 1979.

Shaban, M.A., *The Abbasid Revolution*, Cambridge 1970.

Sharon , M., *Black Banners from the East*, Jerusalem 1983.

________, "The Development of the Debate over the Legitimacy of Authority in Early Islam," *JSAI* 5 (1984), 121–41.

________, "The Military Reforms of Abū Muslim," in M. Sharon, ed., *Studies in Islamic History and Civilisaton In Honour of Professor David Ayalon*, Jerusalem 1986, 105–43.

al-Shāshī, Abū Sa'īd al-Haytham ibn Kulayb (d. 335/946), *Musnad*, ed. Maḥfūẓ Zayn Allāh, Maktabat al-'Ulūm wa-l-Ḥikam, Medina 1410/1989.

al-Shawkānī, Muḥammad ibn 'Alī (d. 1250/1834), *al-Fawā'id al-Majmū'a Fī l-Aḥādīth al-Mawḍū'a*, ed. 'Abd al-Raḥmān al-Mu'allimī al-Yamānī, Maṭba'at al-Sunna al-Muḥammadīya, Cairo 1960.

al-Shīrāzī, Abū Bakr, *Amālī*, Ms. Damascus, Ẓāhirīya, *Majmū'* no. 63.

Sulaym ibn Qays al-Hilālī (d. 90/708), *Kitāb Sulaym ibn Qays al-Kūfī*, al-Maṭba'a al-Ḥaydarīya, Najaf, n.d.

al-Suyūṭī, Jalāl al-Dīn 'Abd al-Raḥmān ibn Abī Bakr (d. 911/1505), *al-Aḥādīth al-Ḥisān Fī Faḍl al-Ṭaylasān*, ed. A. Arazi, Jerusalem 1983.

________, *al-Durr al-Manthūr Fī l-Tafsīr bi-l-Ma'thūr*, al-Maṭba'a al-Maymanīya, Cairo 1314/1896.

________, *Iḥyā' al-Mayt bi-Faḍā'il Āl al-Bayt*, ed. Muṣṭafā al-Āghā, Dār al-Jīl, Beirut 1987.

________, *al-Jāmi' al-Kabīr*, facs. ed., al-Hay'a al-Miṣrīya al-'Āmma li-l-Kitāb, Cairo 1978.

________, *al-Jāmi' al-Ṣaghīr*, Dār al-Kutub al-'Ilmīya, Beirut n.d.

________, *al-Khaṣā'iṣ al-Kubrā*, Hyderabad 1320/1902.

________, *al-La'ālī al-Maṣnū'a*, Dār al-Ma'rifa, Beirut 1975.

al-Ṭabarānī, Abū l-Qāsim Sulaymān ibn Aḥmad (d. 360/970), *al-Mu'jam al-Awsaṭ*, ed. Maḥmūd al-Ṭaḥḥān, Maktabat al-Ma'ārif, Riyadh 1985.

________, *al-Mu'jam al-Kabīr*, ed. Ḥamdī al-Salafī, Baghdad 1983.

al-Ṭabarī, Abū Ja'far Muḥammad ibn Jarīr (d. 310/922), *Tafsīr* , = *Jāmi' al-Bayān 'An Tafsīr Āy al-Qur'ān*, ed. Maḥmūd and Aḥmad Shākir, Dār al-Ma'ārif, Cairo 1954.

________, *Tahdhīb al-Āthār*, ed. Maḥmūd Shākir, Maṭba'at al-Madanī, Cairo 1981–82.

________, *Tārīkh al-Umam wa-l-Mulūk*, ed. Muḥammad Abū l-Faḍl Ibrāhīm, Dār Suwaydān, Beirut 1967.

al-Ṭabarī, Muḥibb al-Dīn (d. 694/1294), *Dhakhā'ir al-'Uqbā*, Ms. Damascus, Ẓāhirīya, *Majmū'* no. 37, General no. 4808.

________, *al-Riyāḍ al-Naḍira Fī Manāqib al-'Ashara*, ed. Muḥammad Abū l-'Ulā, Maktabat al-Najda, Cairo 1970.

al-Ṭabarsī, Abū 'Alī al-Faḍl ibn al-Ḥasan (d. 548/1153), *Majma' al-Bayān Fī Tafsīr al-Qur'ān*, Dār al-Fikr and Dār al-Kitāb al-Lubnānī, Beirut 1956.

al-Ṭayālisī, Abū Dāwūd Sulaymān ibn Dawūd ibn al-Jārūd (d. 204/819), *Musnad*, Dār al-Ma'rifa, Beirut 1986.

al-Thawrī, Abū 'Abd Allāh Sufyān ibn Sa'īd (d. 161/774), *Tafsīr*, Dār al-Kutub al-'Ilmīya, Beirut 1983.

al-Tirmidhī, Abū 'Īsā Muḥammad ibn 'Īsā (d. 279/892), *al-Jāmi' al-Ṣaḥīḥ*, ed. Aḥmad Shākir and Ibrāhīm 'Awaḍ, Dār Iḥyā' al-Turāth al-'Arabī, Beirut n.d.

________, *al-Shamā'il*, Ms. Damascus, Ẓāhirīya, *Majmū'* no. 83.

Tritton, A.S., *The Caliphs and Their Non-Muslim Subjects*, London 1939.

al-'Umarī, Akram Ḍiyā', *Musnad Khalīfa ibn Khayyāṭ* (d. 240/854), Medina 1985.

al-'Uqaylī, Abū Ja'far Muḥammad ibn 'Amr al-Makkī (d. 322/933), *Kitāb al-Ḍu'afā' al-Kabīr*, ed. 'Abd al-Mu'ṭī Qal'ajī, Dār al-Kutub al-'Ilmīya, Beirut 1984.

van Vloten, G., ed., *Tria Opuscula Auctore... al-Djahiz*, Leiden 1903.

Wahb ibn Munabbih, Abū 'Alī (d. 110/728), *Kitāb al-Tījān Fī Mulūk Ḥimyar*, ed. F. Krenkow, Hyderabad 1347/1928.

al-Wāḥidī, Abū l-Ḥasan 'Alī ibn Aḥmad al-Naysābūrī (d. 468/1075), *Asbāb al-Nuzūl*, 'Ālam al-Kutub, Beirut n.d.

Wansbrough, J., "Gentilics and Appellatives: Notes on Aḥābīš Qurayš," *BSOAS* 49 (1986), 203–10.

________, *Qur'anic Studies*, Oxford 1977.

________, *The Sectarian Milieu*, Oxford 1978.

al-Wāqidī, Abū ʿAbd Allāh Muḥammad ibn ʿUmar ibn Wāqid (d. 207/822), *Kitāb al-Maghāzī*, ed. M. Jones, ʿĀlam al-Kutub, Beirut 1984.

________, (ps.-), *Futūḥ al-Shām*, al-Maktaba al-Shaʿbīya, Beirut n.d.

al-Washshāʾ, Abū l-Ṭayyib Muḥammad ibn Aḥmad (d. 325/936), *Kitāb al-Fāḍil*, Ms. British Museum, Or. no. 6499.

al-Wāsiṭī, Bishr ibn Maṭar, *Ḥadīth*, Ms. Damascus, Ẓāhirīya, *Majmūʿ* no. 94.

Watt, W.M., *Bell's Introduction to the Qur'ān*, Edinburgh 1970.

Wellhausen, J., *The Arab Kingdom and its Fall*, trans. M.G. Weir, Khayyāṭ, Beirut 1963.

Wensinck, A.J., arts. "Community" and "Umma," in H.A.R. Gibb and J.H. Kraemer, *The Shorter Encyclopedia of Islam*, Leiden 1974, 324–25, 603–604.

________, art. "Mawla" in *EI* [1], 3/417.

________, *The Muslim Creed*, London 1985.

Yaḥyā ibn Ādam al-Qurashī, Abū Zakarīyāʾ (d. 203/818), *Kitāb al-Kharāj*, ed. T.W. Juynboll, Leiden 1895.

Yaḥyā ibn Maʿīn ibn ʿAwn al-Murrī al-Ghaṭafānī, Abū Zakarīyāʾ (d. 233/847), *Tārīkh*, ed. Aḥmad Nūr Sayf, Markaz al-Baḥth al-ʿIlmī, Mecca 1979.

al-Yaʿqūbī, Aḥmad ibn Abī Yaʿqūb ibn Wāḍiḥ (d. 282/895), *Tārīkh*, ed. M.T. Houtsma, Leiden 1969.

al-Zabīdī, Muḥammad ibn Murtaḍā (d. 1205/1790), *Itḥāf al-Sāda al-Muttaqīn*, Cairo 1311/1893.

________, *Tāj al-ʿArūs*, Būlāq, Cairo 1307/1889.

al-Zajjāj, Abū Isḥāq Ibrāhīm ibn al-Sarī (d. 311/923), *Maʿānī l-Qur'ān wa-Iʿrābuhu*, ed. ʿAbd al-Jalīl Shalabī, ʿĀlam al-Kutub, Beirut 1988.

al-Zaylaʿī, Jamāl al-Dīn ʿAbd Allāh ibn Yūsuf (d. 762/1360), *Naṣb al-Rāya li-Aḥādīth al-Hidāya*, Dār al-Ḥadīth, Cairo 1938.

al-Zubayr ibn Bakkār al-Qurashī, Abū ʿAbd Allāh (d. 256/869), *al-Akhbār al-Muwaffaqīyāt*, ed. Sāmī al-ʿĀnī, Maṭbaʿat al-ʿĀnī, Baghdād 1980.

________, *al-Muntakhab Min Kitāb Azwāj al-Nabī*, ed. Sukayna al-Shihābī, Mu'assasat al-Risāla, Beirut 1983.

General Index

In the arrangement adopted here, the Arabic definite article (*al-*), the transliteration symbols for the Arabic letters *hamza* (') and *'ayn* ('), and distinctions between different letters transliterated by the same Latin character (e.g. *d* and *ḍ*) are ignored for purposes of alphabetization. An effort has been made to indicate the sorts of themes discussed under the names of the various traditionists and authorities indexed, but it should not, of course, be assumed that all the persons named actually did discuss the issues or hold the views later attributed to them.

'Abbād ibn 'Ubayd Allāh ibn Abī Rāfi', and attitudes to black slaves, 83–84

al-'Abbās ibn 'Abd Allāh ibn Mi'bad, evidence on Prophet's perception of future, 26

al-'Abbās ibn 'Abd al-Muṭṭalib
and splitting of land by act of God, 59; children predicted to rule the Arabs, 103; references to Arab ethnicity, 17, 115

'Abbāsids, 3, 17, 26, 34
as basically Arab regime, 118; importance accorded to Persians among non-Arabs, 76–77; conflicting interpretation of Arab, non-Arab influences, 41, 42; motives behind revolution, 2; recruitment of Turks to fight against Khārijites, 111; significance of Persian support for, 122; threatened by Zanj revolt, 86; traditions enhancing role of Persians, 68

'Abd Allāh ibn Abī Bakr ibn Muḥammad ibn Ḥazm, traditions on assimilation of Copts, 70

'Abd Allāh ibn 'Āmir, and traditions on good qualities of blacks, 87–88

'Abd Allāh ibn 'Amr ibn al-'Āṣ *see* Ibn 'Amr

'Abd Allāh ibn Burayda, on Mu'āwiya's promotion of learning, 55

'Abd Allāh ibn Dīnār, on prohibition on naming addressee of letter, 35

'Abd Allāh ibn Sa'īd al-Maqburī, attribution of 'Umar I's pro-Arab policies to Prophet, 31–32

'Abd Allāh ibn Salama, evidence on interpretations of *shu'ūb*, 23

'Abd Allāh ibn Ṭāwūs, and concept of imminent onset of evil, 103

'Abd Allāh ibn 'Ubayd Allāh ibn 'Umayr
and establishment of Quraysh as *Imāms*, 58–59; *see also* Ibn Abī Mulayka

'Abd Allāh ibn Wahb, and assimilation of Copts, 69, 70

'Abd Allāh ibn Yazīd al-Ma'āfirī al-Miṣrī, and assimilation of Copts, 69

'Abd al-Malik ibn Marwān
attitude to dominance of non-Arabs in running affairs of state, 40; difficulties for son of mixed race, 39; non-religious motivation of policies, 119–20; promotion of learning Arabic, 55; significance of separate registers of Arabs, non-Arabs, 30, 117; tradition associating with concept of Arabic as sacred language, 56; traditions on kissing of hands, 34

'Abd al-Muṭṭalib ibn Rabī'a, and tradition of splitting of land by act of God, 59

'Abd al-Raḥīm al-Raqqāṣ, reference to 'Alī's Arab ethnicity, 19

'Abd al-Raḥmān ibn Abī l-Zinād, on prohibition on naming addressee of letter, 35

'Abd al-Raḥmān ibn Hilāl, and fear of internal discords, 102

'Abd al-Raḥmān ibn Jubayr ibn Nufayr, and violation of the Ka'ba, 98

'Abd al-Raḥmān ibn Ka'b ibn Mālik
and assimilation of Copts, 70; evidence on interpretations of *shu'ūb*, 23

'Abd al-Raḥmān ibn al-Mahdī, and Arab attitudes to blacks, 90

'Abd al-Raḥmān ibn Mālik ibn Mighwal, and slandering the Nabāṭ, 79

'Abd al-Raḥmān ibn Mall *see* Abū 'Uthmān al-Nahdī
'Abd al-Raḥmān ibn Shumāsa al-Muhrī, and assimilation of Copts, 69
'Abd al-Raḥmān ibn Yazīd ibn Jābir
and: assimilation of non-Arabs, 72; slandering the Nabāṭ, 79
'Abd al-Raḥmān ibn Zayd, and Arab attitudes to blacks, 93
'Abd al-Raḥmān ibn Ziyād ibn An'am, and customs of the *a'ājim*, 33–34
'Abd al-Razzāq al-Ṣan'ānī
concept of Prophet as messenger to all, 15–16; on differentiation of all *a'rāb* and *ṭawā'if*, 8–9
'Abd al-Wārith ibn Sa'īd, on 'Umar I's promotion of learning Arabic, 54
abdāl, tradition identifying with *mawālī*, 13–14
'abīd ("slaves"), ethnic, racial connotations of term, 80–81; *see also* blacks, slavery
Abraha, campaign against Mecca, 100
Abraham
and significance of marital relations, 122; learns Arabic through revelation, 49–50; wives of, 70, 71, 104
Abū 'Abd al-Raḥmān al-Ḥubūlī, and assimilation of Copts, 69
Abū l-Aḥwaṣ, and tradition on establishment of Quraysh as *Imāms*, 58
Abū l-'Āliya Rufay' ibn Mihrān
and violation of the Ka'ba, 98; and interpretations of *umma*, 14
Abū l-Aswad al-Du'alī, and tradition on threat to Arabs from non-Arabs, 75
Abū Badr Shujā' ibn al-Walīd, and attitudes to non-Arabs, 60–61
Abū Bakr
and: Arab attitude to Turks, 107; love and hatred, 64–65; Prophet's reference to, as "master of the *kuhūl*," 17
Abū Bakra, and Turks/sons of Keturah, 107
Abū l-Dardā' 'Uwaymir ibn Zayd
and: Arab attitude to Turks, 106; unfavourable characteristics of blacks, 78–79: marriage to woman of Banū Layth tribe, 37–38
Abū Dharr al-Ghifārī
and: Arab attitudes to blacks, 88–91; assimilation of Copts, 69; concept of Prophet as messenger to all, 16: slanderous statement about Bilāl's mother, 23
Abū l-Ghayth, Sālim
and: concept of Prophet as messenger to all, 20; disapproval of agriculture as occupation for Arabs, 36; fear of internal discords, 102; violation of the Ka'ba, 96
Abū Ḥamza
association with slandering the Nabāṭ, 80; possible indentification with 'Imrān ibn Abī 'Aṭā, 80
Abū Ḥanīfa
discrimination between Arabs and non-Arabs, 116; non-Arab descent used as argument against, 42; on Arab fiscal policies, 29
Abū Ḥarb ibn Abī l-Aswad al-Daylī (al-Du'alī), and Arab attitude to blacks, 90
Abū Ḥāzim, and interpretations of *umma*, 14
Abū Hurayra al-Dawsī
and: acceptance of Arabic as sacred language, 51, 54–55; Arab attitude to Turks, 107, 108, 109–10; Arabs as untrustworthy, 13; concept of Prophet as messenger to all, 16–17, 19–20; favourable attitude to Persians, Byzantines, 71, 77; fear of internal discords, 101; fusion of Arabs, Islam, 56; identification of Persians with sons of Isaac, 68; integration of blacks into Islam, 87; interpretations of *umma*, 14; imminent onset of evil, 101, 103; loving the Arabs, 61–62; Prophet's repudiation of kissing of hands, 33–34; non-Arab prophets, 72; slandering the Nabāṭ, 79–80; splitting of land by act of God, 59; the last days, 95; threat to Arabs from non-Arabs, 74–75; unfavourable view of Berbers, 78; violation of the Ka'ba, 96–97
Abū l-Ḥuṣayn
and: attitudes to Arabs and non-Arabs, 66; establishment of Quraysh as *Imāms*, 58
Abū 'Imrān al-Jawnī, and Arab attitudes to blacks, 89
Abū 'Iqāl Hilāl ibn Zayd, and violation of the Ka'ba, 97
Abū Isḥāq al-Khamīsī, Khāzim ibn al-Ḥusayn, and attitudes to Arabs and non-Arabs, 64
Abū Mūsā al-Ash'arī
and: Arabs as chosen of God, 59–60; threat to Arabs from non-Arabs, 74; violation of the Ka'ba, 99
Abū Muslim al-Khurāsānī
and promotion of Arabic, 54, 55; reported attitude to Arabs, 41–42
Abū Naḍra, evidence on interpretations of *shu'ūb*, 22
Abū l-Najm al-'Ijlī, expression of anti-Persian sentiments, 25
Abū Qulāba *see* Shayba al-'Absī

Abū Rāfi'
and: attitudes to Arabs and non-Arabs, 62; attitudes to black slaves, 83
Abū Sa'īd al-Khudrī
and: concept of Prophet as messenger to all, 16–17; concept of Turks as eschatological enemy, 108–109; evidence on interpretations of *shu'ūb*, 22
Abū Salama ibn 'Abd al-Raḥmān
and: fear of internal discords, 102; prophetic tradition on ethnicity of black Companions, 56; violation of the Ka'ba, 96
Abū Ṣāliḥ 'Abd Allāh ibn al-Faḍl
and concept of Turks as eschatological enemy, 109; and fear of internal discords, 101
Abū Sufyān
and attitudes to Arabs and non-Arabs, 64–65; Prophet's reaction to slander of Banū Hāshim, 58
Abū Sukayna, and avoidance of Turks, Ḥabasha, 105
Abū l-Sulayl al-Qaysī, Ḍurayb ibn Nuqayr, and Arab attitudes to blacks, 89
Abū Ṭālib, reported inducement to follow the Prophet, 25–26
Abū l-Tayyāḥ Yazīd ibn Ḥumayd, and Arab attitudes to blacks, 91
Abū 'Ubayd al-Qāsim ibn Sallām, on Arab fiscal policies, 29, 115
Abū 'Ubayda ibn al-Jarrāḥ, reported kissing of 'Umar I's hand, 34
Abū 'Ubayda Ma'mar ibn al-Muthannā
and interpretations of *umma*, 15; and concept of Prophet as Arab, 49
Abū Umāma As'ad ibn Sahl ibn Ḥunayf, and violation of the Ka'ba, 97
Abū Umāma al-Bāhilī, Ṣuday ibn 'Ajlān
and: concept of Prophet as messenger to all, 16, 17–18; concept of Prophet's Arab ethnicity, 17–18; interpretations of *shu'ūb*, 23; Prophet's attitude to standing in his presence, 34; the last days, 95
Abū 'Uthmān al-Nahdī, 'Abd al-Raḥmān ibn Mall, on discrimination between Arabs and non-Arabs, 31–32
Abū Wā'il
and: avoidance of Turks, 105; Prophet's attitude to non-Arabs, 79: identification with Shaqīq ibn Salama, 105
Abū l-Yamān al-Ḥakam ibn Nāfi' al-Baḥrānī, and concept of Turks as eschatological enemy, 109
Abū Yūnus, and fear of internal discords, 101
Abū Yūsuf Ya'qūb ibn Ibrāhīm
and Arab attitudes to blacks, 88; and warning against adhering to Khārijites, 92
Abū Ẓibyān al-Janbī, Ḥuṣayn ibn Jundab, and attitudes to non-Arabs, 60–61
Abū l-Zinād 'Abd Allāh ibn Dhakwān al-Qurashī, and concept of Turks as eschatological enemy, 109
Abū l-Zubayr Muḥammad ibn Muslim al-Makkī
and the last days, 95; and standing in presence of Prophet, 34–35; unfavourable view of non-Arabs,78
Abū Zur'a Yaḥyā ibn Abī 'Amr al-Saybānī, and the last days, 95
Abyssinia, Abyssinians
attitude of Arabian Islam to, 121–22, 123; Bilāl as "master" of, 17, 115; descriptions of slaves among, 80–81; no threat posed to Muslim Arabia by, 100; traditions on attempts to assimilate, 71; *see also* Ḥabasha, Negus
Adam, 78
as "master" of mankind, 17; children of, 16
addressees, controversy over naming at beginning of letter, 35, 117
adhān ("call to prayer")
deemed a role appropriate to the Ḥabasha, 87; protest against Bilāl's, because of his black colour
Adharbayjān
fear of Turkish attack on, 107; letter of 'Umar I to, 32; Turkish campaigns against, 108, 110
agriculture, tradition disapproving of, as occupation for Arabs, 36
ahl al-kitāb see People of the Book
Aḥmad ibn Ḥanbal, complimented for not boasting non-Arab descent, 42
'Ā'isha
and: attitudes to black slaves, 83–85; banning non-Muslims from Arabia, 30; concept of Prophet as messenger to all, 16–17; concept of Prophet as messenger to Arabs, 45; rebuke by Prophet for treatment of bedouin, 53; worthiness in marriage, 37, 86
'ajam, a'ājim, 'ajamī practices
described in Qur'ān, 7; in tradition of Prophet as messenger to all, 19; prohibitions on imitations of, 33, 117; Qur'ānic use of *shu'ūb* interpreted as reference to, 20–21; traditions on concept of, as threat to Arabs, Islam, 73–75; *see also* non-Arabs *and individual races*

al-'Alā' ibn 'Abd al-Raḥmān
and: concept of Prophet as messenger to all, 20; banning of non-Arabs from markets, 31; fusion of Arabs and Islam, 121; privileged position of Arabs and Arabic, 57
al-'Alā' ibn 'Amr al-Ḥanafī, and fusion of Arabs and Islam, 57
'Alī ibn Abī Ṭālib
and: Arab attitudes to blacks, 91; attitudes to Arabs and non-Arabs, 65; attitudes to mixed marriage of Arab, non-Arab, 39; concept of equality of race, 68; concept of Prophet as messenger to all, 16; concept of superior status of Arabs, 73; differentiation between Arabs and non-Arabs, 117–18; disapproval of agriculture as occupation for Arabs, 36; discrimination against bedouins, 12; violation of the Ka'ba, 98: fiscal policies, 28–29; insistence on status as *muhājir*, 11; ordered by Prophet to ensure Arabs' well-being, 60; references to Arab ethnicity, 17; reported burning of gypsies, 78
'Alī ibn al-Mahdī, reference to Arab ethnicity of, 19
'Alī ibn Zayd ibn Jud'ān
and: attitudes to Arabs and non-Arabs, 61, 64; fusion of Arabs and Islam, 121
'Alī Zayn al-'Ābidīn ibn al-Ḥusayn
and: concept of Prophet as messenger to all, 16; kissing of hands, 34; tradition on attitudes to black slaves, 85
'Alqama al-Shaybānī, and Arab attitudes to blacks, 89
al-A'mash, Sulaymān ibn Mihrān
and: discrimination between Arabs, non-Arabs, relative to marriage, 39; fear of internal discords, 101; identification of Turks as descendants of Keturah, 104–105; Prophet's attitude to non-Arabs, 79; threat to Arabs from non-Arabs, 74; Prophet's perception of future, 26; violation of the Ka'ba, 99
Āmid, fear of Turkish attack on, 107
'Āmir ibn Ṣāliḥ al-Zubayrī, and discrimination against blacks, 38
'Āmir al-Sha'bī, *see* al-Sha'bī, 'Āmir ibn Shurāḥīl
'Ammār ibn Ghīlān, and avoidance of Turks, Ḥabasha, 105–106
'Amr ibn Abī 'Amr, evidence on interpretations of *shu'ūb*, 22
'Amr ibn Dīnār
and: attitudes to Arabs and non-Arabs, 63; attitudes to black slaves, 84; establishment of Quraysh as *Imams*, 58; fusion of Arabs and Islam, 121
'Amr ibn al-Ḥamq al-Khuzā'ī, and last days, 95
'Amr ibn Ḥurayth, and assimilation of Copts, 69
'Amr ibn Maymūn al-Jazarī
and: attitudes to black slaves, 83; contempt for blacks and Zanj, 86; marriage of Bilāl and brother, 38
'Amr ibn Taghlib
and: concept of Turks as eschatological enemy, 108–109; identification of Turks as sons of Keturah, 108
'Amr ibn Yaḥyā ibn Sa'īd ibn 'Amr ibn al-'Āṣ, and violation of Ka'ba, 99
Anas ibn Mālik
and: Arab attitudes to blacks, 88; assimilation of non-Arabs, 72; attitudes to Arabs and non-Arabs, 63, 64; concept of jealousy as characteristic of Arabs, 13; concept of Prophet as messenger to all, 16–17; concept of Prophet's Arab ethnicity, 17–18; discrimination between Arabs, non-Arabs, relative to marriage, 38; establishment of Quraysh as *Imāms*, 57; loving the Arabs, 62; threat to Arabs from non-Arabs, 74; unfavourable attitudes to non-Arabs, 77; violation of the Ka'ba, 97; worthiness in marriage, 86
'Anbasa al-Baṣrī, and attitudes to black slaves, 83, 124
Anbāṭ *see* Nabāṭ
Anṣār
traditions on: love and hatred of, 64–65; offices pertaining to, 87
apocalypticism
and insecurities, 94–111; in Arabian-Islamic attitude to Byzantines, 123; *see also* eschatology
apostasy
association with occupation in agriculture, 36; sinfulness, after making *hijra*, 10
a'rāb, *a'rābīya*
Arab distinguished, 54; contrasted to those making *hijra*, 10–11; evidence on interpretations of, 120; in depiction of bedouins, 7–9, 10–12; *see also* Arabs, bedouins
'arabī, adjectival use to denote scripture, or language of scripture, 48
Arabia, tradition on banning non-Muslims from, 29–30, 117

Arabic
concept of, as sacred language, 44, 48–53, 50–51, 54–55, 56, 118, 119–20; conflicting traditions on promotion of, 31, 54

Arabs
attitudes to neighbouring ethnic groups: ambivalence, 67–93; and concept of *'ajam* as threat, 73–75; attempts to assimilate, 67–73; concept of bedouins as core of emerging national identity, 120, 125, *see also individual races*: concepts of: as chosen of God, 59–60; as people from whom Prophet descended, 51: discrimination between non-Arabs and: and enslavement, 27–28, 116; and exemption from taxes, 29, 116–17; and rejection of non-Arab habits, 33, 117; by keeping of separate registers, 30, 117; by separate identification of non-Arab forces, 31, 116; equal treatment demanded in Iraq, 23; in differing interpretations of Qur'ān, 7, 19–23; in terms of occupation, 35–36, 117–18; policy attributed to 'Umar I, 116–17; and mixed marriages, 36–38, 116, 118; by banning from markets, 31: recognition of role in Islam, 75–77; traditions on: attempts to assimilate, 68–75; rise to prominence in third/ninth century, 60–61; *see also individual tribes, peoples*: equation with those speaking Arabic, 56; establishment of Quraysh as *Imāms*, 57–58, 59–60, 91; forces separately identified from Islam, 116; fusion of Islam and: and recognition of role in Islam of non-Arabs, 75–77; and rehabilitation of bedouins, 53–54; and traditions on love of the poor, 62; by dropping of polytheism, illiteracy, 46–47, 118–19; by stress on Arabian ethnicity of Prophet, 44–48, 49–50, 118, 120; by elevation of Arabic, 44, 48–53, 55, 56, 118, 120; complexities, 121; concept not present in Qur'ān, 9; dating of, 29–30, 63–64, 120–21; gradual process, 26–27, 29–30, 41, 42–43, 112–13, 115–16; numerous traditions bearing witness to, 56–57, 61–66; recognised in traditions on attitudes to Arabs, non-Arabs, 61–66; significance of battle of Dhū Qār, 24–25; *see also umma, ummī, ummīyūn*; hating, and unsavoury characteristics, 62–66; insecurities: and adoption of bedouin life, 94; and internal discords, 101–102; and role as bearers of new faith, 94–95; expressed in apocalyptic forms, 94–111: polity, and religious position of Islam distinguished relative to slavery, 27–28; relations with Persians: significance of battle of Dhū Qār, 24–25; traditional hostile sentiments, 25: stress on descent, 42–43; traditions identifying Prophet, Companions with ethnicity of, 17–19

al-A'raj, 'Abd al-Raḥmān ibn Hurmuz, and attitude of Arabs to Turks, 109–10

Arṭāṭ ibn al-Mundhir
and: attitudes to Arabs and non-Arabs, 62; violation of the Ka'ba, 98

Arwā bint al-Ḥārith ibn 'Abd al-Muṭṭalib, and ethnicity, 18

Asbāṭ ibn Naṣr al-Hamadānī, interpretation of *ummī, ummīyūn*, 47, 119

A'shā Banī Māzin, and concept of Prophet's Arab ethnicity, 18

'Āṣim ibn Kulayb, and Arab attitudes to blacks, 89

al-Aṣma'ī, 'Abd al-Malik ibn Qurayb
and: Arab attitudes to blacks, 92; attitudes to black slaves, 82–83, 86; banning non-Muslims from Arabia, 30

astronomy
promotion of learning of, 119–20; Prophet's reported commendation of knowledge of, 54–55

'Aṭā' ibn Abī Maymūna
and: fusion of Arabs and Islam, 121; loving the Arabs, 61–62

'Aṭā' ibn Abī Rabāḥ
and: Arab attitudes to blacks, 92–93; assimilation of non-Arabs, 72; attitudes to black slaves, 84, 85; fusion of Arabs, Islam, 57; identifying *abdāl* as *mawālī*, 13–14; integration of blacks into Islam, 87; promotion of learning Arabic, 54–55; scriptural nature of Arabic, 120: policies of 'Umar I reinterpreted as pro-Arabic, 120

'Aṭā' al-Khurāsānī
and interpretations of *umma*, 14; interpretation of Qur'ānic use of *shu'ūb*, 21

'Aṭīya ibn Sa'd al-'Awfī
and interpretations of *umma*, 14; interpretation of Qur'ānic use of *shu'ūb*, 21

'Awf al-A'rābī, and concept of Arabic as sacred language, 55, 120

'Awf ibn Mālik, and concept of Prophet as messenger to all, 16

'Awsaja al-Baṣrī, and attitudes to black slaves, 84–85

al-Awzā'ī, 'Abd al-Raḥmān ibn 'Amr
and: Arabs as chosen of God, 59–60; on assimilation of non-Arabs, 70, 72

Ayyūb ibn 'Utba, Abū Yaḥyā al-Yamānī, and Arab attitudes to blacks, 92–93

Badr, battle of
equal treatment of Arab, non-Arab soldiers fighting in, 30; participation of non-Arabs in Arab army, 75–76
Bahz ibn Ḥakīm ibn Muʿāwiya
association with traditions on Arab attitudes to blacks, 89, 92; tradition on playing of chess, 35
Banū ʿAbd Shams, clan addressed as "masters of the Arabs," 18
Banū Hāshīm
Prophet's response to slander by Abū Sufyān, 58; traditions on: love and hatred of, 65; Prophet's concept of divine choice of, 58
Banū Kināna, and tradition on establishment of Quraysh as *Imāms* of Arabs, 58, 59–60
Banū Layth, attitude to mixed marriage, 37–38
Banū Taghlib
impact of Arab fiscal policies on, 28, 29; rejection of conversion to Islam, 116, 117; traditions on Arab attitude to, 77; tribal associations, 29
al-Barrāʾ ibn ʿĀzib
and: love and hatred of Anṣār, 64; Prophet's policy on clapping hands, 33
al-Barrāʾ ibn Yazīd al-Ghanawī, and threat to Arabs from non-Arabs, 74
al-Baṣra
apocalyptic fear of attack by Turks, 107; attitudes in, toward: Arabs and Arabic, 55; black slave community, 123–24; Nabāṭ, 80; Zanj uprising near, 86
al-Bazzār, and tradition on attitudes to black slaves, 84
bedouins
and differentiation of Arabs, non-Arabs in terms of occupation, 35–36; concept of, as core of emerging national Arabian identity, 120, 125; discrimination against: in tradition contrasting with sedentary peoples, 12; in order forbidding *muhājir* to act as brokers for, 12: pejorative depiction of, 7–9, 10–12, 114; rehabilitation, reconciliation with Islam, 53–54; reversion to life-style of, 11–12, 94; *see also aʿrāb, aʿrābīya*
Berbers
occasional references to, 124; traditions on: identification as descendants of Ham, 71; unfavourable characteristics, 77, 78
Bilāl ibn Rabāḥ
Arabian-Islamic attitude to, 124; black, non-Arab, symbolic ethnic representative, 56, 75, 87; equality notwithstanding non-Arab origins, 20; identification as "master" of Abyssinians, 17; in traditions on attempts to assimilate non-Arabs, 72; protest at call to prayer on account of black race, 21; significance of attempt to marry Arab woman, 118; traditions on marriage of brother and, 38, 118
blacks
traditions on: Arabian-Islamic attitudes to, 72, 73, 123–24; attitudes to slaves among, 82–93; discrimination against, 36; ethnic, racial connotations of descriptions of slaves among, 80–81; expression of contempt for, 86; identification as descendants of Ham, 71; integration into Islam, 86–87; positive qualities, 82–83, 86–88; promise of becoming white in Paradise, 92–93; protest at call to prayer on account of colour, 21; unfavourable characteristics, 78–79; recommendations against marriage with, 38–39; worthiness in marriage, 38–40, 86; *see also ʿabīd*, slavery
blasphemy, Qurʾānic asssociation with *ʿarab*, 8
booty, restriction on entitlement of bedouin Muslims to share of, 12
Bukhārī (language), tradition associating with Hell, 51
Burayda al-Aslamī, and Arab attitude to Turks, 107
Burjān, fear of Turkish alliance with, 107
Byzantines, 30, 72
apocalyptic insecurities relative to wars with, 107; Qurʾānic exegesis depicting, as enemies of Arabs, 26; traditions on: Arab attitudes to, 6, 71, 77, 121–22, 123; attribution of nationalist statements by Prophet relative to, 115–16; defeat of, by Arabs, 26–27; customs of, 33; exhortations to fight against, 106; fear of Turkish alliance with, 107; Ṣuhayb as "master" of, 17; threat to Arabs from, 75; summer campaigns against, 31; threatened defection of Banū Taghlib to, 28; *see also* "Caesar," *raqīq*

"Caesar" (the Byzantine emperor) fall of, promised to Arab tribes by Prophet, 26
caliphs
traditions on kissing of hands, 34, 117; *see also individual caliphs*
Carmathians, attack on Mecca, 101
chess, traditions on playing of, 35
Chosroes
Muʿāwiya compared to, 18; Prophetic tradition predicting fall of, 26

Christ, second coming, Muslim belief in, and traditions on violation of the Ka'ba, 100–101
Christians
accepted as People of the Book, 29; of Najrān, tradition on banning from Arabia, 30, 117
clothing, banning of non-Arab style, 31
colours, use to identify people, in Muslim literature, 14, 15–16
Companions of the Prophet
application of term *umma* to, 9, 14, 15; and concept of Prophet as messenger to all, 16; discrimination between Arabs, non-Arabs, relative to mixed marriage, 37–38, 118; Qur'ānic tradition of equality amongst, 20; traditions associating with Arab ethnicity, 17–18; *see also individual Companions*
conversion, to Islam, Qur'ānic association of resistance to, with *'arab*, 8
Copts
attitude of Arabian-Islam to, 68–70, 121–22; traditions identifying as descendants of Ham, 71

al-Ḍaḥḥāk ibn Muzāḥim, identification of *umma* with Companions, 14, 114
Ḍamḍam ibn Zur'a, and integration of blacks into Islam, 87
Ḍamra ibn Ḥabīb
and: attitude toward marriages with bedouins, 10; warning against adhering to Khārijites, 92
Dāwūd ibn Abī Hind
and: Arab attitudes to blacks, 90; unfavourable characteristics of blacks, 78–79
Dāwūd ibn al-Ḥuṣayn, and attitudes to Arabs and non-Arabs, 62–63
desert-dwelling, dwellers
traditions on: alleged uncouth behaviour, 13–14; depiction as best of people in future, 12; reported commendation by 'Umar I, 32; *see also* bedouins
Dhū l-Nūn al-Miṣrī
and: Arab attitudes to blacks, 93; slandering the Nabāṭ, 80
Dhū Qār, battle of, 24–25
dice, traditions on gaming with, 35
discrimination, racial
between Arabs and non-Arabs: and enslavement, 27–28, 116; and exemption from taxes, 29, 116–17; and rejection of non-Arab habits, 33, 117; by keeping of separate registers, 30, 117; by separate identification of non-Arab forces, 31, 116; equal treatment demanded in Iraq, 23; in differing interpretations of Qur'ān, 7, 19–23; in terms of occupation, 35–36, 117–18; policy attributed to 'Umar I, 116–17; and mixed marriages, 36–38, 116, 118; by banning from markets, 31: recognition of role in Islam, 75–77; traditions on: attempts to assimilate, 68–75; rise to prominence in third/ninth century, 60–61; *see also individual tribes, peoples*

Egypt, conquest by Arabs, Islamicization, 122; *see also* Copts
eloquence, tradition linking with revelation, 49–50
eschatology
in Arabian-Islamic attitudes: to blacks, 122–23; to Turks, 79–80, 108–09, 122–23; in interpretation of civil wars of Umayyad period, 41; *see also* apocalypticism
eunuchs, attitudes to, 80, 81–82; *see also* apocalypticism
evil, concepts of, in traditions on the last days, 95–104

Farewell Pilgrimage *see* Prophet
Farghāna, fighting against Turks in, 110
"forerunners" (*ṣubbāq*) traditions on, and emphasis on Prophet's Arab ethnicity, 17

gaming, traditions on prohibitions on, 35
genealogy, promotion of learning of, 54, 119–20
Ghālib al-Qaṭṭān
on 'Umar I's promotion of learning Arabic, 54; policies of 'Umar I reinterpreted as pro-Arabic, 120
Gog and Magog
concept of, as sons of Japheth, 104; struggle against: and concept of imminent onset of evil, 103, 104; and traditions on violation of the Ka'ba, 100–101; traditions identifying with various non-Arab groups, 71
gypsies, paucity of information on policy towards, 78–79, 124, 125

Ḥabash, Ḥabasha, Ḥabashī
and violation of the Ka'ba, 96–101; term for black slaves, 84–85; traditions on offices pertaining to, 87; *see also* Abyssinia, blacks, Negus, slavery
Ḥabash Banī l-Mughīra, association with tradition on attitudes to black slaves, 84
Ḥabashī ibn Junāda, and tradition of Arabs as chosen of God, 59

Ḥabīb ibn Abī Ḥabīb ibn Zurayq, and tradition on good qualities of blacks, 87–88
Ḥafṣa bint Sīrīn, and violation of the Ka'ba, 98
Hagar, mother of Ishmael, tradition of Egyptian origins, 70
hajīn, offspring of mixed marriage, difficulties for, 39, 118
al-Ḥajjāj ibn Yūsuf al-Thaqafī, 118
conflict with Sa'īd ibn Jubayr, 36; ethnic element in treatment of *mawālī* ex-prisoners, 41; insistence on status as *muhājir*, 11
Ham, sons of
tradition identifying as ancestor: of Copts, Berbers, blacks, 71; of black slaves, 124
Ḥamīd ibn 'Abd al-Ḥamīd, and admiration for Turkish military prowess, 111
Ḥammād ibn Salama, and Arab attitudes to blacks, 93
Ḥamza ibn al-Mundhir, and fear of internal discords, 102
handclapping, attribution to Prophet of recommendation on, 33
al-Ḥārith ibn Suwayd, and violation of the Ka'ba, 98
Ḥarmala ibn 'Imrān al-Tujībī al-Miṣrī, association with traditions on assimilation of Copts, 69
Ḥasan al-Baṣrī
and: banning non-Muslims from Arabia, 30; concept of Prophet's Arab ethnicity, 18, 54; concept of Turks as eschatological enemy, 110; threat to Arabs from non-Arabs, 74: attribution of policies of discrimination to 'Umar I, 117; opposition to mixed marriage of Arabs, non-Arabs, 10–11, 39, 118; policies of 'Umar I reinterpreted as pro-Arabic by, 120; report on dream of Prophet signifying equality of Arabs, non-Arabs, 23; tradition on playing of chess, 35
Ḥassān ibn Thābit, on prohibition of foreign customs, 31
al-Haytham ibn 'Adī
and assimilation of Turks, 71; evidence on Arabian-Islamic attitude to Turks, 122–23
al-Haytham ibn Jummāz, and attitudes to Arabs and non-Arabs, 63–64
Hell
black as the colour of the people in, 78; Bukhārī as language of, 51; created for those who disobey God, regardless of ethnic origin, 92; Persian/non-Arabic as language of, 52
hijra
contrasted to *a'rābīya*, 10–11; of bedouin, sedentary, distinguished, 11; reversion to bedouin life following, 11–12
Hilāl (*mawlā* of Banū Hāshim), and tradition on attitudes to black slaves, 84
Hishām (*mawlā* to 'Uthmān ibn 'Affān), and discrimination against blacks, 38
Hishām ibn 'Abd al-Malik
association with concept of Turks as eschatological enemy, 110; keeping of separate registers of Arabs, non-Arabs in reign of, 30, 117; prohibition on kissing of hands, 117; significance of separate identification of Arab forces, 31; traditions on kissing of hands, 34
Hishām ibn 'Ammār, and attitudes to Arabs and non-Arabs, 65
Hishām ibn al-Ghāz, evidence on interpretations of *shu'ūb*, 22
Hishām ibn 'Urwa
and discrimination betweeen Arabs, non-Arabs, relative to marriage, 38; association with tradition on worthiness in marriage, 86; on non-Arab domination of legal profession, 42–43; tradition on playing of chess, 35
Ḥudhayfa ibn al-Yamān
and: Arab attitude to Turks, 107; concept of Prophet as messenger to all, 16–17; threat to Arabs from non-Arabs, 74, 75; violation of the Ka'ba, 98–99
Ḥudhayfa al-Ṭawīl, and violation of Ka'ba, 98
Hurmuz/Hurmuzān
defeated Persian leader, conversion to Islam, 26; hostile to Arabs, 26
al-Ḥusayn ibn 'Alī
on traditions on playing of chess, 35; tradition on death of, 41
al-Ḥuṣayn ibn Numayr, on marriage of Bilāl and brother, 38
al-Ḥusayn ibn 'Umar al-Aḥmasī
and attitudes to Arabs and non-Arabs, 61, 66
hypocrisy, alleged Arab characteristic, 8, 13–14

Ibn 'Abbās, 'Abd Allāh
and: Arab attitudes to blacks, 92–93; assimilation of non-Arabs, 72; attitudes to Arabs and non-Arabs, 65; attitudes to black slaves, 83, 84, 85; concept of Prophet as messenger to all, 5, 16–17; discrimination between Arabs, non-Arabs, in terms of occupation, 36; equation of Persians

with sons of Isaac, 68; fusion of Arabs, Islam, 56–57; interpretations of *umma*, *ummīyūn*, 14, 47, 118–19; loving the Arabs, 62; *mawālī* servants called by Arab names, 41 n. 70; Qur'ānic use of *shu'ūb*, 21; slandering the Nabāṭ, 80; unfavourable attitudes to eunuchs, 81–82; violation of the Ka'ba, 98

Ibn Abī Laylā, Muḥammad ibn 'Abd al-Raḥmān, on Prophet's attitude to kissing of hands, 34

Ibn Abī Mulayka, 'Abd Allāh ibn 'Ubayd Allāh
and: discrimintion between Arabs, non-Arabs, relative to marriage, 37; Qur'ānic use of *shu'ūb*, 21; violation of the Ka'ba, 98

Ibn Abī Najīḥ, 'Abd Allāh
and: Abyssinian attack on Mecca, 123; interpretations of *shu'ūb*, 22; unfavourable attitudes to eunuchs, 81–82; violation of the Ka'ba, 99

Ibn 'Amr, 'Abd Allāh
and: identification of Turks as sons of Keturah, 108; threat to Arabs from non-Arabs, 74–75; confusion with Ibn 'Umar, 74–75; traditions on: Arab attitude to Turks, 107; condemnation of languages other than Arabic, 52; differentiation between Arabs and non-Arabs, 117–18; disapproval of agriculture as occupation for Arabs, 36; the last days, 95; violation of the Ka'ba, 97, 99: warnings against defection to non-Arab habit, 13

Ibn al-Ash'ath, 'Abd al-Raḥmān, rebellion of, 36, 41

Ibn Isḥāq, Muḥammad
and: Abyssinian attack on Mecca, 123; concept of Prophet as messenger to Arabs, 45; interpretations of *shu'ūb*, 22; Prophet's perception of fusion between Arabs and Islam, 26; violation of the Ka'ba, 99

Ibn Jurayj, 'Abd al-Malik ibn 'Abd al-'Azīz
and: Abyssinian attack on Mecca, 123; Arabic as language of scripture, prayer, 120; attitudes to black slaves, 84; conflicts over entitlement to lead in prayer, 55; discrimination between Arabs, non-Arabs, relative to marriage, 39; equation of *ummīyūn* with polytheists, 47; fusion of Arabs, Islam, 57; integration of blacks into Islam, 87; interpretations of *umma*, *ummī*, *ummīyūn*, 14, 118–19; opposition to mixed marriage of Arabs, non-Arabs, 118; violation of the Ka'ba, 97, 1–2

Ibn Lahī'a, 'Abd Allāh
and: Arab attitude to Turks, 105–106; assimilation of Copts, 70; fear of internal discords, 101

Ibn Mas'ūd, 'Abd Allāh
association with tradition on: Arab attitude to Turks, 106, 108; attitudes to Arabs and non-Arabs, 65–66; concept of Prophet as messenger to all, 19; discrimination between Arabs, non-Arabs, relative to marriage, 39; establishment of Quraysh as *Imāms* of Arabs, 58; identification of blacks as descendants of Ham, 71; identification of Turks as descendants of Keturah, 104–105

Ibn al-Mubārak, 'Abd Allāh
and: assimilation of non-Arabs, 72; concept of Prophet as messenger to all, 16; non-Arab successor to legal authority, 43

Ibn al-Muqaffa', pro-Arab position in conflict with Shu'ūbīya, 43

Ibn Sīrīn, Muḥammad
and: Arab attitudes to blacks, 88–93, 90; Arab attitude to Turks, 106; interpretations of *shu'ūb*, 22; tradition on playing of chess, 35

Ibn 'Umar, 'Abd Allāh
and: Arab attitudes to blacks, 88, 92–93; Arab attitudes to non-Arabs, 73; Arabic as sacred language, 52; attitudes to Arabs and non-Arabs, 62, 63–64; discrimination between Arabs, non-Arabs, relative to marriage, 37; establishment of Quraysh as *Imāms* of Arabs, 58; identification of Persians with sons of Isaac, 68; Prophet's attitude to kissing of hands, 34; unfavourable attitude to *mamālīk*, 81; violation of the Ka'ba, 97: confusion with Ibn 'Amr, 74–75: reported as naming addressee of letter, 35

Ibn al-Zubayr, 'Abd Allāh, 37, 96 n. 8
attribution of ban on wearing of silk to Prophet, 32; rebuilding of Ka'ba, 99–100

Ibrāhīm, son of Prophet, tradition of Egyptian ancestry, 70

Ibrāhīm al-Hajarī, tradition on playing of chess, 35

Ibrāhīm al-Nakha'ī, religious authority in Kūfa, 40

Ibrāhīm al-Taymī
and: significance of battle of Dhū Qār, 25; violation of the Ka'ba, 98

'Ikrima ibn 'Abd Allāh al-Madanī
identification of *umma* with Companions, 9, 14, 114; evidence on interpretations of

shu'ūb, 22; on honest weights and measures, 36
illiteracy, and fusion of Arabs and Islam, 46–47, 118–19
Ilyās ibn Ibrāhīm al-Sīnūbī, in traditions on non-Arab prophets, 72
Imāms, to be from Quraysh, 58, 59–60, 91
'Imrān ibn Abī 'Aṭā', possible identification with Abū Hamza, 80
'Imrān ibn Tammām, and slandering the Nabāṭ, 80
Indians, occasional references to, 78, 124
inter-ethnic relations
 ambivalence in Muslim literature, 67; basis of Arab approach, 67–68; family-based approach in Old Testament, 68; *see also* non-Arabs *and individual races*
Iraq
 Arabian-Islamic attitude to black slave community in, 123–24; discrimination between Arabs, non-Arabs, in terms of occupation in, 36
Irbāḍ ibn Sāriya, and, Arab attitudes to blacks, 88, 91
'Īsā ibn 'Alī ibn 'Abd Allāh al-Hāshimī, and tradition on Arab attitude to Persians, 68
Isaac, sons of
 concept of Persians as, 67–68, 122; unfavourably contrasted with sons of Ishmael, 68
Isḥāq ibn Asad, and assimilation of Copts, 70
Isḥāq ibn Yaḥyā/Abī Yaḥyā al-Ka'bī, and unfavourable attitude to eunuchs, 81–82
Ishmael, sons of
 concept of Arabs as, 122; favourably contrasted with sons of Isaac, 68; tradition ascribing revelation of Arabic language to, 49–50; *see also* Ismā'īl
Islam
 concept of, as universal creed, 72: family-based approach to different ethnicities of faithful, 67–68: fusion of Arabs and: and recognition of role of non-Arabs, 75–77; and traditions of love of the poor, 62; by dropping of polytheism, illiteracy, 46–47, 118–19; by stress on Arabian identity of Prophet, 44–48, 49–50, 116, 118–19, 120; complexities, 121; concept not present in Qur'ān, 9; dating of, 29–30, 63–64, 120–21; gradual process, 26–27, 29–30, 41, 42–43, 112–13, 115–16; initial non-national character, 118; not present at outset of conquests, 112–13; numerous traditions bearing witness to, 56–57, 61–66; through elevation of Arabic, 44, 48–53, 55, 56, 118, 120; through emphasis on Arabian ethnicity of Prophet, 120; significance of battle of Dhū Qār, 24–25; and rehabilitation of, reconciliation with bedouins, 53–54; gradual nature of process, 26–27, 29–30, 120–21; and separate identification of Arab forces, 116: struggles with Turks, 108: traditions reflecting integration of blacks into, 85–87: *see also umma, ummī, ummīyūn*
Ismā'īl
 concept of Prophet as messenger to descendants of, 45; *see also* Ishmael
Ismā'īl Abū Ma'mar ibn Ibrāhīm ibn Ma'mar, and attitudes to Arabs and non-Arabs, 65
Ismā'īl ibn 'Ayyāsh, and attitudes to Arabs and non-Arabs, 65
Ismā'īl ibn Muḥammad al-Ṣaffār, and love and hatred of the Anṣār, 64
Ismā'īl ibn Ziyād, and tradition condemning languages other than Arabic, 51
Isrā'īl ibn Yūnus, and recognition of role in Islam of non-Arabs, 75–76
'Iyāḍ ibn Ḥimār, and Arabs, non-Arabs, People of the Book, 76
Iyās ibn Salama, and Arab attitudes to blacks, 89

Jābir ibn 'Abd Allāh
 and: attitudes to Arabs and non-Arabs, 64; concept of Prophet as messenger to all, 16–17; fusion of Arabs and Islam, 61; good qualities of blacks, 87–88; interpretations of *shu'ūb*, 22, 23; interpretations of *umma*, 15; revelation of Arabic to Ishmael, 50; standing in pressence of Prophet, 34–35; the last days, 95; threat to Arabs from non-Arabs, 75: link with Muḥammad al-Bāqir, 119
Jābir ibn Yazīd al-Ju'fī, and recognition of role in Islam of non-Arabs, 75–76
Ja'far ibn Rabī'a, and concept of Turks as eschatological enemy, 109
Ja'far al-Ṣādiq
 and: establishment of Quraysh as *Imāms*, 58–59; integration of blacks into Islam, 87; interpretation of Qur'ānic use of *shu'ūb*, 21; interpretations of *shu'ūb*, 22
Jāhilīya (pre-Islamic times, the "time of ignorance")
 birth in, as blameworthy, 44; merits of precedents from, 39; value of knowledge from, 32
al-Jāḥiẓ, Abū 'Uthmān 'Amr ibn Baḥr
 and: discrimination between Arabs, non-Arabs, relative to marriage, 39; identification of Turks as descendants of Keturah,

104; revelation of Arabic to Ishmael, 50; assimilation of Turks, 71; Arab attitude to Turks, 106; discrimination between Arabs, non-Arabs, in occupations in Iraq, 36: essay on merits of Turks, 111
Japheth, sons of, concept of Turks, Gog and Magog, Slavs, as, 71, 104, 124
Jarīr ibn 'Aṭīya, expression of passage from bedouinism to Arabism, 120
al-Jarrāḥ ibn Malīḥ, and attitudes to Arabs and non-Arabs, 62
Jazīra
fear of Turkish attack on, 107; Turkish campaign against, 108
jealousy, tradition associating with Arabs, 13
Jidda, tradition concering attack on, by the Ḥabasha, 100
jizya ("poll tax"), discrimination in payment required of Arabs, non-Arabs, 29, 115–17
Judaism, Jews
accepted as People of the Book, 29; attitude of Arabian Islam to, 121–22; traditions on: and unfavourable characteristics, 78; banning from Arabia, 30, 117; close relationship with Arabs, Islam, 72

Ka'b al-Aḥbār, 105
and violation of the Ka'ba, 100–101
Ka'b ibn Mālik, and assimilation of Copts, 69, 70
Ka'ba
apocalyptic traditions on violation of sanctity, 96–101; and Arab attitude to Turks, 107; destruction, rebuilding by Ibn al-Zubayr, 99–100
kafā'a principle *see* worthiness
Kahmas ibn al-Ḥasan, association with traditions on Arab attitudes to blacks, 89
al-Kalbī, Muḥammad ibn al-Sā'ib
interpretation of Qur'ānic use of *shu'ūb*, 21; possible identity of, 81
Keturah, wife of Abraham, concept of Turks as descendants of, 71, 104–107, 108
Khālid ibn Ma'dān
and: assertion of national character of Prophet, 119; Arab attitudes to blacks, 91; attribution of pro-Arab attitudes to Prophet, 48; concept of Prophet as messenger to all, 16; unfavourable view of non-Arabs, 78
Khālid ibn Muḥammad ibn Khālid al-Zubayrī, and tradition on attitudes to black slaves, 85
Khālid ibn Sā'id al-Umawī, on significance of battle of Dhū Qār, 25
Khālid ibn Yazīd
and: Arab attitudes to blacks, 90; good qualities of blacks, 88; integration of blacks into Islam, 87
Khalīfa ibn Salam, and assimilation of non-Arabs, 72
Khārija ibn Zayd, on prohibition on naming addressee of letter, 35
Khārijites
criticised for treating Arabs, non-Arabs equally, 42; traditions warning against adhering to, 91–92; recruitment of Turks to fight against, 111
Khazars (Khūz)
occasional references to, 124, 125; prohibition on marriage with, 39
al-Khiḍr, in traditions on non-Arab prophets, 72
khiṣyān ("eunuchs"), ethnic, racial connotations, 80, 81–82
Khulayd al-Baṣrī, and concept of Arabic as sacred language, 55
Khurāsān
Arab attitude to people of, 76; Turkish attacks on, 107, 110
Khūzistānī (language), tradition associating with demons, 51
Khūzistānīs, and concept of eschatological enemies, 79, 110
Kirmān, and concept of eschatological enemies, 110, 124, 125
kissing of hands, caliph's, Prophet's views on, 33–34, 117
al-Kūfa, Kūfans
Arab control of religious authority, 40; association with traditions on attitudes to Arabs, non-Arabs, 60–61; objection to judge on grounds of colour, 36, 117–18; occasional references to Christians of, 124, 125
Kurayb ibn Abī Muslim, on discrimination between Arabs, non-Arabs in terms of occupation, 36
Kurds, occasional references to, 124, 125
Kuthayyir ibn Murra, and integration of blacks into Islam, 87

Layth ibn Sa'd, 90
and: assimilation of Copts, 69, 70; favourable attitude to Persians, 76–77
Layth ibn Sulaym, evidence on interpretations of *shu'ūb*, 22
Luqmān
in traditions on attempts to assimilate non-Arabs, 72; recognition in Qur'ān, Arabian-Islamic respect for, 124

al-Mahdī
recruitment of Turks to fight against Khārijites, 111; traditions on kissing of hands, 34, 117
al-Mahdī ibn Maymūn, association with tradition on attitudes to black slaves, 84
Makḥūl al-Shāmī
and: assimilation of Copts, 70, 122; campaigns of the Turks, 108; integration of blacks into Islam, 87
Mālik ibn Anas
and: Arab fiscal policies, 29; assimilation of Copts, 69, 70; banning of non-Arabs from markets, 31; prohibition on naming addressee of letter, 35
Mālik ibn Dīnār, and attitudes to Arabs and non-Arabs, 64
mamālīk ("owned ones"), ethnic, racial connotations, 80–81
Ma'mar ibn Rāshid
and: assimilation of Copts, 70; favourable attitude to Persians, 77
al-Ma'mūn, 111
and: kissing of hands, 34, 117; behaviour of Arab tribal confederations, 42
Ma'n ibn Zā'ida al-Shaybānī, reference to Arab ethnicity of, 19
al-Manṣūr, 80
anti-Persian sentiment in reign of, 25; reference to Arab ethnicity of, 19; discrimination between Arabs and non-Arabs in rising against, 42; recruitment of non-Arabs to army, 41, 111
Māriya, mother of Ibrāhīm, tradition of Coptic origins, 70
markets, banning of non-Arabs from, 31
marriage, mixed
and concept of worthiness, 36–40, 86; difficulties for offspring, 39, 118; discrimination between Arabs and non-Arabs relative to, 36–40, 116, 118; of non-Arabs with Arab women, 55–56; prohibitions relative to bedouins, 10–11; with blacks, recommendations against, 38–39; *see also* women
Marwān ibn Sālim
and: identification of Turks as descendants of Keturah, 104–105; unfavourable view of non-Arabs, 78
Maslama ibn 'Abd al-Malik, separate identification of Arab, non-Arab forces under, 31
Maslama ibn Muḥammad, and discrimination between Arabs, non-Arabs, relative to marriage, 38
mawālī, *mawlā* (non-Arab clients)
in tradition of Prophet as messenger to all, 19; need to be affiliated to Arabs, 41, non-Arabs described as, 7, 13–14; Qur'ānic use of *shu'ūb* interpreted as reference to, 20–21; tradition identifying with *abdāl*, 13–14; rejection of appointment to judgeship, 36, 117–18; *see also* non-Arabs
Maymūn ibn Mihrān, and unfavourable attitude to *mamālīk*, 81
Maysūn bint Baḥdal (wife of Mu'āwiya), references to son's Arab ethnicity, 18–19
Mecca
attacks on: Arabian Islamic fear of Abyssinian, 123; traditions associated with, 99–101: concept of Prophet as messenger to people of, 44–45: pilgrimage to, and tradition associating Arabs with threats to, 13; *see also* Umm al-Qurā
Mihjā, in traditions on attempts to assimilate non-Arabs, 72
Mis'ar ibn Kaddām, on traditions on standing in presence of Prophet, 34
mourning the dead, Arab habit branded as element of unbelief, 13
Mu'ādh ibn Jabal
and: Arab attitudes to non-Arabs, 73; discrimination between Arabs, non-Arabs, relative to marriage, 37; fear of internal discords, 103
Mu'āwiya ibn Abī Sufyān
and: Arab attitude to Turks, 106–107; Arab attitude to Turks, 105–106; attitude to mixed marriage of Arab, non-Arab, 39; conflict with 'Alī, and distinction between *a'rābī*, *muhājir*, 11; non-religious motivation of policies, 119–20; opposition to mixed marriage of Arabs, non-Arabs, 118; pro-Arab policies, 40; promotion of Arabic, genealogy, astronomy, 55; reference to, as "Chosroes of the Arabs," 18
Mu'āwiya ibn Ḥudayj, and Arab attitude to Turks, 106
Mu'āwiya ibn Qurra, and tradition identifying Persians with sons of Isaac, 68
Mu'āwiya ibn Ṣāliḥ, and integration of blacks into Islam, 87
Mubashshar ibn 'Ubayd, and connection of Prophet's eloquence with revelation, 50
Muḍar, tradition on Prophet's concept of divine choice of, 58
muhājir (Muslim who has made *hijra*)
distinction betweem *a'rabī* and, 11; forbidden to act as broker for bedouin, 12
Muḥammad *see* Prophet

Muḥammad al-Bāqir
and: assimilation of Copts, 70, 122; establishment of Quraysh as *Imāms*; evidence on interpretations of *shu'ūb*, 22; link through Jābir to Prophet, 119; revelation of Arabic to Ishmael, 50; transmission of concept of Qur'ān as scripture, 119; unfavourable attitude to *mamālīk*, 81
Muḥammad ibn 'Abbād, and concept of Turks as eschatological enemy, 109–10
Muḥammad ibn 'Abd al Raḥmān ibn Abī Labība, and tradition identifying blacks as descendants of Ham, 71
Muḥammad ibn Abī Razīn, and apocalyptic insecurities, 94–95
Muḥammad ibn Ayyūb al-Riqāshī
association with unfavourable attitude to *mamālīk*, 81; possible identification with al-Raqqī, 81
Muḥammad ibn al-Faḍl al-Khurāsānī, and tradition on fusion of Arabs with Islam, 57
Muḥammad ibn Ḥijāra, and concept of Prophet's Arab ethnicity, 18
Muḥammad ibn Ja'far, and Arab attitudes to blacks, 90
Muḥammad ibn al-Khaṭṭāb, and loving the Arabs, 61–62
Muḥammad ibn al-Munkadir, and good qualities of blacks, 87–88
Muḥammad ibn Muṣ'ab al-Qirqisānī, and Arabs as chosen of God, 59–60
Muḥammad ibn Muslim *see* Abū l-Zubayr
Muḥammad ibn Sawā', on significance of battle of Dhū Qār, 25
Muḥammad ibn Zayd/Yazīd ibn Sinān, and tradition on threat to Arabs from non-Arabs, 74
Mujāhid ibn Jabr
and: concept of Prophet as Arab prophet, 49; concept of Prophet as messenger to all, 15–16 and n. 46; concept of Prophet as messenger to Arabs, 44–45; integration of blacks into Islam, 87; interpretation of Qur'ānic use of *shu'ūb*, 21; interpretations of *umma*, 9, 14; playing of chess, 35; unfavourable attitudes to eunuchs, 81–82; violation of the Ka'ba, 99–100
al-Mundhir ibn Mālik *see* Abū Naḍra
Murji'a, traditions warning against adhering to, 91
Mūsā ibn Abī 'Ā'isha, and unfavourable view of Byzantines, 'Ubbād, 77
al-Muṭarraf ibn 'Abd Allāh ibn al-Shikhkhīr
and Arabs, non-Arabs, People of the Book, 76; and concept of Prophet's Arab ethnici-ety, 18
al-Muṭarraf ibn Ma'qil, and loving the Arabs, 61
al-Mutawakkil, military importance of Turks during reign of, 111
Muṭī' ibn Iyās, references to Abbāsid Arab ethnicity, 19

Nabāṭ (Anbāṭ), occasional references to, 79–80, 124, 125
al-Naḍr ibn Kināna, and establishment of Quraysh as *Imāms*, 58
Nāfi', evidence on interpretations of *shu'ūb*, 22
Nāfi' (*mawlā* to Sa'īd ibn al-Musayyib), and discrimination against non-Arabs, 37
al-Nafs al-Zakīya, rising against al-Manṣūr, 42
Negus, in traditions on attempts to assimilate non-Arabs, 72
noble descent, attacking claims to, branded as element of unbelief, 13
non-Arabs
attitudes to dominance in running affairs of state, 40, 42–43; conflicts over entitlement to lead in prayer, 55; discrimination between Arabs and: and enslavement, 27–28, 116; and exemption from taxes, 29, 116–17; and rejection of non-Arab habits, 33, 117; by keeping of separate registers, 30, 117; by separate identification of non-Arab forces, 31, 116; equal treatment demanded in Iraq, 23; in differing interpretations of Qur'ān, 7, 19–23; in terms of occupation, 35–36, 117–18; policy attributed to 'Umar I, 116–17; and mixed marriages, 36–38, 116, 118; by banning from markets, 31: recognition of role in Islam, 75–77; traditions on: attempts to assimilate, 68–75; rise to prominence in third/ninth century, 60–61; *see also individual tribes, peoples, mawālī*
Nubayṭ ibn Sharīṭ, and loving the Arabs, 62
Nubians, traditions on Arab attitudes to, 73

Old Testament, parallels to tracing of ethnicity along family/tribal lines, 68, 121
Ottomans, Arab attitudes to, 111; *see also* Turks

Paradise
apostates to *a'rābīya* after *hijra* will never enter, 10; Arabic as language of, 50–52, 56,

119; blacks to become white in, 92–93; created for those who obey God, regardless of ethnic origin, 92; "forerunners" as first to enter, 18; "masters" of the people of, 72, 124; white as the colour of the people in, 78

People of the Book (*ahl al-kitāb*)
jizya accepted from, if Arabs, 29; traditions concerning exalted status of, 76; *ummīyūn* differentiated, 46

Persian (language)
association with unsavoury characteristics, 52; speaking of, prohibited, 52; tradition associating with Antichrist, Hell, 51, 52; traditions in favour of, 52–53; demeaning of, and elevation of Arabic, 119

Persians
Arab attitudes to, 60, 71, 73, 76–77, 121–22; attribution of nationalist statements by Prophet relative to, 26, 115–16; favourable attitudes towards, 79; identification with sons of Isaac, 67–68; identified as *'ajam*, 75; in tradition of Prophet as messenger to all, 19; relations with Arabs: significance of battle of Dhū Qār, 24–25; traditional hostile Arab sentiments, 25, 26: strength in 'Abbāsid period, 41, 122; traditions associating with avarice, 77

polytheism, polytheists
asssociation by Prophet with slandering of Arabs, 61; and non-Arabs, 32; dropping of, and fusion of Arabs and Islam, 118–19; rejection in interpretations of *ummīyūn*, 46–47

prayer
conflicts over those permitted to lead in, 10, 21, 55–56; for rain, Arab habit branded as element of unbelief, 13

Prophet (Muḥammad)
and: Arab attitudes to black women, 92; Arab attitudes to blacks, 88–93; attitudes to non-Arabs, 76, 77, 79; attitudes to slavery, 27–28, 82, 83–85; attitude to standing for him, 34–35; concept of Quraysh as *Imāms*, 57–58; connecting eloquence and revelation, 50; discrimination against bedouins, 10–11, 12, 13; interest in astronomy, 54–55; kissing of hands, 33–34, 117; naming of addressee at beginning of letter, 35; policy towards *a'rābī*, *a'rābīya*, 10–11; promotion of learning Arabic, 54; slandering Arabs as polytheism, 61; the last days, 94–95; violation of the Ka'ba, 96–97: attribution to, of: abrogation of ban on intercourse with suckling woman, 33; apocalyptic view of future, 103–104; banning non-Muslims from Arabia, 29–30; identification of Persians with sons of Isaac, 68; injunctions on imitation of *a'ājim*, 117; instructions to merchants on honesty, 36; nationalist statements, 115–16; opinion on playing of chess, 35; prohibition on imitation of non-Arab practices, 33–34, 117; pronouncements on marriage, mixed marriage, 37, 38; slandering the Nabāṭ, 79–80; statements instigating conflict with Persians, 26; traditions on attempts to assimilate Copts, 69–70; traditions on threat to Arabs from non-Arabs, 74; traditions warning against harming non-Muslims, 33; 'Umar I's pro-Arab policies, 31–32, 33; unfavourable attitude to eunuchs, 81–82; unfavourable attitude to *mamālīk*, 81; warnings against Turks, 106–11; view of scriptural nature of Arabic, 120: concepts of: as Arab prophet, 49; as descendant of Ishmael, Arabs, 49–50, 51; as messenger to all, 15–17, 19–23, 48–49, 60; national Arabian ethnicity, 17–19, 118–19, 120: concern to secure preferential treatment for Arabs, 60; equation of Arabs with those speaking Arabic, 56; evidence on attitude to bedouins, 53–54; Farewell Pilgrimage to Mecca: and Arab attitudes to blacks, 90–91; significance of contents, 21–23: fiscal policies, 28–29; perception of fusion between Arabs and Islam, 25–26, 26–27; pro-Arab attitudes: in adoption of Arab hair-style, 47; in dyeing beard, 47; in favouring Arab bows, horses, 48; in order on inscription on signet rings, 48; in promotion of turban, 47–48: reported dream signifying equality of Arabs, non-Arabs, 23; reported satisfaction with outcome of battle of Dhū Qār, 24–25; significance of marital relations, 122

Prophets, traditions on emergence among non-Arabs, 72

qabā'il ("tribes"), Qur'ānic use of term, 7

Qābūs ibn Abī Ẓibyān, and attitudes to non-Arabs, 60–61

Qadarīya, traditions warning against adhering to, 91

Qatāda ibn Di'āma
and: Arab attitudes to blacks, 89; Arabs, non-Arabs, People of the Book, 76; concept of Prophet as messenger to Arabs, 45; dream of Prophet signifying equality of Arabs, non-Arabs, 23; equation of *ummīyūn* with Arabs, 47; interpretations of *shu'ūb*, 21, 22, 114; marriage of Bilāl to

enslaved Arab woman, 38; threat to Arabs from non-Arabs, 74; violation of the Ka'ba, 97
Qays ibn Abī Ḥāzim, and concept of Turks as eschatological enemy, 109
Qays ibn al-Rabī', and revelation of Arabic to Ishmael, 50
Qays ibn Sa'd, and concept of Prophet as messenger to all, 19
Qur'ān
absence of ethnic identification of Prophet, 48, 115; concept of Arabic as tool of revelation, 44, 48–53, 118, 119–20; exegesis: and assertion of national character of Prophet, 119; and concept of national Arabian identity, 44–48, 118; and pejorative depiction of bedouins, 7–9; *'arabī, a'rābī* distinguished, 8–9; concept of Prophet as messenger to all, 15–17, 19–23; of *umma, ummī, ummīyūn*, 7, 9, 44–48, 114, 118–19; and specification of Persians, Byzantines, as enemies, 26: pejorative depiction of bedouins, 114; religious, not racial differences expressed in, 7–9; self-descriptions of, as scripture in Arabic, 119
Quraysh, tribe of
establishment as *Imāms*, 57–58, 59–60, 91; significance of birth of Prophet in, 50; traditions on: love and hatred of, 63–64; offices pertaining to, 87; Prophet's concept of divine choice of, 58
Qurra ibn Khālid, evidence on interpretations of *shu'ūb*, 22

Rabāḥ al-Lakhmī, and assimilation of Copts, 70
al-Rabī' ibn Anas, and interpretations of *umma*, 14, 15, 47, 119
Rabī'a (tribal confederation), as defenders of Islam, 29
Rabī'a ibn Abī 'Abd al-Raḥmān, non-Arab descent used as argument against, 42
Rabī'at al-Ra'y *see* Rabī'a ibn Abī 'Abd al-Raḥmān
Radhdhādh ibn al-Jarrāḥ, and unfavourable attitude to eunuchs, 81–82
Rāfiḍa, traditions warning against adhering to, 91
raqīq (white slaves, usually of Byzantine origin), 81–82, purchase recommended
al-Raqqī, possible identification of him with Muḥammad ibn Ayyūb al-Riqāshī, 81
red and black, interpretations of Prophet's mission to, 14, 15–16
revelation
concept of Arabic as tool of, 44, 48–53, 118, 119–20; tradition linking with eloquence, 49–50
Rūm *see* Byzantines

sābiq, subbāq see "forerunners"
Sa'd ibn Bakr, tribe of, significance of upbringing of Prophet in, 50
Ṣafwān ibn 'Amr, association with traditions on violation of the Ka'ba, 100–101
Sahl ibn 'Āmir, and loving the Arabs, 63
Sa'īd ibn Abī 'Arūba
and: interpretations of *shu'ūb*, 22; interpretations of *ummī, ummīyūn*, 47, 119
Sa'īd ibn 'Amr ibn Sa'īd ibn al-'Āṣ, military justification for 'Umar I's pro-Arab policies, 29
Sa'īd ibn Iyās al-Jarīrī, and interpretations of *shu'ūb*, 22
Sa'īd ibn Jubayr
and: identification of Persians with sons of Isaac, 68; integration of blacks into Islam, 87; interpretations of *shu'ūb*, 21; interpretations of *umma*, 9, 14; dismissal on grounds of colour, 36
Sa'īd ibn Kathīr, and fear of internal discords, 102
Sa'īd ibn al-Musayyib
and: Arab attitude to slavery, 27–28, 82; Arabic accepted as sacred language, 51; concept of Turks as eschatological enemy, 109; discrimination between Arabs, non-Arabs, relative to marriage, 37; favourable attitude to Persians, 76; slandering the Nabāṭ, 79–80; violation of the Ka'ba, 96, 97
Sa'īd ibn Salama, and slandering the Nabāṭ, 79
Sa'īd ibn 'Uqba ibn Salam al-Hannā'ī, and identification of Turks as descendants of Keturah, 104
Sa'īd al-Maqburī
association with fear of internal discords, 102; on prohibition on naming addressee of letter, 35
Salama ibn al-Akwa'
and reversion to bedouin life following *hijra*, 11; and Arab attitudes to blacks, 89
Salama ibn Nubāta, and Arab attitudes to blacks, 89
Ṣāliḥ ibn Abī Ṣāliḥ
and: untrustworthiness with Arabs, 13; violation of the Ka'ba, 97
Ṣāliḥ ibn Kaysān, and tradition on rehabilitation of bedouins, 53, 120

Ṣāliḥ al-Zubayrī, and worthiness in marriage, 86
Sālim ibn 'Abd Allāh ibn 'Umar
and concept of Prophet as messenger to all, 20; establishment of Quraysh as *Imāms*, 58; on *a'rābī* leading *muhājir* in prayer, 10
Salm ibn Qutayba, and slandering the Nabāṭ, 80
Salmān al-Fārīsi
and: attitudes to non-Arabs, 60–61; entitlement to lead in prayer, 55–56; mixed marriage of Arabs, non-Arabs, 55–56, 118; prayer for protection against non-Arabs behaving like Arabs, 14; repudiation of mixed marriage, 37–38; unfavourable view of Byzantines, 'Ubbād, 77: symbolic non-Arab ethnic representative, 17, 20, 56, 75; Prophet's comment on, as one of the "people of the house," 76
Samarqand, fighting against Turks in, 110
Samura ibn Jundab, and tradition on threat to Arabs from non-Arabs, 74
Sayf ibn 'Amr (Sayf ibn 'Umar?), and unfavourable view of non-Arabs, 78
sedentaries
bedouins distinguished, 11; testimony of bedouin against rejected, 12
Seljuks, Arab attitudes to, 111
sensuality, covert, alleged Arab characteristic, 13
al-Sha'bī, 'Āmir ibn Shurāḥīl
and: Arab attitude to slavery, 27–28; Arab attitudes to blacks, 88–89; marriage of Bilāl and brother, 38; prohibition on intermarriage with bedouins, 10–11; role in Islam of non-Arabs, 75–76; slandering the Nabāṭ, 79; tradition on playing of chess, 35; warning against adhering to various sects, 91–92
Shaddād Abū 'Ammār, and tradition of Arabs as chosen of God, 59–60
shafā'a ("intercession")
Prophet's: denied to those who cheat Arabs, 61; granted to the Arabs, 94
al-Shāfi'ī, Muḥammad ibn Idrīs
and: Arab attitude to slavery, 27–28; Arab fiscal policies, 29; attitudes to black slaves, 85; discrimination between Arabs and non-Arabs, 116
Shaqīq ibn Salama
and: identification of Turks as descendants of Keturah, 104; threat to Arabs from non-Arabs, 74: identification with Abū Wā'il, 105
Shayba al-'Absī, and Arab attitude to Turks, 107; evidence on interpretations of *shu'ūb*, 22
al-Shaybānī, Abū 'Abd Allāh Muḥammad ibn al-Ḥusayn
and: discriminatory practices between Arabs and non-Arabs, 117; naming addressee of letter, 35
Shem, tradition identifying as ancestor of Arabs, Persians, Byzantines, 71
Shī'a, pro-*mawālī* position, 41
Shibl ibn al-'Alā' ibn 'Abd al-Raḥmān, and fusion of Arabs, Islam, 57
Shu'ayb, and concept of Turks as eschatological enemy, 109
Shu'ba ibn al-Ḥajjāj, and Arab attitudes to blacks, 89, 90–91
Shurayk ibn 'Abd Allāh al-Nakh'ī, on exclusive domain of religious knowledge, 43
shu'ūb, interpretations of, 7, 20–21
Shu'ūbīya, Ibn al-Muqaffa''s pro-Arab position in conflict with, 43
Sijistān, fear of Turkish attack on, 107
slavery, slaves
black: attitude of Arabian-Islam to, 123–24; ethnic, racial connotations of *'abīd*, 80–81; conflicts over entitlement to lead in prayer, 55; discrimination between Arabs, non-Arabs relative to, 27–28, 116: identification as sons of Japheth, 124; tradition on wives permitted to, 82; traditions on attitudes to, 82–85; white, ethnic, racial connotations of *mamālīk*, 80–81; *see also 'abīd*, blacks
Slavs
fear of Turkish alliance with, 107; occasional references to, 124; traditions on attempts to assimilate, 71
splitting of land, tradition of act by God, relative to fusion of Arabs and Islam, 59
sūdān see blacks, slavery
Sudayf
association with uprising of Ibrāhīm ibn al-Ḥasan, 19; reference to al-Manṣūr as "best among the Arabs," 19
al-Suddī, Ismā'īl ibn 'Abd al-Raḥmān
and: discrimination betwen Arabs, non-Arabs, relative to marriage, 38; equation of *ummīyūn* with Arabs, 47; Gog and Magog, 104; identification of *umma* with Companions, 14, 114; worthiness in marriage, 86
Sufyān ibn Sa'īd al-Thawrī
and: Abyssinian attack on Mecca, 123; Arab fiscal policies, 29; discrimation between Arabs and non-Arabs, 116; fear of

internal discords, 101; identification of Persians with sons of Isaac, 68; mixed marriage of Arab, non-Arab, 39, 118; unfavourable attitude to eunuchs, 81–82; violation of the Kaʻba, 99; warning against adhering to Khārijites, 92: non-Arab in legal profession, 43

Sufyān ibn ʻUyayna al-Hilālī
and: assimilation of Copts, 70; attitudes to black slaves, 84–85; concept of Turks as eschatological enemy, 109–10; discrimination between Arabs, non-Arabs, relative to marriage, 38; kissing of hands, 34; revelation of Arabic to Ishmael, 50; worthiness in marriage, 86

Ṣuhayb, symbolic non-Arab ethnic representative, 17, 20, 56, 75

Sulaymān ibn ʻAbd al-Malik, attitude to domination of non-Arabs in affairs of state, 40

Sulaymān ibn ʻAlī, and attitudes to black slaves, 83

Sulaymān ibn al-Arqam, and traditions accepting Arabic as sacred language, 51

Sulaymān ibn Ḥarb, and destruction of the Arabs, 94

Sulaymān ibn Mihrān *see* al-Aʻmash

Syria, Syrians
concept of role in saving Kaʻba from Ḥabasba, 100–101; Arab's fear of reconquest by Byzantines, 123

Ṭalḥa ibn Mālik, and apocalyptic insecurities, 94–95

Ṭalḥa ibn ʻUbayd Allāh, *aʻrāb* urged to fight against ʻAlī by, 11

Ṭalḥa ibn Zayd al-Raqqī, and tradition condemning Persian language, 52; and unfavourable view of non-Arabs, 77

taxation, discrimination between Arabs, non-Arabs, 28, 29, 116–17

Thābit al-Bunānī
and: Arab attitudes to blacks, 93; loving the Arabs, 61; attitudes to Arabs and non-Arabs, 63–64; fusion of Arabs and Islam, 121; establishment of Quraysh as *Imāms*, 57

Thābit ibn Qays, rebuked for slander, 21

al-Thawrī *see* Sufyān ibn Saʻīd al-Thawrī

tribal confederations, Qur'ānic use of *shuʻūb* interpreted as reference to, 20–21

Turks
apocalyptic insecurities related to rising menace of, 104–11; Arab attitudes to Islamicized dynasties, 111; association with Gog and Magog, 104; attitude of Arabian Islam to, 121–22, 122–23, 125; concept of, as sons of Japheth, 104; connotations of *mamālīk* applied to slaves among, 80–81; eschatological context of traditions on, 108; identification as descendants of Keturah, 104–107; traditions on: attempts to assimilate, 71; avoidance of, and avoidance of Ḥabasha, 105: warnings against, 79

ʻUbāda ibn al-Ṣāmit
and: Arab attitudes to blacks, 89; integration of blacks into Islam, 87

ʻUbbād (Christians of Kūfa), traditions on Arab attitude to, 77, 124, 125

Ubayn ibn Sufyān al Maqdisī, and assimilation of non-Arabs, 72

Ubayy ibn Kaʻb, 15
erroneous identification of ʻAbd al-Raḥmān ibn Kaʻb with, 70

ʻUmar (*mawlā*) of Ghufra, and traditions concerning assimilation of Copts, 70

ʻUmar I ibn al-Khaṭṭāb
and Arab attitudes to blacks, 88–89; association with traditions on the last days, 95; attitude to mixed marriage of Arabs, non-Arabs, 10–11, 39, 118; attitude to slave-owning, 82; attribution to, of unfavourable attitude towards Nabāṭ, 80; discrimination between Arabs and non-Arabs, 116–17; fiscal policies, 28–29, 30; interest in genealogy, scripture, 54; non-religious motivation of policies, 119–20; policies reinterpreted as pro-Arab, 30–33, 48, 116–17, 120; policies justified on military grounds, 29; prohibition on enslavement of Arabs, 27–28; promotion of learning Arabic, 54; recommendation of *aʻrāb* for good treatment, 32; reference to Muʻāwiya as "Chosroes of the Arabs," 18; reported commendation of desert life, 32; views on love and hatred of Anṣār, 64–65

ʻUmar II ibn ʻAbd al-ʻAzīz
and: Arab attitude to Turks, 106; assimilation of Copts, 70; attitudes to Arabs, non-Arabs, in affairs of state, 40; attitude to mixed marriage of Arabs, non-Arabs, 38, 39, 118; banning non-Muslims from Arabia, 30; concept of Turks as eschatological enemy, 110; rehabilitation of bedouins, 53; violation of the Kaʻba, 98

ʻUmar ibn Ḥafṣ al-Makkī, and attitudes to black slaves, 84

ʻUmar ibn Hārūn, and traditions condemning Persian language, 52

Umayyad period
basically Arab orientation during, 41; eschatological interpretation of civil wars in, 41; apocalyptic insecurities engendered by collapse of rule, 102–103
Umm Ayman, and tradition on attitudes to black slaves, 85
Umm Hāni', and concept of Prophet's Arab ethnicity, 17–18
Umm al-Ḥarīr, and apocalyptic insecurities, 94–95
Umm al-Ḥuṣayn, and, Arab attitudes to blacks, 88, 90
Umm al-Qurā
association with concept of Prophet as messenger to Arabs, 45; possible identification with Mecca, 45
Umm Razīn, and apocalyptic insecurities, 94–95
Umm Salama, and assimilation of Copts, 70
Umm Sharīk, and the last days, 95
umma, *ummī*, *ummīyūn*
association with fusion of Arabs and Islam, 44–48, 114, 118–19; People of the Book differentiated, 46; uses of: and equation with Arabs, 44–46, 47; and Arab polytheists, 46–47; in *ḥadīth* literature, 47–48, 113; Qur'ānic, 7, 14–15, 44–48, 114; to identify Prophet, 44, 47
unbelief, Qur'ānic asssociation with *'arab*, 8
untrustworthiness, tradition associating with Arabs, 13
'Uqba ibn 'Āmir, and unfavourable view of Berbers, 78
'Uqba ibn Salam al-Hannā'ī, and identification of Turks as descendants of Keturah, 104
'Urwa ibn al-Zubayr
and: approval of bedouins who convert to Islam, 53; attitudes to black slaves, 83–84; avoidance of blacks in marriage, 38; concept of Prophet as messenger to Arabs, 45; imminent onset of evil, 103; worthiness in marriage, 38, 86
'Utba ibn 'Abd al-Sulamī, and integration of blacks into Islam, 87
'Uthmān al-Battī, non-Arab descent used as argument against, 42
'Uthmān ibn 'Affān
and: attitudes to Arabs and non-Arabs, 65–66; Berber viciousness, 78; loving the Arabs, 61; rebellion against, and traditions on Arab attitudes to blacks, 90
'Uthmān ibn Qā'id, and tradition accepting Arabic as sacred language, 52
'Uthmān al-Ṭarā'ifı, and assimilation of non-Arabs, 72

Wahb ibn Munabbih
and: the last days, 95; accepting Arabic as sacred language, 50–51, 119
Wakī' ibn al-Jarrāḥ
and: Arab attitudes to blacks, 90; kissing of hands, 34; role in Islam of non-Arabs, 75–76
al-Walīd I ibn 'Abd al-Malik, 85
reference to Arab ethnicity of, 19
al-Walīd II ibn Yazīd
apocalyptic insecurities engendered by killing of, 102–103; rejection of claim to throne because of mixed race, 39–40
al-Walīd ibn Muslim, and tradition of Arabs as chosen of God, 59–60
Warqā' ibn 'Umar, and concept of Turks as eschatological enemy, 109
Wāthila ibn al-Asqa'
and: Arabs as chosen of God, 59–60; assimilation of non-Arabs, 72
Women
black, traditions on Arab attitudes to, 92; suckling, ban on intercourse with, 33; *see also* marriage
worthiness (*kafā'a*), concept of, in marriage, discrimination between Arabs and non-Arabs, 36–40, 86
Wuhayb ibn Khālid al-Bāhilī, and concept of imminent onset of evil, 103

Yāfith *see* Japheth
Yaḥyā ibn 'Abbād, and interpretations of *shu'ūb*, 22
Yaḥyā ibn Ma'īn, favourable comment on Aḥmad ibn Ḥanbal, 42
Yaḥyā ibn Sa'īd al-Qaṭṭān, and Arab attitudes to blacks, 91
Yaḥyā ibn Sulaymān/ibn Abī Sulaymān, and attitudes to black slaves, 85
Yaḥyā ibn Yazīd al-Ash'arī, and traditions on fusion of Arabs and Islam, 57
Yaḥyā ibn Yazīd al-Sa'dī, and connection of Prophet's eloquence with revelation, 50
Yazīd I ibn Mu'āwiya
reference to Arab ethnicity 18–19; urged to learn genealogy, astronomy, Arabic by Mu'āwiya, 55
Yazīd III ibn al-Walīd, conflict with Walīd II, 39–40
Yazīd ibn Abī Ḥabīb, and integration of blacks into Islam, 87
Yazīd ibn Abī Sa'īd al-Naḥawī, and interpretations of *umma*, 14

Yazīd ibn 'Amr al-Ma'āfirī, and violation of the Ka'ba, 96
Yazīd ibn Ibrāhīm al-Tustarī, and Arab attitudes to blacks, 90
Yazīd ibn Qatāda ibn Di'āma, and traditions on Arab attitude to Turks, 106
Yazīd/Zayd ibn Qays, and fear of internal discords, 101–102
Yazīd ibn Sinān, and threat to Arabs from non-Arabs, 74
Yūnus ibn 'Amr, and Arab attitudes to blacks, 90
Yūnus ibn 'Ubayd, and threat from non-Arabs, 74

zakāt ("alms tax"), discrimination in payment required of Arabs, non-Arabs, 29
Zanj
  revolt of, 86; term for black slaves, 82; *see also* blacks, slavery
Zayd ibn al-Ḥabbāb, and integration of blacks into Islam, 87
Zayd ibn Jubayra, and attitudes to Arabs and non-Arabs, 62–63
Zayd ibn Thābit, reported as naming addressee of letter, 35
Zayd ibn Wahb, and identification of Turks as descendants of Keturah, 104
Zaynab bint Jaḥsh (wife of Prophet), and concept of imminent onset of evil, 101, 103–104
Ziyād ibn Abī Sufyān, differentiation between Arabs and non-Arabs, 117–18
Ziyād ibn Sa'd
  and: discrimination between Arabs, non-Arabs, relative to marriage, 38; worthiness in marriage, 86
al-Zubayr ibn al-'Awwām
  a'rāb urged to fight against 'Alī by, 11; criticised by Prophet for not abandoning *a'rābīya*, 10
al-Zuhrī, Muḥammad ibn Shihāb
  and: accepting Arabic as sacred language, 51; Arabian-Islamic attitude to Copts, 122; Arab attitude to slavery, 27–28; assertion of national character of Prophet, 119; assimilation of Copts, 69, 70; attitude of Arabs to Turks, 109; attitude to mixed marriage of Arabs, non-Arabs, 37, 38, 39, 118; attitudes to black slaves, 83–84; attribution of policies of discrimination to 'Umar I, 117; attribution of pro-Arab attitudes to Prophet, 48; banning non-Muslims from Arabia, 30; concept of Arabic as sacred language, 56, 119; concept of imminent onset of evil, 103; concept of Prophet as messenger to Arabs, 45; domination of non-Arabs in running affairs of state, 40; interpretations of *shu'ūb*, 23; rehabilitation of bedouins, 53; slandering the Nabāṭ, 79–80; violation of the Ka'ba, 96; worthiness in marriage, 86
Zuṭṭ ("gypsies"?), occasional references to, 78, 124, 125